THE MIRACLE WORKERS
America's Psychic Consultants

THE
MIRACLE
WORKERS

America's
Psychic Consultants

JESS STEARN

DOUBLEDAY & COMPANY, INC.
GARDEN CITY, NEW YORK

Contents

Contents

For Maude Robinson, a grand lady and a great psychic, this book is fondly dedicated.

1
The Professionals

As a down-to-earth draftsman, Don La Rosa was very much annoyed with his wife for listening to the strange man next door.

"Wrap up the china because of an earthquake—what rubbish." He gritted his teeth. "Don't tell me what that man says and don't go near him, he's creepy."

"But, Don," she protested, "he's been right about so many things."

La Rosa flung up his arms. "Marge," he said, "I'm beginning to worry about you."

A few days later, on February 9, 1971, at 6:02 A.M., the worst California earthquake in years, rocking the Los Angeles area, centered disastrously in the San Fernando Valley, where La Rosa dwelt so uneasily next to the man who had predicted the quake.

Ten seconds after the last tremor, which flung things about the La Rosa home and shattered his china, La Rosa ran out into the street, and called over to his neighbor, Bill Corrado, psychic extraordinary,

"When is the next earthquake?"

Curiously, Corrado, like other psychics, had foreseen many more implausible events than an earthquake in California—hardly an implausibility considering the explosive San Andreas fault running the length of the state.

But there is something so impersonal about an earthquake that one could well marvel where his warning message came from. Death, accidents, marriage, divorce could already be foreshadowed in the minds of men, and so be capable of being picked up by the delicate antenna of the psychic. But in whose mind was the approaching quake, if not man's?

"How can anybody," asked La Rosa, "predict an earthquake? In order to be a receptor of something you have to get a message from someplace. How can an earthquake tell you, 'I'm coming?'"

Ironically, Corrado did seem to have an earthquake receptor. The Los Angeles psychic first mentioned the quake in early January. "One of Bill's clients," La Rosa recalled, "happened to be leaving, and over the fence it came out that the conversation with the client was about an earthquake."

As the quake approached, Corrado got more specific, La Rosa more scornful.

"At first," La Rosa recalled, "he said before March. About a week later, he was predicting the quake in another week or two, in early February."

As it did millions, the quake gave the La Rosas the shock of their lives. "I was in bed," La Rosa said, "and the first thing I knew there was this rumbling and all three of my daughters jumped in bed with us. I scrambled out of bed, and this thing was still going. The horses back of the house had jumped the corral and were running scared all over the place."

Meanwhile, the Corrado animals were securely bedded

down, and the Corrado china carefully stashed away. Corrado took his own predictions seriously.

As La Rosa had, I wondered how the psychic had tuned into the devastating tremor. Had it been an image, an impression, given in a flash or by meditation? How had it come to him when nobody had even inquired about an earthquake?

"I got the word earthquake first," the thirty-two-year-old psychic explained. "As the time drew near, I became tense and nervous. It disturbed my sleep."

"Did you tell many people about it?" I asked, looking curiously around the La Rosa home for damage.

"Yes, my clients, I wanted to prepare them, as I knew it would center in the Valley, and many of them lived there."

"Does it do any good to tell someone an earthquake is coming?"

Corrado was sure it did.

"I told them to take their things off the walls and not to put them back until fall because of the aftershocks."

There were at least a half-dozen I could recall, including one the following night that shook me up more than the original quake.

"Did you picture the destruction, including the loss of life?"

"No, just a lot of shaking and trembling, and I was doing some trembling myself."

"Did you feel your family would come through unharmed?"

"Yes," he said serenely.

"Then why were you so upset?"

"Just natural human fear. In an earthquake there's nothing you can do, no way you can run."

Corrado publicly predicted another quake in the Southern California area for August, and it came on schedule.

But it was not a very large one, and it didn't do much damage, so there were many who complained about his being wrong.

However, Corrado was complacent.

"I don't want to scare people out of their wits," he said, "nor do I want to see a disaster. I just want to prepare people for problems if I can."

These problems are as broad and manifold as life itself. For with the growing interest in the psychic, a new breed of oracle has come into vogue, the psychic consultants, with Corrado in the forefront of this burgeoning group. They are the last-resorters, generally consulted only when more conventional practitioners—lawyers, doctors, teachers, and parents—have not been able to help. Increasingly, people consult them for every reason imaginable, health, romance, finances, or sheer curiosity. Where once only eccentrics, or the gullible, patronized psychics, captains of finance, college professors, lawyers, doctors, and Indian chiefs now solicit appointments. One may want to know if and when he is getting that job. Another is concerned about an inheritance. Still another asks if she will marry Jack or Joe.

The wise psychic, like the psychiatrist, lets each find the truth in his own way.

"I never tell anybody what they must do, I only advise," says Corrado, "the decision is up to them." Generally the successful psychic consultant builds up his following by word of mouth. Unfortunately, a psychic good for one person is not always good for another.

"Just like my doctor," said one actress client, "he's good for me but not for my girl friend."

In Hollywood, where the film industry has been hurting in recent years, a psychic who can see a job ahead for anybody in the acting profession may quickly acquire a great vogue. Tall, beautiful Eve Bruce, for instance, started a run on Hollywood's Olga Brosten after Mrs. Brosten virtually made a star out of her, psychically.

"Mrs. Brosten," said Eve Bruce, "predicted I would land a job in a week which would be the turning point in my career, and the next week I signed for a part in *The Love Machine.* She then predicted I would have a job on top of a job—a remarkable prediction since I hadn't been working that much—and would have to turn down a very important role. It didn't seem likely. Nevertheless, I was in the middle of *Where Does It Hurt?,* starring Peter Sellers, and was offered a part in *Pancho Villa,* being filmed in Spain. I had to turn it down."

Like other professionals, psychic consultants work by appointment only. But unlike other professionals, many psychics do not have fixed fees, often accepting donations, which might run from two to twenty dollars, or scaling their price to the income of the client.

One day, the young singer Sharyn Wynters, a star of the future, arrived for an appointment with Corrado in a resplendent car costing more than ten thousand dollars. She was greeted by Corrado on his doorstep, had her reading, and was impressed, even shocked, that he could pick up the name of a man she was interested in. She then asked the psychic what she owed him.

"Ten dollars," he replied.

"But I thought you charged twenty," said his satisfied customer.

"I do normally, but you can't afford it."

"Did you see that car I drove up in?" she sputtered.

"Yes," he said, "but you don't own it."

As nearly everyone else, I was impressed by psychic experiences, even the trivial, that had some personal application. I saw a lot of Bill Corrado, among others, as I was researching this work, and so it was only natural, I

suppose, that he should occasionally pick up something
about myself.

"Only last week," he said once, as we were lunching
together, "I read for a pretty girl who is going to work for
you."

My fork stopped in midair.

"What is her name?"

He smiled. "I can't remember."

I had been interested in engaging a researcher on a
part-time basis, but he certainly was no help if he couldn't
remember her name.

"It will happen naturally," he said, "you will just stum-
ble over her."

"Fine," I said, unconvinced.

Two weeks later, I was again with Corrado, when I
drove into Hollywood to drop off a pair of reading
glasses at the studio of a friend, Dr. Paul Thomsen, the
voice coach.

En route, I thought I would have some fun with the
psychic.

"I still haven't stumbled on that researcher you told
me about."

He nodded serenely, "You will."

Finally, we came to a stop before Thomsen's house.

Corrado waited in the car as I crossed the street with
the glasses.

Thomsen was not in, but his piano accompanist was
there, chatting with a pretty student.

As I handed the accompanist the glasses for Thomsen,
she introduced the girl. I didn't quite catch her name,
but suddenly a strong conviction came over me.

I took her by the hand and started for the door.

"There is somebody outside I want you to see."

She was too startled to resist.

As we approached the car in which Corrado was sitting,

his head bobbed up sharply, and a look of incredulity came over his usually phlegmatic countenance.

"That's the girl," he cried.

"Why, Mr. Corrado," she echoed in surprised recognition.

They were soon shaking hands, and talking like old friends.

And so I found my assistant as Bill Corrado had predicted. Her name was Ginette Lawson, and she, as it turned out, was ideal for the job.

As most psychics, with the notable exception of the Dutchman Peter Hurkos, who developed a sixth sense after a fall on his head, Corrado has been noticeably sensitive since childhood. At the age of six, he foresaw the imminent death of his own father. He mentioned it casually to his mother and grandmother, in his native Cleveland, Ohio, and both tried to hush him up.

A week later, his mother was widowed and he orphaned. At twenty-eight, his father was killed in an automobile accident.

When I first met Corrado, he was not yet a professional psychic. He had been working at physical therapy to support himself, and he read the cards for his friends for amusement, though they were not always amused at what he told them.

Friends had encouraged him to become a full-time psychic, but he didn't like the idea of charging to help people, but then fate stepped in to make up his mind. He was in an accident, and his back injured so he could no longer work at his job and support himself. He decided he was being shown the way.

Better educated than most psychics, as a former Catholic seminarian, Corrado's strange power to diagnose human ailments often caused him to speculate where this gift came from. And with his Catholic background, he recalled what Christ had said about others doing what He did with the help of the Father. That, he decided, must be it. Without being spiritual, without feeling this gift was God's, he conversely could do nothing.

Yet he balked at the priesthood, and there is nothing namby-pamby about him. He likes to take a drink on occasion, and, as a single man, to seek out the opposite sex. Outwardly, he is not much different from ordinary people. With his rugged face and frame, he looks the professional baseball player. Other psychics are similarly unspecialized in appearance. Spiritualist Richard Ireland of Phoenix could be mistaken for the manager of a supermarket, Irene Hughes, the Chicago psychic, might be a music teacher. Florida's Anne Gehman looks like an attractive suburban matron, Hollywood's Doug Johnson, a professor of English at a small college, New York's Marie Welt, a Fifth Avenue beautician, Maude Robinson of Norfolk, a dowager duchess.

And just as the biblical prophet had no honor in his homeland, so have few contemporary soothsayers, including Corrado, found recognition close to home.

Accordingly, when Faye Cohen, a Hollywood store manager, was having trouble with her fiancé, and her friend Millie suggested she discuss it with her boy Billy, Faye thought her friend suddenly bereft of her senses.

"You mean Billy your son?"

"Yes," Millie said, "he's a psychic."

"And what is a psychic?"

"He sees things. Try him." She shrugged. "What can you lose?"

So Faye sat down one afternoon across from psychic Bill Corrado, still seeing him as the child she once knew, and watched curiously as he spread a deck of cards out on the table.

"What are you doing that for?" she demanded.

"Just to relax and detach myself a little."

Abruptly he looked up, and took his attention from the cards.

"You will not marry this man," he said.

"What man?" she asked.

"His children don't want the marriage. As a matter of fact, he is being influenced by Barbara."

Faye Cohen's jaw dropped. "Barbara is his youngest daughter," she acknowledged. "He said if I would sign one of those premarital agreements, his daughter would approve his marrying me."

Corrado shook his head.

"You are going to marry a man named Al."

Faye laughed. "Billy," she said, "I know Jerrys, and I know Bobs, but I don't know any Als."

"You will," he promised.

A few months later, she met an Al, and disliked him at sight.

But Al was persistent, and she finally agreed to a date. On their third date, he proposed.

"This guy must be sick," Faye told a neighbor, "three dates and he asks me to marry him."

She asked Bill for his impression of Al.

"Does Al go to real estate school?" he said.

She blinked. "Yes, Billy."

Bill was introduced to Al without being identified as a psychic.

"You're having problems in school," he told Al without preamble. "You have to read a paragraph several times before it goes into your head."

It was Al's turn to blink.

"I was just telling a friend of mine that," he said.

After Al left, Faye looked at the boy who had grown up to become a psychic.

"Well?"

This was now July, and Faye had known Al for about six weeks.

"You will be married to Al before the end of December," the psychic said.

"Never," said Faye. "He's forty-seven, and never married, an unknown quantity."

"He is a good man, and a good provider."

"What else?" asked Faye.

"You will receive eight gifts, near the end of the year."

"I have a birthday in November," Faye said, "and there's always Christmas."

He shook his head. "It's neither of these."

On December 5, Faye and Al were married.

They had been married five months at the time we sat together in her attractive living room discussing Corrado.

"How about those eight presents?" I asked.

Her eyes roved proudly around her apartment.

"They're all here somewhere, the eight wedding presents. Gold-plated silverware, salt and pepper shakers, crystal, silver breadbasket, cigarette lighter, an urn, gold menorah (candlesticks), and a salad bowl."

She was a believer now.

"You need a personal experience yourself to accept the psychic," she explained, echoing other converts.

In retrospect, she saw where Bill had been psychic even as a child. "When Billy was six or seven years old," she recalled, "his mother and I would be going somewhere, and Billy would say, 'I know where you're going,' and he would be right."

She could laugh about it now.

"I told his mother, 'Millie, your kid knew everything we were doing, and we thought he was nuts.'"

Like other successful psychics, Corrado is similarly clairvoyant, telepathic, and precognitive, the whole adding up to what the popular spiritualist Richard Ireland calls extrasensory perception or ESP.

"Anything beyond the perception of the five senses," says Ireland, "may be considered ESP—the miracles of the Bible, the visitation of spirits, premonitions, dreams, hunches, prophecy, and some exceptional talent—the inventive genius of an Edison, the verse of a Shakespeare, the music of a Beethoven."

As one who has amazed millions over television with his own ESP, Ireland has frequently assessed the various powers psychic consultants use in their work:

"Thought transference directly from one mind to another without employing the physical senses is telepathy, and it indicates mental powers transcending the mechanics of the brain.

"The awareness of distant objects or events outside the physical senses—sight, hearing, taste, touch, smell—is clairvoyance. And the spontaneous awareness of distant events through recognized sensual channels is clairvoyant vision. Prophecy or precognition provides a glimpse into the future that startles reasoning—impossible but true."

Psychic healing, as reflected in the Bible, rounds out the psychic's arsenal.

The psychic quality is not limited to professional psychics. In childhood, before training in logic and reasoning, children show strong intuitive impulses. Many adults, too, appear to have an atavistic hangover from a primitive time when man needed his instinct to survive in a hostile world. Some observers feel the psychic faculty may be reviving currently because man is once more in peril, this time from his own destructive thinking.

With ordinary adults, there must be a motivation, generally of a traumatic nature, to bring out a psychic ability. An emotional crisis, for instance, may trigger a psychic experience, like a son being wounded in a far-off battlefield and a mother tuning in that very instant. But the professional psychic needs only a focal point to function at will. A person, an occurrence, even a thought can touch off a psychic impression, since the psychic's subconscious, delicately tuned, is plugged into what humanist C. G. Jung called the Universal Mind. Even so, how is a psychic able to tune in on the unknown, and predict earthquakes, wars, disasters, political elections, death, even romance and marriage?

"The future is out there waiting," says Corrado, "or I could not see it."

Others are not as sure that the future is fixed. But nearly all psychic consultants agree that a Divine Intelligence rules the affairs of man. Without the spiritual, without some feeling of soul consciousness, the psychic factor seems a frivolous gift, in a class with sleight of hand. It is also not very durable. For as they abuse this gift, pressing for their own material advantage, coddling their vanity, psychics invariably dwindle in effectiveness. On the other hand, through dedication to others, many psychics are more effective with time. "As I mellowed," observed New York palmist Marie Welt, "I began to pick up things about people I couldn't possibly have seen in their hands."

Douglas Johnson's development came with giving of himself, though he had an early interest in spiritualism, the philosophic concept that the spirit not only survives after death, but takes a continuing interest in human affairs.

Different psychics have different starting points.

Johnson was sitting on a park bench in Minneapolis when, he reports, he looked up and saw a figure standing there. It was so real it seemed that he could reach out and touch it. By itself, the vision was not terribly dramatic, except for its message for him, a message not fully appreciated until years later.

"I was told to open myself up, not put any limitations on myself or the world around me."

Johnson's may have been a purely subjective experience, culled out of his own subconscious. Even so, it had its purpose, preparing him for what he was to do with his life, though psychic healing was about the last thing he would have previously thought possible for himself.

Believing anything was possible seemed a step toward making it so. Years later, when he was a psychic in California, a woman telephoned in unbearable pain. Johnson had no idea what the physical problem was. But he got into his car and drove out to her home. Even as he was driving he mentally cast a "healing" light around her.

"I put no limitations on the thoughts I sent out."

On his arrival, the woman was still in pain. But Johnson became instantly aware, as he entered the house, of a spirit force so overpowering he could almost touch it.

"Have faith in your own power to heal," he said, "and help will come."

He passed his hand over her, and she could feel the vitalizing heat.

"I feel warm," she said, touching her face.

"Good," he said, glad of a positive reaction.

As he left, telling her she would be well, the woman saw a hazy figure standing just inside the door.

The figure looked for a moment like Jesus. The lips moved, and a voice said:

"With faith in the Father, you have the power to heal yourself."

The pain suddenly left her. She slept well and in the morning she was brimming with healthy optimism.

As he became more confident, Johnson found he could function extemporaneously. He could pick up illnesses on

walking into a room, getting an unhealthy vibration. He
could see auras, shadowy ectoplasmic formations emanat-
ing from the body, which in their depth and color gave
him indications of the individual's state of well-being. For
his own peace of mind, he frequently had to shield himself from these vibrations, as there was little he could do,
anyway, without the person wanting to be helped.

Johnson's healing gift manifested itself outwardly.
And in the material world in which he functioned this was
indeed a boon. For his was a facility that excited confidence, since there was obviously something happening of
a physical nature that skeptics could perceive if not understand. Johnson's hands, as they passed over the anat-
omy, gave off a sensation of heat apparent not only to the
person he was healing but to others in the room.

He worked casually and easily, never raising his voice,
always stressing that the person was healing himself with
the help of Spirit, which he equated with God, Divine Intelligence, the Universal Mind. Such was his own wish to
help everyone that he never failed to respond to a plea for
help at social gatherings where he was a guest. One particular evening, a young law school graduate, Mary Anna
Anderson of San Francisco, mentioned she had broken a
small bone in her foot, and it had not properly healed.

"I cannot run," said this athletic girl, "because of the
pain when my foot touches the ground."

The shoe was soon removed, and the healer looked at
the injured foot with practiced eye. There was no out-
ward sign of any discomfort, but as Johnson's hand
passed lightly over Mary Anna's foot, it suddenly halted,
and he said:

"This is where it hurts."

She nodded.

"Exactly."

As he had done so many times, Johnson called on Spirit

to intervene. Curiously enough, he did not refer specifically to the break, but invoked an overall healing to mend whatever needed mending.

The ritual took but a few minutes.

When it ended, Mary Anna gingerly pressed her foot to the floor.

"It feels all right," she said, "but then it only bothers me running."

That same day, she ran on the hard-packed beach along the Pacific for more than a mile at a brisk pace.

She returned with a bright smile.

"I can't believe it," she said, "not even a twinge."

A week later, she was still running, and still no pain. Whatever Doug Johnson had done, it had worked.

Johnson has by no means had an uninterrupted run of success. But no psychic, whether trying to heal the body or the emotional nature of man, is perfect. If he is right 75 or 80 per cent of the time, his ratio of success is certainly better than the average in other professions priding themselves on being scientific. But when a psychic is wrong he is very wrong, almost disastrously so, for people who make a practice of visiting psychics usually take their advice seriously and follow it implicitly.

But responsible psychics, regardless of the information flow, normally refrain from anything that will needlessly upset a client. Reputable psychics, like astrologers, stay away from predictions of death, even when they see it clearly. In special circumstances, where a death has already been discounted emotionally, they may describe what they see only if they think it might help.

"Have I time to set my affairs in order?" one elderly gentleman asked psychic Maude Robinson of Norfolk, Virginia.

"More than you think," she replied, "so enjoy yourself."

Just as some psychics take a positive approach in handling the death aspect, others inexcusably blurt out whatever passes through their heads, doubly compounding their misjudgment at times by being completely wrong.

The reverberations can be horrendous.

One day, I received a telephone call from a friend, a well-to-do matron, with considerable background and education. I immediately detected from her voice that she was unstrung. And no wonder. Counting on an afternoon's entertainment, she had visited a well-known Los Angeles seeress, and listened amiably as the lady psychic discussed her children, almost perfectly appraising their talents and personalities. She was still beaming as the psychic reviewed her life, again appearing to tune in perfectly, and was hardly prepared for the shocking statement that followed.

The psychic, reading from cards spread out before her, suddenly burst into tears.

"I don't know how to tell you this," she cried.

The smile froze on my friend's face.

"You must tell me."

The psychic sobbed, "Pray for your husband, pray night and day."

"Tell me what you see," my friend implored.

"You will be coming into a large sum of money soon," the psychic said.

"Where is this money coming from?"

Perhaps realizing she had gone too far, the psychic tried briefly to get on to a positive approach.

"Tell your husband to get a thorough physical examination. He is a sick man. Otherwise," she resumed her moaning, "he will be a dead man in September."

Since this was already August, my friend felt a tremor through her body. She was so overwrought that she had consciously to hold herself erect or she would have fainted.

"What can I do?" she pleaded.

"Pray," the psychic cried, "and get him to a doctor before it is too late."

As my friend told the story, I was tempted to get the psychic on the phone and dress her down. But the damage was already done, and it was imperative, I thought, to minimize the whole affair, rather than exaggerate it with recriminations.

"She obviously doesn't know what she's talking about," I said.

My bluntness seemed to take her out of shock.

"Why do you say that?"

"If she foresees his death," I said, "what is the point of praying or having a medical examination?"

She didn't seem to get my point.

"If you're going to inherit, he has to die," I said, "so she's obviously working you up about nothing. And when the event doesn't happen, as it won't," I threw in encouragingly, "she'll take the credit, saying her prayers or the examination spared him."

Like most people, the wife was ready to believe the worst.

"What shall I do?" she said. "We have had the most wonderful marriage."

"Don't do anything," I said. "You'll only alarm him needlessly."

"But it's been years since he had a physical checkup."

At thirty-nine, the husband looked in excellent condition, and I saw no reason for alarm.

"He should be examined," she said. "I'll never forgive myself if I don't at least do that."

"Then get him to a doctor without telling him about the psychic," I said.

Actually, by tactfully suggesting a medical examination, the psychic could have taken the positive approach, suggesting difficulties that could be overcome, and not paralyzing her subject with the specter of death.

A few days later, as August went into September, I learned the husband was undergoing about every test imaginable. Unfortunately, in trying to persuade him to go to a doctor, the wife had divulged what the psychic had told her.

"She didn't exactly say it was you," she comforted him.

"Where else," he replied with grim logic, "is the inheritance coming from?"

As September dragged on, he showed signs of weakening, but only because of the ordeal of tests for every conceivable illness.

"If I survive this," he sighed after a particularly irritating ulcer test, "I don't think I'll ever die."

Unlike Caesar's Ides of March, the month of September came and went without the predicted demise, and when I saw him last, the husband had successfully negotiated another birthday, and was none the worse for wear. He seemed to have taken the whole sorry affair in good grace.

"You can't buy that expensive gown," he good-naturedly chided his wife, "until you come into your inheritance."

It would have been understandable, I thought, had he changed his will. But several good things, at least, came of the misadventure. He did get a badly needed checkup, gave up smoking and drinking, went on to a regular exercise routine, and seemed in better health than ever before.

There was another positive outcome.

The wife, a psychic buff, gave up psychics for an afternoon's entertainment.

The responsible psychic consultants leave their clients feeling better than when they find them, and move with skill and prudence to help those who so trustingly consult them. And the fields in which they function, as noted, are unlimited—financial, physical, social, emotional. In the financial area, for instance, the John Contes of Los Angeles had been told by realtors that the Holmby Hills house they had up for sale could bring no more than $325,000, which seemed sizable enough, yet hardly represented the intrinsic value of this California showplace.

Mrs. Conte, respecting the intuitive, asked psychic Bill Corrado for an opinion, without mentioning the realtors' estimate.

"You will get four hundred and fifty thousand," the psychic said without hesitating, "and I see the purchaser as a lady from an eastern state, somebody you haven't met yet."

Several weeks later, after Mrs. Conte had rejected several offers, the house was sold to a woman from Philadelphia. The price? $450,000, minus of course the broker's commission.

Like other professionals, psychics have their specialties. Just as Doug Johnson accomplishes healings, Florida-based Anne Gehman solves crimes, locates missing people, and gives spiritual comfort to those for whom there is no other help. Widely publicized, she has done much to popularize the psychic consultants by giving readings to all and sundry. She has experienced about every form of psychic adventure herself. In astral flight, a projection, this Orlando psychic has several times been on the moon. Before the first successful moon launch, she was often asked for her impressions of the moon surface, as engineers and others from the nearby Kennedy Space Center flocked curiously to her doorstep. And she closed her eyes and described her subconscious flights into space, almost as an astronanut would.

Once, following the flight of Apollo XI, she was talking

with friends when a space engineer coolly dropped a
small piece of cylindrical metal into her hand.

As the object touched her hand, she felt, suddenly, as
if she was surrounded by a capsule and was launched
like a rocket into space.

She looked up with a smile, and said:

"I feel like I'm going to the moon."

The space engineer gave a startled laugh, then explained.

The piece of metal thrust into Anne's hand was part of
a metal bar taken to the moon and back by the Apollo XI
astronauts. It was later melted down into coinlike sou-
venirs for space personnel.

With man's venture into outer space, his interest has
developed commensurately in an inner space of the mind
which seems to express the infinity of the universe, and
offer some explanation of our relation to this universe. As
is their custom, the so-called scientists, observing the rise
of the psychic operator and his growing public acceptance, have toiled in their laboratories to prove or dis-
prove the existence of psychic phenomena in terms of
their own scientific reference, testing psychics under conditions obviously limited in motivation and scope. Glee-
fully, they look for variations in brain waves, blood pressure, and heartbeat as the psychic hopefully responds to
their suggestions, perhaps guessing a card or inventory-
ing the inside of a file cabinet.

But experiments, as were noted by the late psychic Edgar Cayce of Virginia Beach, have little to do with the
psychic's natural function. In real life, not the laboratory,
do the greatest of the psychics fulfill their mission: in ac-
complishing healings, preparing their subjects for the future, good or bad, and, above all, in establishing by their
very gift the manifestation of an orderly, knowledgeable
universe in which man comes to know his purpose as he

tunes himself in to that universe. In tuning into this divine order or intelligence, the psychic consultants often perform what seem miracles to the ordinary person unaware of the latent powers of the universe.

Whatever the psychic principle at work, its workability never ceases to amaze me. One day in June 1971, I received a telephone call from an old friend, the plastic surgeon Dr. Cadvan Griffiths, of Beverly Hills, whose patients came to him from the four corners of the earth.

"I have bad news," he said. "Chester is in St. John's Hospital in Santa Monica, and I'm not sure he'll make it."

Eight-year-old Chester, the youngest of the Griffiths, was my godson, and my friendship with the parents preceded even their marriage some eighteen years before.

"What is wrong?" I asked with a throb of concern.

"Nobody seems to be sure," said Van Griffiths, "except there is a softening of the bone."

I knew the boy must have had the best medical attention, but I said almost automatically:

"Has he been checked out in every way?"

"Oh, yes," the father said, "everything has been considered, osteomyelitis, tuberculosis of the bone, arthritis, lupus, leukemia—even histiocytosis X."

"Has he had a biopsy?" I asked.

"Several," in a tired voice, "and they didn't turn up anything."

That afternoon I visited Chester at the hospital.

I was shocked at the change in the boy. His face was the color of parchment, his arms and legs like sticks; the knuckles of his hands seemed to have disintegrated under his skin, where his bones had spontaneously fractured without precedent injury. Yet, despite his fragile appearance, he appeared in lively spirits.

"Jess," he said, using my first name as usual, "nobody seems to know what they're doing."

"You'll be all right, Chester," I said reassuringly.

His face grew pensive. "I want to go home and be with the others," he said, referring to two older brothers and a sister.

We visited for a while, but he tired rapidly, giving me a listless good-by as I left. He seemed to be including me with the other grown-ups making things so difficult for him.

From the hospital, I proceeded to the Griffiths' home, and reported that I had found Chester anxious to go home.

"They have to make a few more tests," Van Griffiths said, "and remove some more bone."

"Maybe he'd be better off if they left him alone," I said.

Van sighed. "We tried that, too, but he just got worse."

His wife, Barbara, added, "Van has been in touch with his medical friends all over the country, hoping somebody might come up with a definite diagnosis."

Van gave me a wan smile. "It's pretty hard to treat something when you don't know what it is."

With a hesitant look at her husband, Barbara said to me, "Do you think it possible a psychic might pick up something?"

I shrugged. "It's always a possibility, and what can we lose?"

I turned to Van, recognizing of course that he was in a delicate position as a practicing physician, and knowing that while his wife had an interest in the psychic, he was a rigid nonbeliever.

He returned my gaze evenly. "I'd be willing to listen to anybody."

His wife squeezed his arm.

"Psychic Bill Corrado," I said, "has had some success

tuning in on obscure ailments, and Doug Johnson has had good results with psychic healing."

Corrado obviously seemed the less drastic of the alternatives.

"He doesn't necessarily have to see the boy," I said, "but it might help."

I phoned Corrado the next morning.

"I had an emergency reading last night," he said wearily.

"You have another emergency now," I said.

He groaned. "Who is it?"

"My godson," I said, "nobody knows for sure what's wrong." I had decided against giving Corrado a clue.

There was a pause, and I could sense that he was concentrating on the other end of the line.

"How old is he?" he asked at length.

"Eight."

He seemed to be lining the thing up in his head. "It's a bone condition, isn't it?"

"That's right."

"A softening of the bone, the marrow is affected."

"There seems to be some softening."

He was breathing deeply into the phone.

"He's got a virus, and it's leeching the calcium out of his blood."

"Are you sure of that?"

"That's what comes to me."

"Will he get better?"

"Yes, after a while, quicker if they take him out of the hospital and leave him alone. The tests are only demoralizing him."

I wondered if he could pick up any specific therapy.

"Yes," he said, "Calcium D, large doses of Calcium D."

"And what," I asked, "is Calcium D?"

"I don't know," he said, "it just came to me."

Later that day, I passed on the information to Dr. Griffiths.

"That's curious," he said, "there has been one theory that perhaps a virus was at the seat of the problem."

"Have you heard of Calcium D?" I asked.

He checked over the pharmaceutical records. "There is a Di Calcium, calcium with vitamin D, and it's indicated for some bone conditions."

Chester left the hospital in a few days, the tests still inconclusive. He was put on a regimen of vitamins and Di Calcium, a product of Spencer, Mead. He showed instant improvement, and soon gained ten pounds. But his progress was short-lived. One day, he went into a fever, suffered a drop in energy, with all the symptoms he had shown before.

"That's to be expected," Corrado told me. "But eventually he will be strong enough to overcome the virus once and for all. But when he gets overtired, or his resistance is low, the problem will recur."

When I passed on the information, I was surprised to learn that there were plans for Chester to return to the hospital.

"We can't leave any stone unturned," his mother told me. "A doctor friend back East phoned last night, and said he had a case with similar symptoms—multiple cysts of the bones with enlargement of the lymph nodes, spleen, and liver—which had responded to massive doses of penicillin and tetracycline."

"Have you mentioned it to Corrado?" I asked.

"No," she said, "we are a medical family, and we would never forgive ourselves if we overlooked knowledgeable medical therapy."

I felt a certain frustration, thinking the youngster had stood about all the experimentation he could.

Corrado was equally disappointed. "The boy will react

badly to the antibiotics," he said, "and they will be discontinued after the second round."

Back into St. John's Hospital went poor Chester.

And again, just as Corrado had predicted, there was an adverse reaction to the antibiotics and they were discontinued.

Chester was brought home, but this time with the promise of no more biopsies, blood tests, or injections. "So far," his doctor father said grimly, "only Corrado has been right all along."

Just being home, without the threat of medical attention, seemed to improve Chester's well-being.

But Corrado had one more suggestion to speed the boy's convalescence.

"It would help," said he, "if he got a healing from Douglas Johnson."

He knew Johnson only slightly, and his impression was purely psychic in this instance.

I assured the Griffiths that Johnson was a simple, unpretentious man whose approach was not calculated to upset anybody. And so Johnson was invited into the Griffiths' home.

I could see that he made a favorable impression. He was soft-spoken, conservatively dressed, and, as noted, looked as if he belonged on a college campus.

After we got through dinner he was ready for Chester.

The boy, still pale and wan, was brought out in his pajamas, and we adjourned to a small room. The other children were curious, and Johnson had no objection to their presence.

"Just don't say anything," their mother admonished.

Chester sat on a couch next to Johnson, who smiled at him encouragingly.

"Are you a doctor?" he asked Doug.

"A sort of painless one," I said.

I had seen Johnson work before, and it was no different now. His voice was almost a monotone as he called on the forces of the universe to assist in the healing he was now attempting. "Let him be whole and well," he said, "making use of the healing forces that are within him."

His hand meanwhile passed over the boy's face and body as if it were a Geiger counter, picking up the trouble areas. He nodded affirmatively from time to time, as if he had tuned into the expected.

"He will be all right," he said. "Spirit will have no trouble healing him. He wants to get well."

Young Chester's eyes bulged as he hung on every word of the psychic's. And now, with Johnson's hand near his face, his cheeks took on an unaccustomed color.

"I feel warm," he said.

"That's good," Doug Johnson said gently. "You're reacting well."

The others in the room, including the children, also mentioned they were getting warm. Johnson nodded, as if gratified at this result.

He placed his hand on the boy's head, and patted it a few times.

"Okay," he said, "that should hold you."

In the next weeks the boy's progress was steady. His appetite improved, his listlessness disappeared, and he could hardly be restrained from exercising. He was back in school, and the moment he got home, he grabbed his field hockey stick and began playing in the yard. He was on large doses of Di Calcium and vitamins, and that was all.

One day, perhaps three months after my visit to the hospital, he came to visit me. He was still thin, but active, and in ebullient spirits. In three hours he didn't sit down once, and he was raring to go when his parents finally collected him for the drive home.

"He is better than ever," his mother said.

His father, as a physician, was more reserved.

"He seems to be recovering," he said. "His bones seem firmer."

"Between them," I said, "Corrado and Johnson seem to have done the trick."

He smiled thinly.

"Well, with everything that's gone into the boy, it's hard to say precisely where the recovery came from. But I am certainly grateful for their efforts."

2
The Psychic Denominator

Thou hast hid these things from the wise and prudent, and hast revealed them unto babes.

—Matthew 11:25

Metaphysical teacher Ralph Winters said to his twelve-year-old son, Robbie, "Max Freedom Long, age eighty. What do you pick up on him?"

The boy, just finishing up a Mind Dynamics course on the development of psychic awareness, answered without hesitation:

"Bone cancer."

Without the slightest conscious idea of what ailed the octogenarian occultist from Vista, California, the youngster had accurately tuned in on him from his own home a hundred miles away in Los Angeles.

In San Rafael, California, ten-year-old George Afremow, recently graduated from a similar course, went into his *alpha* brain levels, invoking his slumbering subconscious, and located a leak in the hull of a yacht tied up in nearby Sausalito, a leak which had defied the exploratory efforts of skilled marine engineers.

"I wanted to help the owner, Mr. Patrick [business tycoon William Penn Patrick]," George explained.

I had my own experience, too, when another graduate, twenty-eight-year-old John Burnham, a San Francisco accountant, turned to me one night at a psychic demonstration, and said, "Give me the age and sex of anybody you know well, and I will tune in."

In seconds he was accurately describing that person's physical and emotional nature, correctly diagnosing an abdominal ailment, and implanting the suggestion that this person change doctors so she could be promptly healed.

Twenty-four hours later the twenty-five-year-old subject of the reading, some five hundred miles away, unaccountably went to another physician, and two weeks later, a disorder troubling her for months apparently yielded to treatment.

Through an alpha-wave technique of visualization and imagination, taught in a few days, I observed where ordinary people were able to detach their subconscious mind from their conscious and momentarily perform as if they were professional psychics.

After taking the alpha-oriented Mind Dynamics class myself, I was able, given only the name and age of a twelve-year-old boy, to tell that he was suffering from asthma and reversed vision, reading abnormally right to left.

Subsequently, before a group of doubting Thomases, given only a woman's date of birth, I correctly identified the individual and saw a deep religious experience which would reshape her life. A daughter confirmed this spiritual experience of her mother only four days before.

In time, presumably, everybody will be more or less psychic, and it will be commonplace to telepathize to the moon, Mars, and Venus. Obviously there will be some people more psychic than others, just as some play the piano, write, sing, or juggle better. Meanwhile, observing the psychic quality in action, it becomes obvious that the best professional psychics are the simplest people of scant intellectuality, since the intellectual reflects the conscious mind, and the psychic functions out of a subconscious, free of deliberate and rational thought. Knowing this, psychics make a real effort to detach their conscious mind and insulate themselves against an individual's wishes, hopes, and anxieties which might influence a psychic reading. To attain a clear subconscious channel, Hollywood's Doug Johnson concentrates on articles belonging to the subject, Bill Corrado on a battered deck of cards, Maya Perez holds a person's hand to get a vibration through which the subconscious can flow. Others go about it differently. Maria Moreno slips into trance and calls on her spirit guides, Helen Stalls closes her eyes and thinks of God, Marie Welt plays her searchlight over the lines of the palm, Vera Winston reads from the Psalms, and Maude Robinson recites them out of memory.

Some psychics, healers for instance, appear to make things happen; others are content to be mere channels, as in predicting the future, usually stressing the optimistic, but like twelve-year-old Robbie Winters, ten-year-old George Afremow, and the older Burnham, all have a desire to help their fellow man.

One celebrated crystal gazer, on the contrary, is so inflated with her own importance, so intent on headlines, that she scatters her predictions around like buckshot. She is generally wrong, but so prolific that some predictions inevitably materialize. So lacking in taste is she that she bragged about predicting Marilyn Monroe's suicide, the Kennedys' assassinations, yea, and even De Gaulle's assassination before he succumbed to old age. She was four years premature on the 1971 California earthquake, but took credit anyway. Meanwhile, her psychic aware-

ness has dwindled to a point where a schoolboy can out-
predict her. She is right about 10 per cent of the time.

Beset by similar self-indulgence, a well-known psychic
sleuth became so venal that he demanded a two-thou-
sand-dollar fee before he would discuss the case of a missing child with the distraught parents. The last time I saw
him perform publicly he couldn't have told what time it
was sitting on a clock.

In a world of materiality, seeking to maintain their own
spirituality, many psychics are confused as to the price
they should put on their services—if any. Most are all too
aware of the danger of prostituting themselves for money.
But the real peril lies in attitude, not in payment itself. "I
never turn away anybody in need," Doug Johnson points
out, "and if they can afford to, they pay what they like.
This is something for them to think about, not me."

Maria Moreno, the Mexican medium, most recently of
Los Angeles, once raised her prices, and her gift left her.
In consternation, she dropped her fee to three dollars,
hardly enough to support herself.

"I can't take any chances," she told me, "of losing my
power to help people."

Aside from Jeane Dixon, the realtor-psychic from
Washington, D.C., few psychics have earned any great
sums, and even her psychic income comes chiefly from
books and lectures, which flow out of her as endlessly as
her predictions. The Dutchman Peter Hurkos commands
a fancy figure for individual readings, and his manager
makes sure that he doesn't waste his talents on the poor,
but even so he is hardly in the financial category of doctors or lawyers. And some say, underlining the point, that
as Peter's price goes up, his psychic ability goes down,
gain being a very conscious consideration that so often
subordinates the subconscious.

Many psychics feel their information comes from an

omniscient Universal Mind. But, actually, psychics don't concern themselves as much as the so-called scientists with where the gift originates. They look to the Bible for evidence that this power is God-given, quoting the Greatest Psychic of all as he said that others can do as He with faith in the Father.

However, even believing as they do, psychics have freely co-operated with investigators to test the source of their information. Minnesota-born, sandy-haired, fortyish Doug Johnson, curious about his own gift and the spirits that apparently hover about him, welcomed research efforts that might indicate why he was more psychic on some occasions than others. In one experiment, while permitted to function spontaneously, he collaborated with Los Angeles parapsychologists Louise Ludwig and Eloise Shields to determine whether his information came from other minds—telepathy—or from an outside agency.

"Mrs. Shields and I set up three different situations," Louise Ludwig said. "In one the subject was in the room with Mrs. Shields or myself, in another the individual for whom the reading was being given was not present during the sitting, but was known to the experimenters. Doug Johnson in that instance might conceivably get his information from the parapsychologist who knew the subject but not directly from the mind of the sitter."

In the third controlled situation, Louise Ludwig asked a friend to bring an object belonging to somebody she didn't know.

In all situations, the psychic's response was similar.

"As far as our figures went," Mrs. Ludwig said, "Doug Johnson was equally accurate in all three cases. It didn't seem to make any difference at all."

It also didn't make any difference what kind of object he psychometrized. "In some cases we would just write the person's name on a piece of paper and this would represent the object or personal possession he would normally hold."

The advice that came from Johnson was invariably spontaneous and useful.

"He predicted for a friend of mine," Mrs. Ludwig recalled, "that her business would be sold, and he correctly named the brokerage firm that would handle the sale (possible power of suggestion). But he named a competitor as having some connection with the whole thing (which couldn't possibly have been suggestion), and this too proved true. He also gave her business advice that was very helpful and which seemed very unlikely at the time. And everything turned out as he said."

Psychometry presents obvious pitfalls, since an object through which the psychic is tuning in could conceivably be associated with several people who may have handled it.

Holding an object which Mrs. Ludwig had given him, Johnson discussed in detail an injury to the owner's right leg, specifically the knee. He said it was an old injury, which no longer bothered the person, and which wasn't noticeable in walking.

Knowing nothing about such an injury, Mrs. Ludwig couldn't appraise Johnson's accuracy at the time. She checked later with the woman who owned the object, and found that the description fitted an old football injury of her husband's.

One test was revealing in illustrating how Johnson picked up his impressions. Mrs. Ludwig brought an object belonging to a friend, who was not there. Johnson immediately saw a girl. He felt her father had been dead a long time, which was true. He said that her father had lived in a small town when she was young, not true. He said her father had had something to do with a railroad, and then changed this, saying only it was somebody close to her during childhood. He then made it more specific, saying it was her uncle.

"The fact of the matter was," Mrs. Ludwig observed, "that this woman's grandfather had owned a railroad, and her uncle had worked for it. Her father had not."

Johnson had trouble describing the railroad right-of-way. The parapsychologist, knowing the railroad, told him to picture the people living alongside the tracks.

Johnson concentrated.

"Oh," he said, after a few seconds, "they look Mexican."

And so they did, for the railroad was in Mexico.

When wrong, psychics can often be very wrong, through misinterpreting their own impressions.

A psychic giving a reading for youthful Bob Dursi of Manhattan Beach, California, warned of an accident with a purple car. The suggestion took the pleasure out of Dursi's driving for the next few weeks. Then one day, while playing a coin-machine game featuring miniature racing cars, Dursi accidentally collided two cars, one with a highly improbable color—purple.

Another psychic foresaw an early marriage for a young lady. Since she was already married and had no intention of divorce, she became anxious about her husband's health. She could have spared herself this concern. The husband left her for somebody else, which the psychic hadn't clued her in to, and the young lady, on recovering from her shock, remarried.

Knowing numerous psychics as I do, I have received many unsolicited readings. Some vividly indicate the frailties of these psychics. One day, a woman phoned as I was finishing writing a book on drugs (*The Seekers*). A psychic had instructed her to say that I should give up the book, incompleted, and leave California, otherwise something terrible would befall me.

The following day I heard from the great lady herself.

"You had better do as I say," she said, "for when I clearly foresee an event I am never wrong."

I suppressed my annoyance.

"If you accurately foresee something, how then can it be avoided?"

She found the convenient loophole invoked by many psychics to cover their mistakes.

"Some events are fixed, others subject to change if the individual will heed the warning."

"Nonsense," I said. "You are trying to dramatize your ego at my expense."

"I am never wrong," she insisted.

"You are asking me," I pointed out, "to disregard not only my contractual commitments, but to push aside a project which has a message I thoroughly believe in: that the continued use of drugs by our young people could become a national disaster."

"I must tell you what I see," she said.

"Why?" I said. "I haven't asked your advice."

"I offered it," said she, "because your writings have done much for psychics."

"And of course I should write about nothing but psychics?"

"That is what my information tells me."

I felt a rising irritation.

"Stop playing God," I said, "and concentrate on other people's needs, not your own need for self-importance."

As she broke into tears, surprisingly, I could not help but think of St. Paul's injunction:

"And though I have the gift of prophecy, and understand all mysteries and knowledge; and though I have all faith, so that I could remove mountains, and have not charity, I am nothing."

To be of practical value, a professional psychic should

be accurate at least 75 or 80 per cent of the time, a percentage corresponding favorably with the efficiency of other professional consultants. Those claiming to be correct at all times are automatically suspect, for like others, the psychic's performance is often affected by his state of mind and body.

There are ways, nevertheless, that the individual can gauge the effectiveness of a psychic reading.

"If a psychic can pick up on my past and present," said one psychic buff, "telling me things about my life that nobody but myself could possibly know, then he may be sufficiently tuned in to forecast my future."

Some psychics give themselves a more stringent test—feeling they are tuned in only when they can pick up on a client's reason for the consultation.

"Why have I come to you?" a Washington businessman asked Norfolk psychic Maude Robinson.

"Money," she replied.

"How much money?" he inquired.

"Five hundred thousand dollars," she said. "You want to know if the bank will loan it to you. They will."

And so they did.

Because of their extreme sensitivity, psychics are more vulnerable to their environment than other people—hence the protective shields they put around their minds. Generally, a psychic's first reading of an individual is his best, for as he gets to know somebody on a conscious level, he picks up conscious impressions which may block the subconscious flow.

Professional psychics beware this hazard, particularly in reading for one another. Once, Bill Corrado was checking with Akashan, Hollywood's "telephone psychic," on a personal court action against an insurance company.

"How will it turn out?" he asked.

Akashan foresaw a rosy conclusion.

Corrado checked the source.

"Akashan, are you in the thinking business?"

Corrado, as it turned out, prior to the settlement, was able to detach himself sufficiently to turn down a four-thousand-dollar out-of-court offer, because, as he told me, he saw the figure 13.

The settlement came to thirteen thousand dollars.

The ability of psychics varies day to day, just as that of other creative people—inventors, writers, artists—who depend on the inspirational flow of the subconscious. And it also varies with the subject, some apparently being better channels of the psychic energy than others.

"I've learned to think of this ability as a talent like any other," said Louise Ludwig, onetime president of the Southern California affiliate of the American Society for Psychical Research. "It seems to come and go. They are often confused between their own ideas and the psychic impressions they get. It becomes a continuous struggle not to do this."

She recognized that psychics have bodies as well as minds, in speculating about off and on days. "They may not be feeling well, or they may be emotionally upset, and consequently don't seem to do as well, though this is not always the case."

A subject's disbelief or lack of rapport, contrary to what many parapsychologists believe, has little to do with the effectiveness of a reading. Longtime supper club readers, such as Maya Perez and Marie Welt, accustomed to the skepticism of sophisticated audiences, have reached prophetic heights in responding to this challenge.

One evening, I was receiving a reading in a New York supper club from psychic Maya Perez, when my companion, a free-drinking businessman, butted in.

"Why do you listen to that junk?" he sneered.

The psychic turned on him, eyes flashing.

"You could very well listen. You are running around with other women, and your wife is going to leave you."

"It will never happen," he said, startled in spite of himself.

"Oh yes, it will," she said, "and you will end your days alone, in a miserable hotel room."

The sneer had left his face, and he looked at her uncertainly.

"My wife and I will always be together," he said.

"Just remember," she enjoined, "and mend your ways."

He turned to me angrily. "Let's get out of here."

That evening was never discussed between us. But a couple of years later his marriage of thirty years broke up. Three years thereafter, the rest of the prediction was fulfilled. He was found dead in a bleak hotel room of a heart attack.

Is it better, seeing something, not to reveal it, or to reveal it in such a way that it may conceivably be of benefit? One night, a psychic told a young woman I know to be especially loving to her father for the next few months.

The implication was obvious, but instead of being affronted, the woman took the psychic's advice, and when her father passed away months later, she had the satisfaction of knowing she had helped make his last days happy.

The clairvoyant reader at best can only prepare the subject for an event. How much a psychic should divulge is an ethical consideration each psychic must work out, always considering that he may be psychically inaccurate. Happily, this will never be a problem for Marie Welt, the optimistic reader, who has read for thousands in New York supper clubs. For in all her years of peering into people's palms, Marie Welt has never told anybody anything bad.

"If I see something that isn't good I keep it to myself. If I see a little brightness, I tell them."

A Roman Catholic priest gave her perhaps her greatest testimonial. Clad in ordinary street clothes, he called on her one night, and was promptly told that he was a clergyman, that he was a good influence on many people, particularly the young, and that he was there out of curiosity.

"I am a priest," he acknowledged, "and I did come here to find out why so many young girls in my parish are coming to you instead of me."

He smiled ruefully. "I found out. You give them hope, and a feeling of purpose." He took her hand. "We are both trying to do the same thing. Carry on."

I have no idea what Marie Welt's batting average is, her percentage of accuracy, so to speak. But she has been wonderfully specific at times, both as to the nature of a predicted event and its timing. Once, when I was a newspaperman, she said that in two days I would receive a call to do a book, and this call would alter my career, taking me out of newspaper work.

"You are hardly giving yourself room for reasonable error," I smiled.

"Some things," she said, "I see as probable, and they may or may not happen, but others I know will happen."

It happened in two days, as she said, and in time turned out as foreseen.

Though now officiating at Manhattan's La Veranda Restaurant, for years Marie spread her good tidings at New York's Fifth Avenue Hotel, where she received the seekers and the curious. It was easy for her to separate the two, but she put each equally at ease.

"Sit down," she said cheerfully one night to a dark-haired young man who approached her uncertainly. "And let me tell you about yourself."

Her little searchlight played over the lines of his hand.

"You are interested in a young lady with the initial E."

A look of quickened interest came into the young man's eyes.

"This girl," Marie went on, "has a problem with her legs."

The young man nodded.

"You are right on both counts," said he, "the girl's name is Evelyn, and she has difficulty walking."

Continuing to peer into his hand, she saw the initials C and G, which turned out to be his own—Charles Gerber.

So far she had only told him what he knew—including a business affiliation selling advertising time on radio.

"I see you changing your job," she said, "and marrying E."

The young man left the cocktail lounge with a light heart.

She saw no more of him for weeks. Then one night, he returned with a lovely young girl, slim, of medium height, with light brown hair. She was on crutches.

This was Evelyn, and she, too, wanted a reading.

Marie made her comfortable.

"This is painless," she said, "relax."

The psychic smiled as she concentrated on Evelyn's hand.

"I have good news for you," she said. "You will walk one day, unaided. But I see a series of operations first, they will be successful."

She continued:

"I can see C and G in your hand, the initials of the man you will marry—Charles Gerber."

They left arm in arm, eyes shining, thanking Marie profusely, as though she were responsible for their happiness. She did not see them for months. Then, one night, they again came in together, but now Evelyn was using only one crutch in walking.

"I had surgery as you predicted," she cried, "and look what it has done."

Marie was as optimistic as ever. "You will have additional surgery, which will further correct your condition, and you will be married shortly to C and G."

Two months later they were back, and Evelyn was proudly wearing a ring on the third finger of her left hand. One more prediction had come through. They were now man and wife.

Evelyn had discarded her crutches, and was walking with two canes.

"You will eventually use only one cane," Marie Welt said, "then discard that one, and walk with barely a limp."

The bride looked at her hesitantly.

"Will I be able to have children?"

"Definitely," said Marie, accenting the positive as usual. "You may have a miscarriage or two, but you will finally have a healthy, normal baby."

Many months passed, and one day Marie received a baby announcement card, with no name or address, just a little blue ribbon attached. Whoever had sent the announcement through the mails had apparently figured she was psychic enough to know whose baby it was. And she was. For she knew instantly that the Gerbers had a bouncing baby boy, and mother and dad were doing fine.

The announcement, from out of town, revealed that still another prediction had come true. Gerber had changed jobs and was working in the Chicago area.

There was a postscript to this happy tale. One evening, Marie Welt looked up from her table and saw the Gerbers coming towards her.

Evelyn was walking vigorously without canes, with a hardly discernible limp.

They had come in to express their gratitude.

"Marie," said Evelyn, her eyes misting. "I owe you so much. You gave me the hope to go on."

As a "cold reader" Maya Perez was once in Marie Welt's category, able to turn on instantly. After I had written the book *The Door to the Future*, describing psychic Jeane Dixon's presidential assassination prediction, interviewer Long John Nebel had invited me to bring the Washington psychic onto his New York radio show.

"Jeane Dixon can't tune into anything on demand," I said. "Let me bring Maya Perez along, too."

As predicted, Mrs. Dixon could muster no predictions on the spot.

Long John turned a skeptical eye on Maya Perez.

"And what *don't* you predict?" he asked.

Maya didn't mince any words. She predicted for Long John himself.

"I see you changing to a bigger station within a year with three times the money."

"Nonsense," said he, "there's no bigger station, and I'm staying here."

Eight months later, he had moved to NBC's New York outlet, and there was no larger broadcaster than the National Broadcasting Co. The salary? Exactly three times what it had been.

Madam Perez' psyche was usually best with people she had no conscious knowledge of. She was at her best, I thought, when she wasn't even trying. Living in Balboa, California, she had consulted a chiropractor, Dr. John Evers, in neighboring Costa Mesa. As Evers touched her, she looked up and said, "You are a natural healer."

The chiropractor gave her a perfunctory thank-you.

As he pressed her shoulder, she added, "You were in a different profession once. You took care of the dead."

His hands stopped in their tracks.

"I was an embalmer for thirteen years," he said.

"You were also in the priesthood," she went on.

Evers smiled uncertainly.

"I studied for the priesthood for four years."

As he went back to his manipulations, his patient said casually, "Your mother is in this room with you. Her name was Collins, was it not?"

His jaw dropped.

"That was my mother's maiden name."

He drew back the least bit.

"Who are you?" he demanded.

She laughed, "I am a sensitive, a psychic, I communicated with you as you touched me."

Before the treatment was over, the sensitive had told Dr. Evers he was a fortunate man. "Everything you touch," she said, figuratively, "will turn to gold."

After this consultation, the chiropractor consulted with her. His questions concerned practical affairs. Once he inquired about a property he was considering buying with three associates, principally as a tax write-off.

"Buy it," she said, "you will make a great deal of money with it."

Evers got his group to go ahead with the project.

"We picked up about sixty acres in Oceanside, California, all oceanfront property," Evers said, "and sold it within six or seven months." He smiled fondly. "Because of Maya we made a profit of nearly a half a million dollars."

Like other creative people, psychics vary in the way they dial in their subconscious.

Bill Corrado, at thirty-two, is a psychic of the first magnitude, but as a Cancer, astrologically, with a chart dominated by water signs, he is highly impressionable, often taking on the subconscious desires of his subject.

Similarly, his subconscious is sometimes blocked when the subject is blocking subconsciously. Consequently, he can read some people more clearly than others, even tuning in through them into friends or relatives of theirs whom he could not read as well for directly, as in the case of a young Los Angeles couple, Patrick and Lorin Hurley, for whom he read separately. With Lorin, Corrado saw immediately the whole flow of her life. With Pat, the readings were spotty, inconclusive, the psychic feeling that Pat was unwittingly blocking. However, ironically, Hurley didn't block out his wife, who came in on a clear channel.

"He couldn't tell me much for myself," said the thirty-five-year-old Hurley, "except that I would in time leave my temporary bartending job, which I loathed."

But even before Corrado read for Lorin Hurley he had tuned into her problems via Pat.

"Your wife has a good deal of pain in the lower back," he told Pat Hurley. And so she had, presumably from a car accident that had involved her spine.

"Tell her to go to a gynecologist," he said, "she has an ovarian cyst." And so she did, giving her a sharp referral pain.

When Lorin had her reading she was affected spiritually as never before. "As a Catholic, I felt for the first time the closeness one should feel in the confessional. I felt I could say or think anything and he would understand and commiserate."

During that first reading, in May of 1968, Corrado was reassuringly candid.

"You are going through nine years of hell," he said. "But when this is past, beginning in 1971, everything will turn out as you want."

As he had already told her husband, Corrado urged Lorin to make an appointment with a gynecologist for a checkup.

"But it's my lower back that's been bothering me," she said. "I've been going to a chiropractor."

"Stop going," he said, "and that pain will disappear in a week."

When she took his advice, and the pain vanished, Lorin paid a visit to the gynecologist.

"He found the cyst where Bill said it was," she observed, "but he said it was innocuous."

Yet Corrado had told her she was going to require surgery in this area in a year and a half or two years at the most. As much as she respected Corrado, Lorin felt he was wrong this time, particularly after the clean bill of health from the gynecologist.

"I thought there was no way I would need surgery."

But Corrado had not only picked up the disorder that was to lead to surgery, but the attending pain, which he felt, sympathetically, in his own lower back.

Lorin herself didn't feel the pain for a year. Then she discovered she had a kidney stone. When they operated, the surgeons found what Corrado had guardedly warned about. The kidney stone had passed but the doctors came upon a malignant growth in the uterus.

A hysterectomy was performed in November of 1970. Corrado had encouraged Lorin to proceed with the surgery. "It is the end of your health problems," he told her. He was right again, the cancer had crystallized, and was contained.

Lorin now regarded Corrado as something of a demigod. She didn't dare make a move without him, a circumstance he discouraged, as he wanted her to run her own life.

"Twice a year is enough for a reading," he said, "enough for insight and direction."

With a few readings, nevertheless, Corrado had completely revitalized Lorin's life. Before she met Corrado, she kept to the house, seeing nobody but her husband, not having enough interest or energy to get out and do anything.

Corrado, at that first reading (her first trip out in weeks), told her some woman was going to offer her a job.

She was skeptical.

"I never leave the house or see anybody," she told her husband. "Where is this woman coming from?"

One day the phone rang. It was a friend asking her to manage a food shop in downtown Los Angeles.

She didn't take it, because she didn't drive, but it was added proof that Corrado was attuned to her affairs.

And so he became priest and psychiatrist combined. "I tell Bill everything. Things I wouldn't tell my husband—that's how much faith I have."

Born a Catholic, she had early left the Church. Corrado influenced her to go back to it, for the spiritual support she so obviously needed.

"I had put God down, I had put everybody else down. Everything was one big garbage pail. Consequently, my marriage was a garbage pail, unproductive and purposeless, even though Pat and I never had overt difficulties. But I wasn't contributing the way I should. I'd get up in the morning and go to bed at night, I never had any interest in anything. But this man with his pipeline to God made me believe that life was not just vegetating. I got interested in myself, in doing things. I started painting pictures, crafting with wood, knitting. I started thinking of Pat and his needs, and of other people's, instead of just sitting around feeling sorry for myself.

The change was gradual, but now she regards each day as a challenge.

"I find myself counseling friends as Bill did me. Not once did he preach. He would suggest, and let me find for myself that it worked. Like the business about the Church. He didn't press it, and so I got curious about how it would help, when it hadn't helped before. So I received Communion, and went to confession, for the first time in twenty years. It was different now, because I believed in God, and it had new meaning."

As vital as these changes were, they proved, moreover, that Corrado could find a clear channel in one person through which he tuned into the affairs of other people. From Lorin's testimonial it became apparent that Corrado worked best with people whose subconscious merged with his for an exciting jaunt into the Universal Mind.

In reading Lorin, the psychic saw that her husband would not get another job, despite a solid background in acting and real estate, until he left his bartending job on the Sunset Strip.

A week after Pat left the restaurant, he had his first job offer. And other predictions for Pat, in reading Lorin, began to turn out.

"Bill," said Lorin, "forecast by June 1971 a complete change for Pat, with his teaching real estate, and that is what he is doing." Corrado had also said that Pat would go to computer school in November of 1970, but she thought this unlikely. "No way, you don't realize how Pat hates computers."

But that November, not even aware of Corrado's prediction, Pat applied for computer instruction at the Automation Institute in Los Angeles. And on December 1, he started the course. Corrado was one day off.

On timing, which is usually difficult for psychics, operating outside our concepts of time and space, Corrado is invariably right on with Lorin. "If he tells me February," she observed, "it is February, and if he tells me August, it is August. He has never been off. If he says a year and a half, it's a year and a half."

Through Lorin, other messages came for relatives and friends. In May of 1970, the psychic foresaw a fire, with the injured, Lorin's mother-in-law, Mrs. Cecilia Hurley of the San Fernando Valley, and Lorin's nephew Craig, fourteen.

"Bill," said Lorin, "saw it happening the second week of July."

As the elder Mrs. Hurley had planned a bus trip with her grandson at that time, Lorin told her of the prediction and advised her to be careful.

The grandmother remembered the warning. As some children near her on the bus began playing with lighter fluid, she carefully slipped into her fur coat, and placed herself between her grandson and the other children. "Just as she did so," Lorin said, "a lighter can blew up and the boy playing with it was burned. The fluid sprayed all over my mother-in-law's arms and her coat caught fire. The flames were quickly put out. But if she hadn't had her coat on, her arms would have been burned badly."

But Craig had gone unharmed.

However, back home a few days later, Craig and two other boys were roasting marshmallows, when a marshmallow caught fire and lighted on Craig's arm. He was only slightly singed, but the forecast was fulfilled.

Corrado had a more serious warning for the mother-in-law—again through Lorin.

"I see a dark-skinned man with gray hair and a younger man bringing danger to your mother-in-law," he said. "Tell her to be careful."

The mother-in-law was working then for an optometrist in nearby Huntington Park.

"Two months later," Lorin said, "a couple of armed Mexicans held up the optometrist's office. One was a swarthy gray-haired man, the other about eighteen. They forced my mother-in-law and the doctor to lie on the floor, and held a gun to the back of her neck. They told the doctor if he didn't turn over the money they would blow her brains out. The kid kept saying, 'Let's kill them, let's kill them,' and the older man said, 'No, I'll tell you when to kill.'"

In the end, the bandits took their money, and went off. The warning may have helped the older woman to go along with the incident and not make a false move.

Just as a psychic may misinterpret his own impressions, so may a subject confuse what he or she is told.

Corrado picked up a health problem for a lawyer around Lorin, and asked if she had a lawyer.

"Yes," said Lorin, "Irving ——."

"Tell him to be careful," Corrado said, "I see a bad heart attack, he could die."

Lorin knew two other lawyers well, Kenny ——, who lived with Irving, and John Lane. The three lawyers were all quite close to each other and her.

But she felt she knew which one it was. "I called Irving and told him to please go to a doctor and have his heart checked."

Irving had no misgivings about his heart, and with some justification.

"But two weeks later," Lorin said, "Kenny called to tell me that John Lane had died on his way home from a basketball game, apparently of a heart attack."

3
The Guiding Light

In the delicate area of personal guidance, no counselor—psychiatrist, lawyer, clergyman, vocational guide—has the impact of the psychic consultant, for he combines the functions of all with a unique gift of his own—the ability to peer into a client's past, present, and future without asking a single question.

Who but a psychic could have foretold for businessman Mark Annau that he would suffer sharp financial reverses in 1964, that his parents would be on the sick list in 1965, that there would be danger to his person in 1967, that he would redeem himself financially, and that his ailing parents would come out from Montana in 1970 to be near him in California?

With these readings the Reverend Douglas Johnson braced Annau for events to come and made it possible for him to better handle good fortune and adversity.

"But Doug Johnson's greatest aid to me," Mark Annau decided, "has been in helping me to put up with day-to-day problems. When I become discouraged, he has a mar-

velous gift for calming one down, being such an un-
complicated person himself, when it comes to getting at
the heart of one's problems."

Before Annau was ready to accept Johnson's philosophic
offerings he had to be won over by the spiritualist's
psychic ability. "It was amazing," said Annau, "how he
would read things into my life and predict things in my
future and they would come true."

In 1963, when Annau gave up a hotel operation in San
Francisco, and took a job in the Los Angeles area, the
association began. He met Johnson in a casual way, so-
cially; otherwise, he probably would never have consulted
him. Like the majority of people, Annau found it hard
to reconcile the psychic to a rational frame of reference.
However, he was the type that pragmatically accepted
anything which proved itself. And that Johnson had certainly done with him.

"In 1964," he recalled, "shortly after I moved to Los
Angeles, Doug predicted a terrible money loss for me,
and much ado with lawyers. He didn't say why—just a
problem. It seemed impossible at the time. But an investment I had in San Francisco unexpectedly turned sour,
and it ended up in much litigation and cost me a lot of
money plus mental strain."

As this was Johnson's first effort, Annau was not prepared for the event, and consequently didn't profit psychologically.

In January of 1965, Johnson advised Annau to be on the
alert for the sudden illness of his parents. In May of 1965,
his mother and father were hospitalized after their car
overturned in an accident. Visually, Doug had seen them
in the hospital, accounting for his interpretation. But
where Annau was concerned, it was right on.

"In giving me a clue to the future," the businessman
said, "he braced me for disaster."

But Johnson had an even greater counseling weapon—
he held out hope when others took a pessimistic view.
After the auto accident, Annau's father suffered a stroke,
and the doctors ruled out a return to productive living.
Johnson ruled otherwise. He said the father, then living in
Great Falls, Montana, would in time come out to California and recover.

For a while, it looked as if the doctors knew better.
"My father was in the hospital for four years," Annau
said, "using up all his savings. Yet, when everything
looked blackest, when he was completely helpless, Doug
Johnson said he would get better out here in California.
The doctors disagreed."

Annau made one of the Johnson predictions materialize. He brought his parents out to Southern California in
November of 1970, finding a place and fixing it up for
them, after convincing his mother it was the right step.

But the second prediction is coming true irrespective of
him. "Dad's progress since they came out six months ago,"
said Annau, "has been ten times what it was in Montana. The hospitals are so impressed with what he has
been doing in the way of restored movement that they
are giving him full physical therapy to try and make
him a complete person again."

Speechless for years, his father is articulating once
again, though his speech is slurred. He is able to sit up
and watch television, and take a lively interest in the
activity around him.

"The doctors can't believe the progress he's made at
his age," Annau said.

Johnson remains more optimistic than anybody else.
The father is still chair-bound, but the psychic says he
will walk again. Others are not as sure.

"The doctors don't think there's enough muscle structure left after years of being bedridden," Annau said doubtfully.

As he spoke, Annau looked around the Hollywood bar which Johnson had predicted he would buy. "But who," he shrugged, "knows better than Johnson?"

There is a rational aspect to the Johnson therapy. "From the hope Doug gave me I got the strength to do what had to be done for my father."

Meanwhile, Annau was busy with his own life, most of it predicted by his counselor extraordinary.

After San Francisco, Annau joined a business firm in Los Angeles through the auspices of a friend. And so it came as a jolt when Johnson said this man was about to die. The prediction was made in May of 1965, and a month later the friend was dead. The death was cushioned by the prediction, which prepared Annau emotionally for the event, giving him time to consider his position.

Johnson saw Annau offered a job in Texas, but not taking it.

"I was offered a position in Houston, with the copy machine outfit I was working with in service management," Annau said. "But I turned it down."

Johnson next prepared his client for a transfer to the firm's home office in Chicago, but predicted he wouldn't stay. In five months Annau left the company and returned to Los Angeles, joining another copy machine company, Xerox. Johnson still saw changes. In eight months Annau went with Litton Industries, and was happy at last. But Johnson advised him not to get too set.

"With the recession," Annau said, "I lost the job—the first job I ever lost."

But it was all good experience for something else. Johnson saw him going into business for himself, and soon, with a friend, Annau began acquiring business properties, including the bar he now operates in Los Angeles.

Johnson's counseling extended to every area of life.

In January of 1966, the psychic cautioned Annau, who was traveling a lot, to be particularly careful in the next few weeks. The warning did not make him nervous, merely watchful, but, stored in the subconscious, it would come to the surface at the first sign of danger.

Four or five weeks later Annau was in a plane bound for Houston. The night was foggy, and the pilot, overshooting the runway, desperately yanked the big jet up to avoid a crash.

"Everybody on the plane was hurled to the floor," Annau recalled. "It was a terrifying experience."

Annau was only shaken up. For even in falling, his subconscious had prepared his body for danger.

Johnson's work has made a convert of Annau. "Like so many people," he said, "I couldn't accept something that I knew nothing about. But now I've done a complete turnaround. There's nothing occult about it really. It's down to earth.

"When I was having all these job problems, transfers, no job, Doug reassured me by always seeing another job around the corner. And he was always right."

As events occurred as predicted, Annau gradually got the idea there was an order in his life, and that he might as well accept it. "When I was having trouble with that lawsuit he had predicted, he told me it would be resolved, but it would take two years, so I should relax. As I am normally an anxious person, this tended to settle me down and make life tolerable."

A major result in the end was the evolution of the man himself. As he became aware of a larger order around him of which he seemed a part, material things lost some importance, particularly when one's actions seemed to have little to do with the ultimate result. "Observing Johnson changed my life style," Annau said. "Previously, I was very ambitious for the success I found so elusive. But it somehow doesn't seem to matter anymore. All that really matters is that we do our best, for others and ourselves. That's Doug Johnson's philosophy, and it's now mine."

Many of the people seeking out psychic consultants are shrewd professional people who are themselves paid for giving out advice. In a way, they are pioneers, helping to establish the practical use of the psychic.

"I'd stand on my head if I thought it would help," said Victor Dobrin, the well-known Los Angeles attorney. "I believe in being pragmatic."

Nevertheless, Dobrin might not have gone to Corrado if the psychic hadn't first gone to him about a legal matter. As the two men sat across from each other, Corrado nonchalantly crossed his legs, and said to the older man with hawklike features:

"You have two children going to Europe?"

Dobrin nodded in surprise.

"My son Jon Marc, seventeen, and Christine, nineteen, are interested in going to the American College in Paris. But I don't think Christine will qualify."

"Why not?" Corrado asked.

"Because the school requires a foreign language, and she doesn't have one."

Corrado shrugged slightly.

"They'll take both children."

The lawyer looked at him suspiciously.

"How do you know?"

Corrado didn't seem to hear the question.

"Around June first, your son will meet a girl with a name like Lisa. He will become so attached to her he may not want to go to Paris, but he will."

Dobrin began to look around nervously.

"How do you know all this?" he asked.

Corrado's blue eyes twinkled. "I'm a psychic."

Dobrin looked at him doubtfully. "You could still be wrong," he said.

"Just tell your daughter to apply for admission, immediately. She will be accepted."

The father passed on the advice. But even when Christine was accepted he wasn't particularly impressed, until his son Jon Marc, on June first, met not Lisa, but Elsa, and was loath to leave her for his European trip.

In consulting Corrado subsequently, curiosity was clearly one of Dobrin's motives. "I knew what a lawyer could do, or a doctor, an engineer, a judge, or a teacher. I didn't know what a psychic could do, but I knew enough to know it would be different."

And different it was. That first reading was so unusual that it became a memorable day in the lawyer's life. The attorney was fearful about his first visit to a psychic, as many people are, sometimes with justification.

"Tell me something good," he said.

Corrado shrugged. "I get what I see."

"Well, if you get something bad, forget it."

"You have another daughter," Corrado said, "and I see an operation for her."

"I don't want to hear about it," Dobrin said.

"It's just minor surgery for a female problem, nothing to get concerned about."

At that time, the daughter, Lynn, twenty-two, was living with her husband at an Air Force base in Southern California. She seemed in perfect health. "But a month later," Dobrin said, "she went to a doctor, and he said she required a minor operation. But Bill was right, she had her operation, and that was the end of it."

Corrado also predicted Lynn's divorce, though not right off.

"Shortly after the operation," Dobrin said, "Lynn's husband was transferred to a base in Alaska, and she went along with him. I thought they were getting along fine. But a few weeks later, in July, Corrado said Lynn would be leaving her husband in August, but wouldn't file for divorce until later."

On a Saturday morning, August 29, the lawyer was sitting in Pupi's, a Hollywood coffee shop, when he got a call. It was Lynn, wanting him to pick her up at Los Angeles airport.

At the airport, she blurted out tearfully, "I've left Tony, but I'm not going to divorce him right away."

Despite Corrado's prediction, the breakup had come as a surprise to the lawyer.

And this rather surprised me, since Dobrin now consulted Corrado regularly. But as a lawyer, Dobrin was typically skeptical of anything which wasn't backed up by prima facie evidence.

"He could be correct," the lawyer explained, "but if it's what you don't really expect, you don't give it much credence, particularly if it's something you don't want to hear. I buried his prediction away in my mind because I didn't think it would come to pass. And I remembered it only when she got on the telephone."

At this point, Dobrin was more concerned about his children than himself.

He had learned from Christine, then at school in Paris, that because of a chronic menstrual problem doctors wanted to perform exploratory surgery and perhaps a hysterectomy.

He called Corrado and the psychic discouraged surgery.

"Tell her not to be concerned, her period will occur within six weeks."

Dobrin relayed the information to his daughter. "Just sit tight," he wrote.

In four weeks she had her period.

In December 1970 Dobrin joined his children and traveled with them to Israel. Meanwhile, Christine's problem recurred, and they decided to go to the Sea of Galilee, where there were special baths for female complaints. "In order to take the baths," Dobrin said, "permission was needed from a supervising doctor. This doctor asked Christine all kinds of questions and suggested she go back to Paris and let them perform the operation. This she was reluctant to do."

Back in Los Angeles, Dobrin contacted Corrado, and was reassured. "Corrado said the problem would be straightened out if she would go to a chiropractor and start taking vitamin E immediately. He said it would take four to six weeks to clear up fully."

He passed on the information to Christine.

"Certainly, what Corrado was recommending was nowhere near as drastic as what the doctors prescribed and we could always come to that if Corrado's advice didn't work."

So Christine went to a chiropractor in Paris, and took vitamin E. "As a result," said Dobrin, "the period came as predicted, she lost weight, and is very pleased with herself."

Had Dobrin put any questions to the psychic for himself?

"You don't ask him questions. The first half hour he talks to you and tells you everything. He covers about every thought in your head."

The attorney had been to Corrado perhaps a half-dozen times, and telephoned frequently when something special was on his mind.

"Sometimes," he grinned, "I've sneaked in appointments by taking him out to dinner."

Had he used the psychic in his own legal practice?

"Well, I don't ask him how to conduct a case. I went to law school for that, and trained in the court of hard knocks, but I occasionally ask about the outcome of a case."

He cited a case. "I had a very substantial negligence action involving an old woman who was hit on a crosswalk. We were having difficulty trying to settle the case and as the woman was over seventy-five years old, I was concerned about her staying well long enough to reach a protracted trial date. As a matter of fact, the insurance company was stalling so they wouldn't have to settle the case."

Dobrin sought outside professional opinion as to the case's potential. "I went to Melvin Belli and Lou Ashe's law office and asked for an evaluation of the case. They said it was worth fifty thousand dollars."

After checking with his peers, the lawyer checked with Corrado.

"Corrado said I would get considerably more than that, and that I would have my settlement within a month."

And who was right?

"Two weeks after my discussion with Bill the case was settled—for seventy-one thousand five hundred."

Dobrin was more impressed than he cared to admit at the time.

"This resolution of the case, as foreshadowed by Bill, was truly remarkable. From a legal standpoint, they could have forced me to a trial which would have delayed any settlement for months, perhaps even years, what with the crowded court calendar."

And by that time he might have lost his elderly client.

Dobrin had come to rely on Corrado in his own life. At one point he was short on cash. Some old investments had turned sour, and he had loaned out a considerable amount of money which was slow coming back. One outstanding debt was for fifteen thousand dollars. Dobrin had been hoping to get this money back in time to help pay for his children's schooling abroad. However, the prospects weren't encouraging, as his debtor, an old friend, was constantly dissipating his income on the races.

"It looked hopeless," the attorney said, "but Bill Corrado didn't think so. He just looked off into space, and said, 'You are going to be paid back this money quite unexpectedly, as the result'—here even Corrado blinked—'of a horse race.'"

Dobrin's jaw dropped. For the man who owed him the fifteen thousand owned a racehorse which was running that week in San Francisco.

The attorney said nothing to his friend about Corrado's prediction, but his interest was additionally piqued when his friend told him that he was placing a large bet on his horse in the upcoming race. The odds were thirty to one against a victory at post time.

"The horse came in first," Dobrin recalled, "my friend made a killing, and I got my fifteen thousand, all in one fell swoop. That's predicting for you."

As a trial lawyer who had made rules of evidence his guiding star, Dobrin had tried to apply a similar yardstick of logic to measuring the psychic. It didn't wash.

"Philosophically," he observed, "there's a school of thought that says the logic you have is not necessarily the logic that is applicable to the event happening. In other words, you might have to use a new principle of logic, different from the cause-and-effect of ordinary living, to figure out your relationship to God and your own destiny pattern."

Corrado's foreshadowing of the future tended, for instance, to modify the attorney's feelings about free will.

"I am more or less committed to the destiny concept, since I can't find any logical way of talking myself out of the inevitability of events that can be effectively foreshadowed."

He didn't seem like a fatalist.

"In the process of everyday living, you have to take a dozen twists and turns whether you want to or not. You can never be sure which turn furthers destiny, as even the best psychic may be fallible. So we have to keep trying, as the twisting and turning may be the experience we are here for."

But those events Corrado saw correctly in their conclusion appeared unavoidable to him.

"Is it possible," I asked, "that you made a number of things happen yourself through Corrado's suggestion?"

"That," he said, "is a question worthy of a parapsychologist. Am I to believe that I could cure my daughter's menstrual problem through talking about it when the doctors couldn't help her? Or that I could influence that nag, lucky to finish a race before, to finish first, when I couldn't even talk like a horse?"

Even if a man does live his life to arrive at a fixed destiny, how then are psychics able to perceive this destiny?

Dobrin had wondered, too, about this. He had been impressed by a movie which seemed to offer a clue. "The analogy they used was that if you were able to reach a high enough point you could see the different phases of an event sprawled out before you, like a man walking, for instance, from point A to point B. You have a knowledge he is going to reach point B because that's the line he is walking in, and his progression appears to be inevitable. There is nothing in his way, no pitfalls, no stumbling blocks, and if there were, you would also see them, and so be able to bring them into focus."

"You're going against your own premise," I said, "trying to frame the psychic experience into a logical pattern without reference to unknown factors, which could very well supply the answer."

"I was just creating a hypothesis," he said, "an analogy. The psychic is actually on a higher mental level. If his mind power is sufficiently developed, then he is at a summit where he can see the whole panorama of events shaping the individual's destiny. And the higher his elevation, the more he sees."

An interesting concept, it recalled a clairvoyant reading that the late Edgar Cayce had given years before for a Hollywood producer working on a picture in London. The reading had been requested by Harry Goetz, then a Paramount executive, for the producer, who was suffering from a stomach disorder. At the time appointed for the reading, a foursome, including the late producer Leland Hayward, Goetz, and the subject of the reading sat around playing contract bridge in a suite in London's Savoy Hotel. Meanwhile, back in Virginia Beach, the Sleeping Prophet had nodded off to sleep in his effort to tune psychically into the subject.

"Cayce," Goetz said, "opened the reading by saying, 'A Good Hand.'"

Cayce's secretary, Gladys Davis, busily transcribing each word that came from the seer's mouth, thought that Cayce had made a reference to the subject's hand or palm.

Not until a copy of the reading was sent to Goetz, as the person requesting the reading, did it become apparent what Cayce was really referring to.

"At the very time Cayce was beginning the reading in his little room three thousand miles away," Goetz said, "my friend the producer had bid and made a grand slam in bridge—the perfect hand."

How then had Cayce seen this hand?

Had his spirit, his soul force, the ethereal entity that was the envelope of his physical body, made an astral projection through space, or had he, like a radio receiving set, somehow set his frequency at the precise vibration necessary to tune into that hotel room in London?

Like other professional counselors, psychic consultants frequently have difficult clients. But they are no problem to the well-balanced psychic.

"If there wasn't something wrong with some of them," observes Norfolk's Maude Robinson, "they wouldn't be coming to me."

One day, she opened the door and a woman of fifty stood framed in the doorway.

The visitor ran her eyes imperiously over the unprepossessing figure in an ordinary housedress.

"You don't look like you could tell me anything," she said at last.

"Do you have an appointment?" Maude asked.

"No, I read about you, and drove all the way from Massachusetts and now I'm sorry."

"Would you like to come in?" Maude said.

The woman shrugged. "I don't see what for, what can you tell me?"

"Why don't you try me?"

"All right, tell me something."

"You have been married three times, is that not right?"

"That's a good guess," the woman said grudgingly.

"And each time you married for money, but you didn't get any."

The woman's eyes sharpened. "What makes you say that?"

"Because you were divorced each time for the same reason—adultery."

The woman's eyes dropped.

"May I come in?" she said. "I do think you can tell me whatever I need to know."

Maude Robinson is a counselor extraordinary. She not only reads for the distressed and lonely, but befriends them as well, often invoking Scripture, usually a Psalm, to help tide them over the rough spots.

She has counseled thousands over sixty years, and she can recall even Edgar Cayce, near death in 1945, asking what she could foresee for him.

Maude Robinson had known Cayce only slightly, speaking to him as he talked to the flowers in his garden, encouraging them to grow, but she felt the mutual rapport of spiritually oriented psychics.

"Mr. Cayce," she said then, concealing her emotion, "I can't tell you anything you don't know for yourself."

And so Edgar Cayce recognized with a sigh the message this kindly woman had for him.

Despite advanced age, Mrs. Robinson has never turned down a request for help and her fee system would horrify any respectable accountant. She not only feeds many of her clients, but will take five dollars from one, and give it to the next.

She explains with a laugh, "That's one way of showing them that God is listening."

She has been called "the poor man's psychiatrist" because she listens so well.

But when she talks, it is to awaken that faith in God that she considers man's greatest resource.

Significantly, Maude's regulars stress how good she makes them feel, rather than the predictions she makes. Psychically, she analyzes the various relationships that are important to her clients, giving them new insight into the attitudes of people close to them.

When she first came to Maude, auditor Thelma Boykin had gone through a rocky marriage, was uncertain about her financial future, and felt she had made a mess of her life.

"My husband had just left and with it went everything I had in a material way. My children believed after I remarried that I did not love them any more. Consequently, they remembered only the bad things, not the affection I had shown them even after they had grown up."

In the very first reading, Thelma Boykin was struck by Maude's immediate grasp of her situation, including her remarriage to a man her children didn't care for.

"She told me that I had done the best I could for my children and that she would help bring them back to me. She explained that my daughter was very bitter over my second husband, but that in time she would understand and love me, as well as realize that she was wrong in condemning me for my seeking my own happiness.

"She told me to keep in touch with my son in Texas, even though I believed that he didn't care about me and that he would come to my Virginia Beach home, and tell me that he loved me, though I hadn't heard from him in years."

It really didn't matter, pragmatically, whether the psychic influenced the event, or merely foresaw it.

"In April of 1971," said Thelma Boykin, "my son arrived in Virginia Beach to visit me. I had not seen him for thirteen years."

Once more unmarried, she has also re-established a good relationship with her daughter, as the psychic had foreseen.

"My daughter is so close to me now that she will turn

down a date to be with me. She also has told me that I
have a home with her anytime I want to quit work, and
that any man she might marry would have to understand that 'Mama' will have to live with them.

"Of course I have no intentions of living with her, if she
marries, but it is heartening to know she cares for me
again."

Maude Robinson was clearly the catalyst that helped
bring this reunion about, telling her "people" to discard
false pride and take the first step. "The Lord," she says,
"despises a stubborn man."

The offer of love so often brings a like response.

"Christ," Maude tells the loveless, "rejected, scorned,
spat upon, held out his hand in love, to teach man that
his strength came in loving."

Thelma Boykin could have heard similar counsel in the
nearest pulpit. But what minister could describe the man
that would fill a woman's emotional void, predict when he
would arrive, and how the meeting would take place?

Maude had clearly proved herself with Thelma Boykin.

"Maude," Thelma said, "told me of a man that would
come to the Virginia Beach hotel where I was employed,
and said that he would love me very much and I would
love him. He arrived in 1966, as she said, and we went
together for three wonderful years."

Once a psychic has proved herself, the danger is not
that the subject will not believe, but that he will place
entirely too much reliance on the psychic. But Maude
Robinson is careful not to manage her people, merely
giving them sufficient confidence to draw on their own resources.

"I have gone to her with tears in my eyes," said Thelma,
"and I come out laughing. Because of her support I have
gone about my work as if nothing was bothering me,
and pretty soon it wasn't."

Even her success as the first woman auditor of the celebrated Cavalier Hotel in Virginia Beach, she attributed to her metaphysical mentor. She had been working in the hotel's accounting division when she was asked to take over the auditor's post. It was a big promotion, and called for great responsibilities.

"When the owner offered me the job," she said, "I told him it was too big for me."

The owner said he was impressed by her efficiency and diligence. He wanted her to reconsider.

Thelma asked for one hour to decide. "I called Maude immediately. She said that I could do the job, as it had never been done before, and she would stand behind me. That's all I had to hear."

And so Thelma Boykin accepted this new opportunity. "I worked long hours to learn the things I didn't know about the job, but they weren't tiring hours, for I felt that someone—the man who gave me this chance and Maude —cared."

Besides, Maude had never been wrong about the hotel. "Some time before, she had told me the hotel manager was going to die, and he was in the prime of life, and never sick. He died shortly after that. I also remembered that she had told me to look for an unexpected promotion, so I guess I was destined to make her prophecy come true."

In the area of usefulness, psychics put no ceiling on the scope of their work. Medium Anne Gehman of Orlando, Florida, is equally adept at solving crimes, finding missing persons, foreshadowing marriages and divorces, tuning into ailments, or predicting elections. It all comes out of the same universal bottle, says the lady who told the Canadian press that their bachelor Premier, Pierre Trudeau, would take a wife young enough to be his daughter.

Through a friend, I had met this pretty spiritualist
when she was a "spook-in-residence" in the spiritualist
community of Cassadaga, Florida. For this friend, Joan
Scott, a fashion model, she had foreseen the major de-
velopments in her life—the birth of a child, when Joan
felt she would never have another, divorce, business ven-
tures, and a drastic change of residence. "It made a believer out of me," said Miss Scott, who had a reputation
for not believing what she couldn't put in the bank.

Even the skeptical news media grudgingly acknowledged a prophet in their home country.

A reporter for the Orlando *Sentinel*, Jean Yothers, decided that Anne Gehman had X-ray eyes. How else could
she see so clearly into the minds and bodies of people
who came to her—not to mention those she didn't even see
in person?

Jean Yothers was enough of a reporter to pass her information on to her readers and let them judge for themselves:

"A Daytona Beach woman, being read by Anne, was
surprised when informed that she had a large mass in a
certain area of her body and was advised to see a doctor.
The woman took the advice, though she had been experiencing no discomfort. She was X-rayed and found to
have a massive tumor which required surgery. The
woman's physician was amazed at the medium's ability
and contacted her.

"They now have a close association, the physician
sometimes sending patients to her."

In the pursuit of missing persons, Anne Gehman ri-
valed the late Florence Sternfels (Florence Psychic),
often used by New York and New Jersey police to track
down missing people.

As the newswoman noted, Anne was helpfully precise:
"A distraught mother, questioning Anne as to the

whereabouts of her missing daughter, was directed to
the town and address where she could be found. 'And she
needs you desperately,' Miss Gehman added. The mother
took a bus to the out-of-state town mentioned. Her
daughter was at the address given. She was alone with a
tiny baby, deserted by her husband."

While Anne Gehman has a facility for doing various
things psychically at different times, there are psychics
who put it all together in one reading. With equal ease
Kay Carment of Virginia Beach, wife of a navy captain,
passes from a health reading into previous reincarnations,
and then into the future. It is all there in one package, if
that is what is wanted.

"She told me I was going to get a divorce," said
one brunette divorcée triumphantly, "and I got it."

For an equally attractive divorcée, she foresaw a new
boyfriend, which was not unusual, but also named him,
which was unusual, since the divorcée at that time knew
nobody by this name. She met him quite accidentally
weeks later, and almost jumped into his arms.

Kay is an extremely personable lady, and when she
told me that I was a writer in a past life, probably in the
Victorian period, I mumbled something about having
been told once I was the English poet Robert Browning.
She didn't seem impressed.

For my always flagging energy, she recommended
seven hundred units of vitamin E—doubling a medical
prescription—and a large dosage of vitamin A for my
eyes.

All this, she said, she saw psychically. And since she
had predicted so many romances and divorces correctly,
I went from her house directly to the drugstore.

As for my private life, what there was of it, she saw
me meeting a wondrous blue-eyed girl in latter 1971, and
marrying again during the first four months of 1972.

"You will travel all over the world with her," she said, "and she will be a real companion to you."

It was the pleasantest reading I had received in weeks, and I felt better for it, even if it didn't work out.

As an aficionado of psychics, I am ever aware of the guards they frequently put around themselves. Psychics, like psychiatrists, prefer to keep a gulf between themselves and their clients, maintaining a proper detachment. However, this is obviously difficult within the intimacy of the family circle or among close friends. And a psychic revelation, despite all precautions, sometimes creeps in.

At dinner one night, with psychic Bill Corrado, I noticed that he seemed unduly preoccupied.

"Anything wrong?" I inquired.

His normally bright blue eyes were dull and glazed.

"My stepfather," he said, "he's going to have a heart attack."

I had just met his stepfather, visiting from Cleveland, Ohio, and he had seemed in fine spirits.

"It's going to happen," Corrado said glumly, "two months after he's back home." And of course it did.

Another time, he saw an attempted suicide, the slashing of wrists, on the part of a relative, and he was morose for days—until it finally happened.

"Couldn't you have warned against it?" I asked.

He shrugged. "I really don't ever see anything unless it is going to happen."

"Then what good is it to know?"

He smiled grimly. "At least, I was able to prepare others in the family, and so the blow was softened." His dark brow knit in a frown. "And also they were a lot more compassionate, since they realized she couldn't really help herself."

These impressions presumably come to Corrado in not

closing himself off when not giving a reading. However, he is so close to his family he can't always resist tuning in.

One day, in June of 1971, as his brother Frank pulled up in the driveway, Bill got the distinct impression of an accident. The impression stayed with him, and he decided to speak to his brother about it.

"Please be careful," he said, "I see you ramming your car into the back end of another car."

Frank made a face. "Don't tell me those things," he said.

"I am just telling you so you will try to avoid it." Or, he might have added, be prepared for it.

A month later he again mentioned his foreboding to his brother. "It is getting closer," he said, "be careful."

In August, Friday the thirteenth, Frank cracked his car into the rear end of a parked car, and flew through the windshield. Bleeding profusely, he was taken to the hospital, treated, and released. The warning had not altered his destiny pattern.

In the beginning, Corrado was as remarkable with me as with most people. But as time progressed, he often seemed to see for me what I wanted rather than what was there. One night I mentioned that my brother was in intensive care in a New York hospital, and that I had negative feelings about his recovering and making it out to California to stay with me.

I asked, perhaps unfairly, what Corrado saw.

"I see him coming out here," he replied.

"You are picking up my wish."

"I don't think so," he said.

"That's the problem," I said. "You're thinking about it, and I have a feeling here." I pointed to my solar plexus, where I occasionally registered intuitive feelings.

"I'm afraid," I said, "he is not going to make it."

My brother passed away that night, and twenty-four hours later Corrado called. He had picked up what had happened.

"I guess you were right," he said.

"You were trying to be a friend," I said. "Thank you for that."

Spiritualist Doug Johnson, too, picks up impressions about people close to him. As a child he saw his own mother's death, and later pinpointed his father's death to the day. However, this information slipped in spontaneously, before he had learned to close off his subconscious.

Trying not to get too close to their subjects, many psychics discourage regular repeat sessions, not wanting to take over anybody else's life.

"How many things happen in the average life every month or so?" said Johnson. "There just isn't anything new to tell most people—and besides, the reading is chiefly designed to help them help themselves."

Unlike some colleagues, Marie Welt, the supper club psychic, doesn't bother with philosophic arguments trying to explain what she is doing. For Marie her gift is very much like that of others with a special facility. "One person has a flair for the piano or violin, another writes beautifully or invents things that make life easier. I happen to be psychic, because, I suppose, God wanted it that way."

She has developed a compassion for people, and her readings reflect a concern which, paradoxically, has an impersonal quality—essential in cutting off emotionally from a subject.

"When I look at a person's palm," she said, "I just forget who and what they are. It could be my own husband, and it wouldn't make any difference."

Oddly, her husband, Jack Welt, a former business executive, is a strong skeptic, even though Marie has read for him accurately a number of times. They had been married some time when she first read for him in June 1946. He was at loose ends after four years with the Marine Corps, and couldn't locate a job that suited him. Watching him prowl about the house, Marie decided that if she could help strangers, she could certainly help her own husband.

"Coming home from a night of readings, I found Jack very despondent and decided to read him. He agreed, though he wasn't very enthusiastic."

As usual, she took out her little searchlight and flashed it across the palm, better to read the lines and mounds, which are, in her case, predominately a psychic channel.

As she peered into his hand, her face lit up.

"Jack," she said, "within ten days you will hear from a man with the initials J.W., and he will have a job for you."

"But those are my initials," her husband replied doubtfully.

"They are also his initials," she said.

"And what's more," she went on, "I see you going to a place with the initial L, which will be instrumental in your getting this job."

Within three days, Jack Welt received a call from a friend telling him that Hunt Foods, in California, was hiring salesmen for the New York area. The friend gave Jack a number to call. It was the Hotel Lexington. The man interviewing job applicants was a Jules Womack.

As Marie had predicted, Jack was offered the job, and he took it. He stayed with the company fifteen years, in time becoming a field supervisor. Eventually, he left the company and began scouting around for another job. But he was now at an age where new jobs were scarce.

Marie decided it was time for another reading. "He was

getting a little edgy and I knew this would stop as soon as he got out of the house."

So she sat him down, reminding him how effective that first reading had been.

She frowned as she held his hand.

"You won't be hired for two months, Jack, so you might as well enjoy yourself for a while."

"Not for two months?" he growled.

She shrugged. "I can only see what's there. I can't make it happen. You'll have to be patient, Jack."

"So tell me about this big job, already."

"It's not a big job," she said, "but it will be a job you will like. You will be connected in some way with a governmental job, with"—she paused—"a New York City bureau or agency."

"Never," said Jack. "Not in a million years."

Not long after this session I met Jack. He was a pleasant-faced, middle-aged man who smoked cigars.

He was also, as I found out, an inspector for the New York City Department of Licenses—a job he enjoyed for the next five years.

4
Business as Unusual

"If they're so psychic, why aren't they rich?"

I have heard this hundreds of times, and the answer is obvious to anybody who knows anything about psychic affairs and the need for a higher motivation.

Yet, as a lark, I have seen the one and only Akashan, Hollywood's telephone psychic, hit four out of four races at California's Santa Anita track, including a horse, as I watched, who paid sixty-two dollars for a two-dollar ticket to place. However, I question whether he could do this regularly for profit. Otherwise, I am sure, he would have an easier time with his first-of-the-month bills. And I have seen other psychics, who wouldn't think of playing the market for themselves—psychics such as the spiritually oriented Marie Blieckers of New York—counsel their clients profitably from time to time. One client I know saved tens of thousands of dollars when Madam Blieckers, overruling his broker, frightened him out of the market in the spring of 1969, just before it fell off so precipitously.

A psychic can ordinarily do little for himself in a fi-

nancial way, since, as noted, the thought of gain clouds
the subconscious. But psychics have made fortunes for
others, and are consulted on a regular basis by businessmen, who often reap the fruits of this labor, without having the chivalry to acknowledge it.

For their clients psychics have spotted mines and oil
wells, found buried treasure, advised profitably on real
estate and other business transactions, counseled successfully on jobs and job opportunities.

Once, on a national television show, Bill Corrado was
asked how many oil strikes he had a part in.

"I hit nine wells out of nine," he said.

He has also located gold and silver mines, and a cache
of buried treasure.

At the same time he was doing all this he was having
trouble paying the mortgage on his home in the San
Fernando Valley, and was driving a used car that gave
no assurance of reaching its destination.

His standard fee is twenty dollars, but when the client
can't afford it, the readings are less or free. Since he
can only handle three or four readings a day, five days
a week, he is fortunate to clear two hundred dollars a
week, even when his clients are making thousands out of
him.

On one occasion he even predicted the precise number
of barrels that would be brought in daily from a well.
And for this he received his regular twenty dollars and a
bonus—lunch.

Unlike a geologist, Corrado doesn't have to stir out of
his house to find oil, nor does he have to see his client
in person. One time the entrepreneur picked up the phone
and called Corrado across the country.

Corrado saw a strike with two different amounts.

"He said," an associate recalled, "that this particular
well would have a capacity of thousands of barrels a day,

but for some reason only four hundred barrels a day would be taken out."

At the time the entrepreneur and his group had been drilling four to five weeks. Corrado said they would hit in four or five days. Three days later they had a gusher. But in that state, regardless of capacity, a well's output was limited to four hundred barrels a day.

In locating his first wells Corrado had amazed a businessman by scanning some geological maps and picking out the sections where he held oil leases—one in Southern California, another in Northern California.

After drilling began in the north, they asked the psychic to take a look at the south section.

A geologist was already on the ground when the psychic arrived. He watched curiously as Corrado briefly examined the terrain, pointing out where the fault lines were, on which side of the fault the oil was, and how deep they would have to drill—3,500 feet.

"What kind of a geologist is he?" the geologist inquired.

"He isn't," the entrepreneur replied.

"Then what is he?"

"A psychic."

The geologist's eyes bulged.

"That," he said, "is crazy."

Nevertheless, the well came in, as predicted.

In another venture, poring over some mining maps at home, Corrado predicted that his principal would hit a silver vein in two weeks. The strike occurred thirteen days later.

Not all of Corrado's wells were gushers.

In Wyoming, where he actually visited a field, Corrado had told the oilman that a certain well would yield but thirty-five barrels a day—hardly commercially productive.

"The output began at thirty-five barrels a day," Cor-

rado recalled. "Then it went down to ten, and then three.
I felt something was blocking the oil from coming out. So
they pulled out the pipe and probed around. They found
the pipe full of paraffin, keeping the oil from coming up."

The paraffin was burned out, but then the hole closed
up again, and the flow again diminished.

With Corrado now back in Los Angeles, the entrepreneur put through an emergency call.

"I told him," Corrado said, "that the hole was not big
enough—they would have to fracture it. But it was too
expensive a procedure for a potential of only thirty-five
barrels a day."

The entrepreneur was not entirely ungrateful. When a
copper or silver mine came through, or a gusher, he
helped Corrado with medical bills for his family, an oc-
casional mortgage payment, and even collaborated with
a Toronto banker, who also consulted Corrado, to permit
the psychic to buy a relatively new used car.

"He was very generous," Corrado decided.

Businessmen will generally hire a psychic consultant
only after he has read for them personally, convincing
them of his powers.

William Penn Patrick, the head of Holiday Magic, a
cosmetic firm, had his first psychic reading from Corrado,
and became a convert, hiring the psychic on the spot.

Corrado had not only tuned into Patrick's various problem situations, but, equally impressively, had turned to
the millionaire's chauffeur, and said, "That man's a relative
of yours, isn't he?"

The chauffeur was Patrick's brother-in-law.

Even when a business reading isn't scheduled, it sometimes comes through unexpectedly, as the psychic isn't
at all sure what will flash through his subconscious until
he concentrates on his client.

One distinguished lady had gone to Corrado out of

curiosity, and sat spellbound as the psychic discussed her
husband's bank back in the Middle West, an affiliation
which few of their California friends knew about. Even
more remarkably, the problem Corrado got into had not
yet been brought to the husband's attention, though it
was on its way to becoming a full-blown scandal.

Although the husband was a director of the bank, he
was a full-time diplomat and international lawyer, and
had left the management of the bank in what he thought
were capable hands.

"At this point," said the distinguished lady, who pre-
ferred to be anonymous, "there was no reason for us to
have any concern for the bank. Yet Corrado told me my
husband was going to have this associate off his back
soon, and we didn't even know then there was anybody
on his back. But two or three weeks later, the president
of our bank got himself—and the bank—into hot water."

When reports of misplaced funds confirmed Corrado's
reading, the harried husband, an unbeliever until then,
suggested that his wife go back for another reading. By
this time the bank affairs were so tangled that nobody,
leastwise the directors, knew where anything stood.

The second reading began with a business question.

"I asked Corrado how the bank problem was going to
come out," the wife said, "and he said there was going
to be a waiting period of a year before everything was
settled."

"Why," I asked, "would there be a waiting period in
the rehabilitation of a bank?"

A look of distaste clouded her elegant features.

"Because the president of the bank had drained the
bank of its assets. He had formed another company and
had used the bank's assets, borrowing money from the
government and other banks."

"He wasn't stealing, just borrowing?"

"His loans were enormous," she explained, "and loaned to friends with no collateral."

"What stopped the bank from going under?" I asked.

"The Federal Reserve," she replied, with a frown. "I think if the Federal Reserve hadn't stepped in, it would have gone under." But, as Corrado had said, it still took a year for the bank to get back on its own.

"Had Bill Corrado said there would be a change in bank administration?"

"I'm not sure. He did say this man would be gone." She sank back in a chair, and sighed.

The interview was over—or nearly so.

In what way, then, had Corrado been helpful?

"Actually, it helped my husband, because he didn't panic. I told him Bill had said that everything would be all right, and he was inclined to believe him because he had been so right in the first place."

Her husband had never been to a psychic. But he could hardly resist at this point.

His wife smiled faintly. "Yes, he went, and Bill told him practically what he had told me."

In the work Corrado performed in the business area, I have seen no abuse of his powers which could lead to the eventual loss of these powers. His only motivation, as in other matters, is to help the person who comes for help. And this has been his strength.

But in the long run, I wondered, even if a psychic didn't profit himself, wouldn't this emphasis on the material be detrimental to the presumably spiritual channel through which the information came?

Corrado himself doesn't think so.

"As long," he said, "as I am trying to help people, and they are trying to help others, I see no problem. If they are functioning out of greed, I don't think I could get anything for them. I would feel blocked."

With some business people he has a better rapport than others. He had a very good feeling, for instance, about the ruddy-faced man, with the sandy hair, who had come to him to find out about a union election.

It was no ordinary election, to be sure. With some 3,600 members, Local 683 of the Film Technicians Union in Hollywood was a very powerful unit in the IATSE (International Alliance of Theatrical and Stage Employees), and Corrado's visitor, Robert Robertson, president of that local, was in a struggle for control of this union.

"My concern," said Robertson, "is to give the union back to the members."

The union machine, controlled by a paid business agent, had been in power for twelve years. It appeared unlikely that any reform movement could derail this machine. A special election for business agent was coming up on October 17, 1970, with ten candidates, including the incumbent and Robertson, the principal challenger.

Corrado appeared to completely misread the situation.

"I see three men running for the job," he said.

Robertson thought he might be misinterpreting.

"Perhaps," he said, "there will be three leaders in the voting?"

Corrado shook his head.

"No," he said, "I see three running. Persevere and you will be successful, not only in being elected, but in strengthening the union, and putting the membership first."

Told there were ten men in the running, Corrado didn't alter his prediction.

"I see three candidates," he insisted, "and you shall win."

At this point, Robertson might have been forgiven for wondering what he was doing there.

However, he was impressed by the fact Corrado had picked out the name of his principal opponent. And then, as Corrado kept insisting he saw only three candidates, it occurred to Robertson that the psychic might be foreshadowing the regular election of officers, which was to follow the special election within a short time.

The main election, offering a general slate of officers, was scheduled for January 2, 1971, and whoever won as business agent in October would still have this additional challenge ten weeks later.

And this was exactly what happened.

With ten candidates, the vote spread was so thin that nobody could beat the incumbent—the machine candidate. He polled six hundred votes, Robertson was second with three hundred votes.

Robertson continued the campaign vigorously, remembering what Corrado had said. As the second election neared he consulted Corrado again, pointing out that his rival had twice as many votes as he in the previous balloting.

Corrado's opinion didn't change.

"You will win comfortably," he said.

"Will it be decisive?" Robertson asked, wanting a mandate that would make his job easier.

Corrado shook his head.

"No, but it will be sufficient."

"How about the rest of my slate?" Robertson asked.

"Most will be elected with you."

Robertson left, far more optimistic than when he had arrived.

Meanwhile, the new election seemed to line up as Corrado had foreseen.

There had been four candidates, not three, as the psychic had visualized. But Robertson had managed to eliminate one rival by offering him another spot on the slate.

And so then there were three.

The election was bitterly contested.

The incumbent maintained his original strength with 619 votes. But Robertson more than doubled his earlier tally, with 679 votes, a plurality of sixty, a comfortable 5 per cent margin. And he carried the slate with him— eight out of eleven officers.

Shortly after Robertson took over a business agent in April of 1971, I had lunch with him. The opposition was still so active that he was walking on eggshells.

"I have to give Corrado credit," he said, "but in the last analysis I had to evaluate everything that he said. So in the end the decisions were my own."

"Were you encouraged by what he told you?" I asked.

"To be perfectly frank, I was not only encouraged but influenced by his prediction. He inspired me with confidence, and this, to a certain extent, helped bring it about."

Had he any qualms about consulting a psychic?

He shook his head.

"Corrado came well recommended. Besides, many businessmen rely on intuition, and are psychic in this sense. There is an inner or guiding voice in all of us. We have to be made aware of it, and Corrado did that for me."

I was impressed by the thought he had given to his own role in the ultimate result.

"Your intuition then was part of the whole picture?"

He nodded. "I had an intuitive feeling about Corrado, and this was decisive in not only taking me to him, but in my accepting what he said."

Robertson was looking confidently to the future. He had

been elected to a two-year term and had some time to established himself and his administration.

"What will happen after that?" he had asked Corrado.

"After a slow start, due to your adversaries still working against you, you will gradually gain the confidence of the great majority," Corrado said. "And then with the membership realizing you are working in their behalf, you will win the next election decisively."

Many of those who habitually visit psychics are certainly prone to suggestion. But by and large, they represent a cross section of the population, which is no less impressionable than they are.

Tom Robbins, at twenty-one, was admittedly a material-minded young man interested in Number One. His ambition was to make a million dollars before he was thirty. He was all business, and business was his all. He was in jewelry, designing and manufacturing, with offices in New York and Los Angeles. Tom hadn't got his million yet, but he was on his way. He was sure of it because of what the medium Maria Moreno had told him, while visiting in New York. Tom had never before sought business advice from a psychic. Admittedly, it was against everything he thought about bending life to his will, and against his background. "I'm from a Philadelphia Jewish family which frowns on this type of thing."

So why did he look up Maria Moreno?

He was curious and a friend had said she had told her all kinds of personal things that nobody could have possibly known about.

The reading was an experience.

"One of Maria's guides, an oriental doctor, came through and gave me a health reading. The doctor—through Maria—gave me a thorough 'examination.' He said I'd had my adenoids out as a child, which I had, and had my skull X-rayed, which was done for braces. And that was all that was ever done to me, and he was right. He said I had excellent health, which would be hard to ruin, and I would live very long."

Maria had mentioned an uncle, and said correctly that he had had a heart attack, which he had concealed, as he felt it would threaten his job.

"Tell him to take vitamin E," she said.

This the uncle promptly did, after hearing from Tom how his secret heart attack had been revealed.

But all this was dross to Tom.

"How about business?" he asked. "There's a recession, and I'm hurting."

Maria Moreno switched to another guide, Pepe, a hunchback lawyer, and as Pepe emerged in her subconscious, her bodily form changed accordingly—her back becoming twisted—and the mood turned businesslike.

"You will be successful," she told Tom. "You will form a business dynasty, and visit the White House. You will be very wealthy and win international awards."

This was fine, thought Tom, beaming, but how about next month's rent check?

Oddly, what had impressed him most was her statement that he lived alone with a big black dog, whose name began with S. Tom's black Labrador was called Sam.

Pepe, unlike Clarita, Maria's permanent guide, and her various medical guides, was quite specific.

"Do you know a Mr. Green?" Maria asked for Pepe. Tom thought hard.

"If you don't know him, you will meet him soon," Maria went on, "and he will help you directly in a business way."

Ransacking his memory, Tom finally came up with a Mr. Green, an executive with Swank jewelry.

The next day he showed up fresh-eyed and bushy-tailed at the Swank offices.

"Mr. Green," he said, "I have just been to the psychic Maria Moreno, who said a Mr. Green would help me in my business—and you're the only Mr. Green I know."

Mr. Green smiled at the young man, amused perhaps by a new sales approach.

Tom had dramatically drawn out the story.

"What did he do?" I asked.

"He doubled the usual order," Tom said enthusiastically, "and made a prophet out of Maria Moreno."

There had been more predictions.

"She told me I would be in Jamaica in three days on a business trip. Nothing could have been farther from my mind. But an editor of *Vogue* magazine—their belt and handbag editor—called and said:

"'We're going to Jamaica,' she said, 'and change these buttons into earrings, can you go?'"

Tom was delighted.

"Four days after the reading, I wound up in Jamaica—I got the buttons and they made beautiful earrings, and it all worked out."

Maria had admittedly been a big help.

"Put it this way," Tom said. "I got a ten-thousand-dollar excess from Swank at a time I was in the dumps about business."

One order hardly seemed a career, but nothing could stop Tom. He was sold on his future, Maria having confirmed what he already thought himself.

"Maria Moreno," he said, "was the first medium I'd ever met who wasn't a fake. I've had these idiotic experiences where you pay somebody some money, and they pretend they're in communication with the other side. But with Maria, I really felt I was speaking to a spirit through her, and that the spirits were coming through to me. And the spirit told me things—zap, zap, zap—that Maria herself had no business knowing. No generalizations, no maybe, just one specific right after another."

To most people, a job is as important as any business. Consequently, this is a major area for psychics, even when the client has another reason for calling.

Helen Caron had to be prodded by a friend into her first session with psychometrist Doug Johnson. A registered nurse at the Kaiser Hospital in Fontana, California, she took a dim view of Johnson's reported healings, but finally made an appointment because of a marital problem.

"If ever a life needed changing, it was mine," Helen recalled. "I had been married twice to the same man, and he had our two older children. I didn't even know where they were. And I felt incapable of raising the one boy I had with me. I was completely negative."

Now, six years later, sitting with her, it was hard to believe this had been the case as she proudly watched her youngest boy, Ronnie, thirteen, playing on the beach.

"You certainly seem positive now," I said.

She smiled. "Doug Johnson got me thinking that maybe there was more to living than grousing about it."

In the beginning she had been anything but favorably impressed. "He picked up my watch," she said, "and told me I had to close doors on the past, that I wouldn't know happiness until I changed my attitude and lived for the present."

While his words didn't impress her, his sincerity did. So, subsequently, when a job problem presented itself, she called him for advice. She had applied for a transfer, from the hospital proper, where she was working nights, to the hospital emergency room, and had been told she would have to rotate shifts with two other nurses.

"The change meant a lot to me, but I couldn't take the

job if it meant rotating; my baby-sitter could only work nights."

But after speaking to Johnson on the telephone, she promptly regretted it.

"When I hung up I was about as mad as a hornet. None of it seemed possible. He not only told me that the rotating didn't apply to me, despite what the other nurses had said, but said my superiors would offer me a raise."

That night, at the hospital, she told another nurse what the psychic had said, and the two were laughing about it when the clinic supervisor walked in.

"Are you Caron?" she asked brusquely.

Helen Caron nodded.

"Why," the other continued, "all this fussing about this job?"

"I just can't rotate with the others," Nurse Caron said.

"Well, who said you had to? We need one nurse steady, and that's you."

And then, as Helen Caron's jaw dropped, the supervisor added:

"And if it's of any interest, you will be getting more money with this job."

Helen Caron was now a convert. The new job was hardly as important as believing in the rest of Doug Johnson's message—that with hope and prayer, and some positive thinking, one could climb out of the doldrums.

"Doug made me realize that my responsibility was to do the best I could where I was, to show the boy I had with me that he was loved."

Johnson even worked successfully with the boy. He had learning problems at school, even though he had an unusually high IQ. But with special attention, supervised by the psychic, this problem diminished, along with teacher complaints.

In some respects, Johnson is better than any vocational

guidance counselor. For one thing, he doesn't have to see the person he is counseling. At the request of Joe, a hospital orderly confused about his career, Helen Caron had agreed to ask Johnson what he saw for him.

Told that Johnson often got his psychic vibrations by tuning into personal objects, Joe gave the nurse a pair of scissors. Helen kept the scissors overnight, agreeing to take them with her for her appointment the next day.

"Joe was so keyed up about going to medical school in South America that I couldn't refuse him, even though I had tried to talk him out of studying there. I had known him for five years, as an orderly and a pre-med student, and I knew he couldn't be budged once he made up his mind."

But in the morning, as she drove to her appointment, Helen forgot the scissors.

After her own reading, however, she told Doug Johnson about Joe, pointed out that she had carried his scissors around for hours, and wondered if Johnson could pick up any lingering vibrations.

The psychic smiled. "I'll give it a try."

"Doug had never seen Joe," Helen recalled, "and didn't know anything about him. But he immediately told me how stubborn he was. He asked if he was a Virgo, which he was, and said his biggest problem would be his stubbornness, which I felt was the case."

She asked if Johnson saw Joe studying in South America.

"I don't see him leaving his present area, and he would be handicapped if he went through with his plans, since he doesn't speak Spanish."

On her return Helen was tempted to tell Joe that a diagnosis of acute stubbornness had been confirmed, but dismissed this as negative.

"You are not going to South America to study medi-cine," was all she said.

Joe smiled unexpectedly. "My wife and I were just dis-cussing today that maybe I should go closer by, like Loma Linda."

In some instances, Johnson handles the job problem from the wings. Beverly De Crescent had become dis-contented with her secretarial job one August, and had sent out résumés to major firms in her Ontario, California, area. Her qualifications were excellent, and she expected an immediate response.

She was disconcerted when Johnson saw no immediate change for her. And even more disconcerted when he appeared to be right. For months she checked with him by phone. "Towards the end of the following January," she said, "he started saying that a job change would be coming up."

In February, she received a telegram from a company executive asking her to call the personnel manager for an appointment for a certain day, as the interviewer would only be available that day. But Beverly's boss was leaving town that day and she was too busy to take time off. She phoned, explaining why she couldn't go for an interview.

In her dilemma, she also phoned Johnson.

"Relax," he said, "you will get the job anyway."

She didn't believe him. But the next day the personnel manager called back and said the interviewer was im-pressed by her sense of responsibility. They would see her at her convenience.

The subsequent interview was satisfactory, and she was offered the job, but the personnel manager balked at the salary she was asking.

Wanting the job, she was tempted to accept the lesser salary. But Doug Johnson insisted she would get what she wanted and so she held out.

"Several days later," she recalled, "the personnel manager called me again and said that they had had a special meeting of the Salary Review Board and decided they would meet the salary."

It did seem the company was going to a lot of trouble for a secretary. But there was a reason, as Beverly learned on the job.

"The company made this special effort because they had just commenced an Air Force contract and the position was secretary to the Air Force liaison officer. It was he who insisted they hire me."

Johnson had also predicted she would like her new boss. At first she had difficulty adjusting to his style of doing things, and wondered whether she—and Johnson —had made a mistake. "But eventually he became one of my favorite people. And though he is no longer in the Air Force, we still communicate frequently."

Beverly liked her new job, and was grateful to Johnson for encouraging her. But as before, she was dubious when, eight months later, he saw her changing jobs.

"I have no intention of leaving," she said.

Doug had this reassuring word. "You will not be leaving the company, but working for a different department."

He saw the change as imminent.

And so she was prepared when it happened.

"Within a couple of weeks," Beverly said, "our office was notified that I would have to be replaced by a Civil Service secretary. But, as Doug said, I continued with the same company in a different capacity."

Through sessions with psychics who have encouraged them in their endeavors, many businessmen have become architects of their own success.

When Mario Pacini, a paint and art supply dealer of Newport Beach, California, met the sensitive Maya Perez, he was thoroughly demoralized. He had recently gone through a severe financial crisis. He had not only lost his lifetime savings, but had been cheated in an oil deal by a man he had trusted. "He took the last money I had," he said, "and flew the coop."

Though Pacini had retired with a comfortable sum when he first moved to California, he was now forced back into business to satisfy his creditors and support his family.

"I could have filed for bankruptcy," he said, "but I wanted to sleep at night."

Pacini seemed a practical man to me, of medium build, sharp eyes, and an incisive way of talking. I was surprised he could have been taken in so easily.

"This man," he explained, "rented one of my apartments, and was a minister of sorts. He was always talking about people helping one another. And I believed him."

He was about ready to give up on the human race—and himself—when he met Maya Perez. By telling him a few things that came true, she got his faith moving in the right direction.

"She got me to praying to help my business improve, and constantly talked about the turn in the road."

It was good psychology, but why should Mario Pacini believe her, when his trust in somebody else had just been so badly misplaced?

Mario Pacini smiled indulgently.

"She proved herself."

And how was that?"

"She pinpointed a number of things she couldn't have consciously known about. She described my mother and my sisters who are back East, and my sisters had never been West. She said my oldest sister was having a heart problem, and a couple of months later, we got a letter about her heart trouble."

All this had nothing directly to do with business, but it did make Pacini responsive when she urged him to pray for success, a course which simultaneously freed him of debilitating rancors.

Even more influential were her predictions. Three years ago, when he was a distributor for a paint company, she predicted that he would be in the paint manufacturing business. This was hard to believe, as there seemed no rhyme or reason to it. But today he is manufacturing paint and thriving at it.

"I represented this eastern firm for nine years," he explained, "and they had promised they would never have another distributor in my area. But they sent out two more distributors and these fellows reaped the harvest of my years of labor."

Mario Pacini reacted with all the fire and fury of his Latin heritage. "I decided then and there to have my own company. I copyrighted my own labels, manufactured my own paint, and now I'm competing successfully with those people—just as Maya Perez said I would."

She had also told him he was going to be an inventor, which seemed far out, even though he had gone to an engineering college for a while and had a penchant for the mechanical.

And now, as unlikely as it seemed, he has invented a number of things—one, a novel lighting system for Christmas trees.

After his Christmas light was registered in the patent office, he came up with a disposable ashtray for airplanes.

"We were negotiating," Pacini said, "when the recession hit the airlines, and they pulled in their belts."

Maya Perez has told Pacini that both inventions will be produced commercially, and so he is confidently looking to the future.

Undoubtedly, Pacini had been influenced by the psychic's predictions, but nevertheless the inventions materialized because they were in his future, not because she had encouraged them. Similarly, other psychics have tuned in on inventions without ever having met the inventor.

An elderly Inglewood, California, man, for instance, had invented a convenient folding cabinet for mobile homes, trailers, airplanes. Repeatedly, he seemed on the verge of selling his invention, Japanese manufacturers being particularly interested. But at the last minute, something always happened to spoil the deal. He was thoroughly discouraged, but a psychic would have been the last person he would have gone to for advice.

However, his wife, unknown to her husband, consulted a psychic, Florence Davis of Inglewood. Mrs. Davis immediately visualized the invention, though she had not even been asked about it, and then said almost apologetically:

"I don't like to mention this, but I have to tell the good with the bad. Your husband's cabinet will be sold, but nothing concrete will materialize until after his death, and it will then mean lifelong security for you."

It must have been a blow for the pleasant-faced elderly lady who had been married for forty-five years to the same man. But she reacted philosophically, and was still philosophical as we discussed it together. "My husband hasn't been feeling well for five years. But when Mrs. Davis told me that he had had several heart attacks, I told her that I'd been married to him nearly forty-six years, and knew he'd never had a heart attack. But after that he had a complete physical, with X-rays and fluoroscopes and all, and they confirmed the heart attacks."

And what was the psychic's prognosis?

She sighed unhappily.

"Florence said he would have one attack that would finally take him off."

Well, at least the invention would be there to console her.

She smiled enigmatically.

"Oh, there may be more than that. Mrs. Davis said I had a beautiful life ahead of me and I would get married again."

She flushed under my gaze. "He is a good man, difficult at times, but still a good man, and I care for him, though he has been grumpier than ever lately." But death was as inexorable as taxes, and hadn't the Master said, let the dead bury the dead, and the living get on with life?

"I really don't believe it," the woman said, "but Mrs. Davis did describe the man coming into my life. He would be a kind man, and good to my grandson, who is seventeen, and presently living with me.

She frowned. "This made me feel that it wouldn't be too far off."

Though the good lady put no restriction on me, I decided not to use her name. Her husband might possibly read about himself and have a last heart attack or apoplexy.

For moral support, generally, no psychic can exceed that incurable optimist Marie Welt. And since some sunshine sifts through the dark clouds in nearly every life, this unique psychic is invariably able to tell anybody something good about his career. She once told doubting singer Robert Goulet that he would be doing a show with his wife, Carol Lawrence. A few months later, they were co-starring in a summer theatre production of *I Do, I Do,* in Westbury, Long Island.

Time after time, she gives new evidence of her accuracy in defining an individual's career. One evening, two women Marie had never seen before came into her supper club for a reading.

One was a short, sweet-looking woman, the other a tall redhead.

Marie read the short woman first. "As I took her hand," she said, "I immediately saw she was a very talented person, very artistic."

The woman acknowledged that she was a painter. Marie then picked out the initials N and L in her hand. She was the well-known artist Naomi Lorne.

"I told her," Marie said, "that she would sell a painting to an important politician with the initial R, and one to a big movie star with the initial G."

She then read for the taller woman. She picked out the initials G and E in her palm, standing for the woman herself, Gertrude Eisler. She found her rather depressed, because she had just left her position, but she was able to offer some cheer.

"This very week," said this optimistic psychic, "you will be offered a position with a very important attorney with the initials L and N."

Neither woman knew what to make of it. Marie was certainly pleasant, and they felt better for being told nice agreeable things, but what did it have to do with reality?

Several days passed, and Marie Welt received a telephone call from Gertrude Eisler. She had been offered, and had accepted, a position with a celebrated attorney, author of the best-selling *My Life in Court*—Louis Nizer.

About a month later there was a second call, from Naomi Lorne. She was thrilled and excited. She had sold one painting to an important (R) politician, Governor Rockefeller of New York, and another to a big (G) movie star, Cary Grant of London and Hollywood.

5
Affairs of the Heart

After the astrology class at Carroll Righter's, we were sitting in Schwab's Hollywood drugstore, and the attractive English girl was teasing Bill Corrado about the marriage prediction he had made for her.

"When, oh when, sweet William?" laughed Evelyn Sharpe.

"Pretty soon," the psychic said.

"How soon?"

"Two months or so, maybe less."

Evelyn rolled her eyes dramatically.

"But where shall I meet this paragon?"

Corrado waved an arm casually. "Not far from here, I can almost smell it, it's so close."

"Smell it, is right," the English girl said. "How could anybody meet anybody worthwhile in this area?"

Corrado smiled. "But you will, and it will take care of everything."

"All right, Bill," she said, "if you say so."

I knew nothing of what they were talking about, having just met Evelyn Sharpe that evening.

She was not averse to giving me a fill-in.

"After my divorce, I went to Bill for a psychic reading several months ago, and he told me I would marry again, and he described the man. He would be over six feet tall, black curly hair, thirty-five or thirty-six years old. He would be in business with two other men, and he would have been married before, and have a little girl about five years old."

After being told all this, Evelyn, a jobless singer, asked a very practical question:

"Will this man be able to take care of me and my two children?"

"Very, very well, and he will enjoy doing it."

Evelyn Sharpe smiled happily, and I thought to myself that even if wrong, Corrado had given her one good evening.

She may have picked up my thought, for she said quickly, "Bill has been very good with me. Even before he met me, he picked me up psychically when he was reading for my voice coach. She knew nothing about my plans but Bill said I would be back in Los Angeles from London on March 31, 1969. So she was expecting me on that day and all the time I thought I would surprise her by dropping in."

I wondered how Corrado had even known she existed.

"The voice teacher had known my marriage was on the rocks, and was worried about me. This was during the previous September. As I found out later Bill told her that I would have been already back but was delayed by major surgery in the lower abdomen."

The teacher's first question had concerned that operation.

"Yes," said Evelyn, "I had a hysterectomy. Who wrote you about it?"

"Nobody," the teacher said, and told her English pupil about the remarkable psychic who had revealed all this.

Evelyn couldn't rest, of course, until she met the psychic who seemed to know so much about her. She wangled an appointment with him for two weeks later, not mentioning who she was.

She felt an immediate rapport with Corrado, and he responded in kind. Not consciously identifying her as the English girl he had already picked up on, having never heard her name, he still found that she was a singer, that she had had a difficult operation, that she was having a problem getting over her former husband.

"Let go of the past," he told her, "for you will meet another man who will be the love of your life."

Evelyn felt he was dead wrong at the time, as she thought she would never feel anything like love again.

But Corrado was obviously in tune with her, for a short time thereafter she happened to pass him in her car, and stopped to talk. He looked at the car curiously, and said, "Be sure you keep it locked."

Soon after that, somebody placed two fire bombs in her parked car (which was unlocked), and totally destroyed it.

He saw her again in October of 1969, and realized immediately that she was so depressed that she was contemplating taking her own life. Her career was at a standstill, and she just couldn't seem to pull herself together.

He spoke encouragingly, insisting that he saw a rich, full life ahead for her.

"You just have to get through this time of learning."

Evelyn was sure then, looking back, that the only thing that stood between her and suicide was the slim hope that Corrado might be right.

We were at Schwab's in April of 1970, and by Corrado's reading, Evelyn's knight in shining armor was to make himself known by June.

A month passed without event and Evelyn put the prediction out of her mind, thinking that Corrado had taken this means of buoying up her sagging spirits. On a Sunday, May 10, she had gathered up her two boys, Sandy, eight, and Danny, nine, and was taking them to an ice show, with tickets provided by a friend, comedian Marty Ingels. The children wanted to stop by at a place known as Kiddie-land en route to the Ice Capades, but Evelyn had at first demurred.

"I really didn't think I could afford to take them to Kiddie-land. Then, I thought, well, Marty paid for the tickets, so I'll take them for a few minutes."

And so unexpectedly she found herself in Kiddie-land with her two boys.

Soon the boys were having the time of their lives, getting into everything as quickly as they could. There was no way of keeping up with them as they scurried from one attraction to another.

"My kids," she recalled, "were trying to get into a helicopter, and there was this little girl also going for it. Of course, they got into it because they were bigger than she was. So this big fellow in a white sweater and white trousers and tennis shoes comes rushing over protectively. Then he noticed me standing there, trying to ride herd on the boys, and said:

"'Are these your boys?'

"I said, 'Yes, they are.'

"He was about to say, 'Then why don't you control them? That's my daughter they're pushing.' But his attitude suddenly changed as he looked at me.

"Instead, he said mildly, "That's my little girl with your boys.'"

They talked as the children played, he asked what she did, and she told him that she was a singer-actress, not working at the moment.

As she looked at him, captivated by his charm, humor, and intelligence, she told herself, "My God, can this be the one?" His name was Philip Belous. He was well over six feet tall, his hair was dark and curly, and he operated a clinic with two other men, his physician father and a friend.

She recalled what Corrado had said about the man being thirty-five or thirty-six.

She looked at him appraisingly, then asked suddenly: "How old are you?"

He laughed, it was such an odd question.

"Thirty-five, but I will be thirty-six next month."

He was a Gemini, and she had always loved Geminis. "And your daughter?"

He was amused. "She'll be five next month."

So there it was, right down to the last detail.

Evelyn could hardly contain herself. "I couldn't tell him, you know, that we were going to be married and everything was going to be roses, but I couldn't resist saying, 'You know, I was told I was going to meet you.'"

He laughed when she told him it was a psychic prediction. He didn't believe in such nonsense. He was a very practical man, and knew better.

At any rate, he asked for her phone number, and she gave it to him. He called the next day, and they met for a drink that consumed three hours—until he had to leave, reluctantly, for a business appoinment.

The courtship continued apace. He was strong yet kind, big but gentle. "I was absolutely enthralled with him," she said. "He had qualities I had never found in anyone before."

He was good not only with her but with her children.

She soon forgot her former husband, and plunged into a new close relationship. She was happy for the first time in years.

Two months after they met, they were married in Mexico. Bill Corrado was one of the first to be told about it.

"It was almost," she smiled, "as if he were the best man."

After her marriage, Evelyn took a handsome apartment in Beverly Hills, and gave every appearance of being the perfect suburban housewife. She was grateful to Corrado for giving her the hope to go on when she was in despair, and was virtually bubbling over when I called on her.

"Do you remember," she said, "that evening at Schwab's, with Bill saying that the man was so close by that he could almost smell it happening?"

I nodded.

"Well, Phil, my husband, was born on Laurel Avenue, just around the corner from Schwab's, and his parents still live there."

And Kiddie-land, where it all began, was very close by.

Evelyn wanted me to meet her husband, and he was everything she had said—big, good-looking, intelligent in a practical way. By now, he was familiar with the Corrado marriage prediction, and he found it interesting, particularly since it did seem to have changed the course of his life, too.

But he looked at me earnestly, and there was no questioning his sincerity as he asked:

"Do you really think that people can predict the future?"

Only a direct experience, it seems, is capable of converting skeptics to a belief in the psychic. On the other hand, there are some who believe too ardently, the psychic buffs who go from one psychic to another, generally out of loneliness, hoping against hope that if one psychic doesn't bring some prospect of romance into their lives that another will.

"Three different psychics told me I would meet my new husband in December," a divorcée told me confidently.

"They didn't say what December," I responded, as she gave me a dark look.

Responding to need, there is hardly an area in the sexual spectrum that psychic consultants do not get into. They are constantly asked how long a marriage will continue, whether the partner is faithful, and even the prospects of an extramarital romance or widowhood.

Some of these inquiries are often cloaked in concern. "I am so worried about my poor husband," said one wife. "I just don't think he will last out the year."

"Don't worry your head about it," the psychic replied, tuning in on her secret desire. "He'll be around a long time."

Often, the need has only to be in the client's subconscious for the psychic to tune in.

When she made an appointment with psychic Irene Hughes in Chicago, Fran Sanders, an Encino, California, clothes designer, thought it might be entertaining. She sat quietly, with a watch-and-wait attitude, waiting for the psychic to perform.

The reading didn't get off as she had anticipated.

"Your husband," Irene said, "is having problems with his job and almost had a nervous breakdown in December of 1967. Were you aware of this?"

This was now January of 1968, and so it would seem that Fran Sanders should have known about it if it were true.

"No," she said, "I wasn't aware of any such problems."

"Were you aware," Irene said, "that there was another woman in your husband's life?"

Mrs. Sanders' eyes fell.

"This woman," Irene Hughes went on, "is redheaded and has two children."

Fran Sanders gulped.

"I know of such a woman."

"You have nothing to worry about," the psychic said. "He will never marry her."

The designer bridled. "I have been married to him," she said, "for nineteen years."

Irene Hughes gave her a gentle smile. "Don't be too hard on him," she said, "because before the year is over you will be having a romance with someone, in October to be exact."

"I wouldn't dream of anything like that," Fran Sanders said.

Irene Hughes smiled as if she had heard remarks like this before. "By the way," she said, "if you have any money in the stock market, get out before the middle of nineteen sixty-nine."

The sitting left the California woman rather confused, particularly since she couldn't consciously conceive of an extramarital relationship. Actually, the only thing the psychic had said that she knew to be accurate was that her husband was interested in somebody else, and that, she thought cynically, could be said about any man who had been married for a number of years. What if she *had* described the woman and mentioned her children? That could be pure coincidence. She put the reading out of her mind.

But that fall, back in California, she developed an allergy, and went to an allergist. He was friendly, warm, interested, and before she knew it, the association had gone beyond professional bounds, and that October she was very definitely involved in a close personal relationship.

The relationship ended as quickly as it had begun.

"One day he didn't show up," Fran said. "And I learned later that he had a heart attack."

One year after that first reading, in January of 1969, the designer again looked up Irene Hughes in Chicago.

As she walked through the door birdlike Irene Hughes greeted her with a wan smile.

"You're no longer married, are you?"

The designer shook her head. "Yes, I am."

"Well," the psychic said, "you won't be married by September of this year."

After twenty years of marriage, Fran Sanders had decided there wasn't much point in breaking things up, so the prediction only amused her.

She was also told that her own business was good and would expand, and she was again reminded about a stock market slump.

Again, she received the psychic's advice with a grain of salt.

But that September, she impulsively walked out on her marriage and began arrangements for a divorce. The marriage that would never end was finished. Skeptics might say she was influenced by the psychic, but Fran Sanders made her decisions her own way in her own time.

"I didn't even pull out of the market like she said," she observed wryly, "and I lost nearly everything."

Irene Hughes was able to pick up problems involving Fran Sanders' friends, problems that Fran didn't even know about, making one wonder whether friendship, too, isn't a matter of like-minded people being on the same psychic frequency.

On that last visit in 1969, as Fran started to walk out

the door, Irene Hughes stopped her. "There's a girl who could be your daughter, with long, dark hair, between nineteen and twenty-one, who is pregnant right now. She will have either an abortion or a miscarriage."

All the way back on the plane, Fran racked her head as to who this could be. She finally decided that she didn't know anybody who fitted this description. When she finally landed at Los Angeles International Airport, her girl friend of many years was waiting to pick her up. As they collected the bags, and went for coffee, she noticed her friend had been crying.

"What is wrong?" she asked.

The friend started crying again. "My daughter is pregnant, and I'm taking her away tomorrow for an abortion."

Fran Sanders was shocked. She had known the daughter from birth. She was twenty, lovely, with long black hair, as Irene Hughes had seen. It was clearly incredible.

Almost without exception, people with emotional problems, particularly the sophisticated, have run the gamut of advisers, personal and professional, before they turn to the psychic. But once exposed, they are invariably hooked, and for what they consider very substantial reasons.

"If a psychic can describe the person I am going with," a young lady pointed out, "tell me how I met him, and how I feel about him, I am ready to accept what that psychic has to say about the relationship."

Nevertheless, I wondered why so worldly a figure as John Newland, the distinguished television director of One Step Beyond, had consulted a psychic about his marriage, when he had access to the best professional counselors.

Despite its delicacy, Newland was ready to discuss his

situation, as he felt it was a landmark in a psychic resolution of a complex marital problem.

The Newlands had seemed the ideally married couple, but of course nobody but the wearer knows where the shoe pinches. Newland was fiftyish, silver-haired, handsome, and successful. His wife was charming, attractive, gracious, with a keen humor. It was a pleasure being with them. Therefore, when I heard they were consulting psychic Bill Corrado about their problems, I was rather dismayed.

Eventually, I heard they had separated, and one day John called, and after we had talked briefly about other matters, I asked if Corrado had been of any help in his personal situation.

"Vastly," he said.

And so one morning, at my urging, he came out and we sat looking at the ocean. He spoke nervously, incisively, as if he were a lecturer addressing his class; he was obviously determined that I realize what a vexing problem it was, and how consummately Corrado had handled it.

"I went to Corrado originally," he said, "because my wife had been to him. She got a lot of philosophical things from him. When she related them to me they seemed a bit ambiguous and I had a feeling he was trying to tell her something about our relationship, hoping that she would read into this what he psychically detected as the problem. I felt the ambiguities were intended. And so I went to him for elaboration."

"This was last summer?" I said.

"September or October, I believe. He talked to me about my marriage, which was a remarriage. He told me I would have to go through all of the unpleasantnesses we all dread. I would have to end the marriage. He talked at great length on why it was over. Everything he told me were things I knew and wouldn't admit to myself. He touched briefly on my career and my health. But he really was determined to talk about the marriage."

"Don't you think," I said, "that he took a lot on himself?"

He shook his head.

"I admired his restraint with her and I also admired his directness with me."

I had no idea what the problem was.

"He recognized you both cared for each other?" I said, for something to say.

"Yes, he knew the power of the relationship and the bondage which was not erotic. He also knew the original thought that caused the divorce. By the time she had gotten around to forgiving that vast error of mine, we had disturbed the whole texture of the marriage. We were not relating to each other sexually."

I wasn't quite sure why one needed a psychic to comprehend the void created by the absence of this marital prerequisite.

But Corrado had done more than philosophize, he had also predicted, and what he had predicted had been reassuring to a man with deep qualms about his course of action.

"Corrado told me of her ultimate reinvolvement with another man. She would not stay where she was, but would find another place in the world. She would re-relate, and so would I."

It still seemed to me he was putting excessive reliance on somebody else.

"The thing that strikes me," I said, "is that here you are a sophisticated person, in the true sense of experienced living, and you come to this man who hasn't any experience of the type you describe, having never married himself. And yet you accept unquestioningly what he says."

Newland explained:

"He verbalized what I knew to be true. He didn't urge me to do it, he didn't advise me. He just told me what was so, talking with great detail about our personalities and conflicts, and quite accurately."

His eyes floated distantly out to sea.

"Our relationship had been over for some time, but we were both pretending it wasn't."

"How does one recognize when it's over?"

"When the sexual element of my marriage had been bruised I went through long analytical periods to see why it couldn't be reoriented, and no one could give me an answer. There isn't one."

As an adult male, I had given the usual thought to the proper place of sex in a relationship. "In the last analysis," I observed without originality, "sex between a couple is an expression of their love for each other."

"That element was so bruised by the circumstances of our lives that it lost its spontaneity. I also found when I began to be her friend and adviser, rather than her husband, the virility of the relationship was gone."

I wondered about her position in all this.

"What were your wife's feelings about Corrado?"

He answered indirectly.

"He told me that she was in great danger if we continued to live this way. He saw she was getting ill. And she saw it too."

"Actually," I said, "what Bill did was outline and confirm a situation you both sensed but didn't want to act upon."

Newland held up a finger for emphasis.

"He detected it, sensitized it, and said it. And you

should write about it, and the world should read it, because he dared to take a stand."

It was certainly dramatic.

Despite Newland's experience, I wasn't sure it was wise to allow a psychic to manage one's marriage, even if he could do it better. Nevertheless, psychics do have the insight at times, it seems, to perceive better than the interested parties the true sentiments involved in an intimate relationship. For this reason perhaps, affairs of the heart, more than other concerns, are apt to make psychic-hoppers out of otherwise self-reliant people.

"If a psychic hadn't told me that my husband no longer cared for me," one female buff told me, "I would have never taken the trouble to find out he was cheating on me."

Ironically, those who most frequently consult psychics about romantic possibilities exert very little initiative of their own to bring about rewarding relationships. But some, like Gerri Carson, an attractive Los Angeles divorcée, are seriously seeking help in finding the relationship they want.

For more than a year, Gerri had been checking each new prospect with the psychic Kabrina. Her problem seemed to be married men. She could hardly move without falling over one, and she was beginning to question their intentions. Dan had practically promised he would be hers after his divorce. But Gerri had heard this story before and she took her misgivings to the fair Kabrina, a striking brunette.

And what had Kabrina been able to do for her?

"Plenty," said Gerri. "I went to her about Dan, and she told me he would be getting a divorce. But it wouldn't be for a while, and his wife knew he was dating other girls. She hadn't let on yet, because she was going to lower the boom on him and take him financially. But he wouldn't be marrying me, anyway."

"What else?" I asked.

"Kabrina said that Dan's wife had lovers on the side. But when I told Dan about this, he said it was impossible, and that he would never get divorced now. He thought I was trying to pull something."

But six months later Dan changed his tune.

"His wife came to him then," Gerri said, "and wanted a divorce. She told him that she had a lover and had been having different lovers for the last five years—just like him."

While this checked out Kabrina, what good did it do Gerri?

"If I had listened to her," Gerri said, "I wouldn't have wasted all that time with Dan."

As Dan was on his way out, Gerri became interested in Tom. Tom was also married, but at least he was honest about staying married.

While she wasn't that serious about Tom, Gerri had a certain curiosity. She asked if Tom would rent the house he was interested in, and Kabrina said that it would burn down before he could move in, and she was right.

But there were more exciting things.

"Kabrina said that Tom was associated with a dark-haired man who smoked smelly cigars and packed a gun. She said that if he continued this association he would be liable to be done in."

On questioning Tom, Gerri discovered he was in a shady business, and his associates had already threatened his life.

But Kabrina's great coup came when she said that Tom was not the man for Gerri.

"Did one have to be psychic to see that?" I asked.

"Anyway," Gerri said, "she told me it would last three

months, which it did, and then I would meet a blond man, and this would be a step up."

Sure enough, a blond man turned up, youthful, successful, in the glamorous field of writing, everything a girl could ask for in the way of an eligible male.

Gerri obtained a snapshot of him, and took it to Kabrina.

Kabrina took one look at the picture, and beamed.

"Now, that's the blond man I was telling you about," she said. "But watch out for a married man."

Gerri was as pleased now with Kabrina as she was with her blond suitor. However, there was no need for the warning about the married man, as she was very happy with her new boyfriend. But as the weeks wore on, she got to seeing less and less of him. It disturbed her.

"He was working such late hours, and he would drop over and be so tired he could only stay for a short time. I seldom got to see him after a while, and never got to go out with him in public."

One day, reviewing the relationship, she said to a friend, "Dating him is almost like dating a married man."

The friend looked up startled, "Didn't you know that he is married?"

He was not only married, but he had two small children, and Kabrina had never seen any of it.

Gerri was philosophical. "I guess," she said, "that nobody is right all the time."

Not everybody is as generous as Gerri Carson. Most people who patronize psychics demand more of them than they do of other people, and are disappointed when they don't perform instant miracles. At the same time, because psychics often anticipate problems that haven't occurred yet, they may be disregarded until their predictions eventually prove out.

Only time can determine the validity of some readings.

Psychic Maya Perez was reading once for a group sitting around in a circle. She was making brief remarks about their lives when she came to a fresh-faced girl of twenty, who happened to be there with her mother.

Barbara Rock had been married but a few weeks, and had no qualms about her marriage.

The psychic's dark eyes focused on the newlywed as she told her the last thing a bride would want to hear.

"You shouldn't have married the man you did," she said, "because he studied black magic in a previous lifetime while you were a dancer and studied with the higher gods. He could destroy you." Before this jolter could register, the psychic added that the marriage was inevitable, as it was the girl's karma—the soul debt which reincarnationists believe carries over from one life to another.

The bride was not taken with her reading, and when Madam Perez added that she would have a little baby girl, with blue eyes and blond hair, she said crisply, "I would like a boy."

Barbara Rock paid little attention to the reading, not even bothering to mention it to her husband, but then, unexpectedly, discord began to develop.

"Within three or four months," the young wife recalled, "I was having problems like she had predicted. All of a sudden my husband manifested a violent temper, and it was ruining our marriage. I didn't know what to do, but remembering what Maya had said, I went to her for advice."

Madam Perez gave her two alternatives.

"She said I could leave him or I could help him. If I worked with him and healed him, as she said I was capable of doing, he could come to greatness, personally and professionally."

She looked at the psychic doubtfully. Tom Rock was

twenty-six then, a non-believer in the psychic, and at this point he seemed a typical Leo, wrapped up in his own ego problems to the exclusion of everything else.

Maya Perez' advice was simple.

"Just guide him," she said. "Give him love and attention, and no criticism. Treat him as a child until this period passes."

"When will this period pass?" Barbara asked.

"Not long, everything will soon be all right."

Since this conversation had taken place two years before, I could not but remark on how placid and contented the young wife seemed now. She was sitting next to her mother, Mrs. Evy Ludwig, who had originally introduced her to the psychic, and she was holding a blond, blue-eyed infant in her arms.

"A boy or girl?" I asked.

"Candace is her name," she said.

"And so Madam Perez was right about that?"

The girl nodded. "She was right pretty much about everything."

I marveled that Madam Perez' opening remarks about reincarnation and black magic had not frightened her off.

"Oh, I believe in reincarnation," said Barbara. "It sometimes seems to be the only thing that adds up."

By accurately tuning into the domestic problem, the psychic had won over the girl's confidence when nobody else could have, and so influenced her life.

"My husband wasn't happy in his work, which was the cause of a good deal of his dissatisfaction. He was working in the television studios as a stagehand. The hours were long and he was under tension. But Maya said there would be changes for him, once my attitude changed."

After that second reading, the changes became apparent. The roaring lion became a lamb, and all through Barbara's remodeling herself as the psychic had suggested.

"The first thing in the morning, after I woke up," Barbara said, "I would start thinking positively about Tom. I'd say to myself, there will be no arguments. And no matter what he said, I would preserve this attitude."

"How had you changed?" I asked.

"I'm very critical, I'm a Virgo," she said, "and he couldn't take criticism, so we were working against each other. So I just stopped criticizing. And he stopped being violent."

Not content with reading for the wife, Maya asked to meet Tom. Since Tom was not about to consult a psychic at this point, the meeting was arranged as a social event. Barbara's mother invited the young couple to her San Fernando Valley home one evening while Maya Perez was there.

By now Tom was relaxed, enjoying his marriage, and crediting the transformation in his wife with their new tranquillity and his own transformation.

"He would keep telling me that the little girl he had married had finally matured into a woman, and he was proud of me."

The meeting with Maya was a revelation for Tom.

Though he had become tolerant of his wife's interest in the psychic, he was still not receptive, though not quite as negative as he would have been a few weeks before. He was still essentially discontented about his job, though he had learned to live with it. It was still, however, his chief concern.

Maya Perez was quite hopeful.

"You will leave the work you are now in," she said, "when you meet an older man who will either become your partner in a new business or help you get into this business."

It all seemed remote. Tom had little education or training, he had been working for a pizza store when Barbara

first met him, and his work at the studios was not condu-
cive to anything better. Besides, he knew no older man
who could help him.

The reading had taken place early in 1970. In June of
1970, Barbara and Tom met a successful Southern California businessman, Bob Moore, who was in his forties.
He and his wife took an immediate liking to the young
couple, and proceeded to help Tom get into another
business.

"They started talking together, Bob and Tom," Barbara recalled, "about going into the swimming pool
business. First, they talked about a partnership, and then
about Tom buying his own business."

Bob Moore, in the business of building and servicing
pools, was in a position to help his young friend get off
the ground.

"Bob Moore, as Maya Perez had indicated," Barbara
said, "was able to introduce Tom to the right people, and
so just last month (this was in the spring of 1971) he was
able to start his own business servicing home pools."

Maya had forecast a bright future for the budding
entrepreneur.

"Eventually," observed the proud young wife, "Tom
will start designing pools and building them. He's a
changed person, he doesn't sit around and blame other
people now, he just goes out and does things."

Their whole style of living has changed. Friends she
once disapproved of have melted away, and they relish
each other's company. "When we were first married," she
said, "we always felt we needed people around to enter-
tain us because we couldn't communicate."

They have a giving attitude toward each other. "Tom
was raised a Catholic and I was brought up in the Church
of Religious Science," Barbara said. "Of his own volition,
since the birth of our child, he has come to me and sug-

gested that Candace be raised in Religious Science and that we all go to church together."

This would have never happened six months before. And Barbara gives full credit for the happiness of one growing family to the clairvoyant.

"If I hadn't met Maya at that time, I probably would have left Tom, because I was spoiled and immature. But being made aware of my faults, being able to accept what Maya said by seeing how right she was about everything else, I was able to face up to the problem and work things out. And she did give us a lot to look forward to."

Where the heart is concerned, not everybody listens to the psychics they consult, especially when that advice doesn't suit them.

Having used sensitive Florence Davis herself, Natalie Rehm of Canoga Park, California, a realtor, recommended her for all and sundry problems, including romance or its reasonable facsimile.

Natalie had been concerned for some time about a girl friend who was living with a writer who went on violent drunken sprees. They were not married, and Natalie had urged her friend, an artist, to leave this man, out of concern for herself and her children.

"During his drunken sprees, which would last for days," Mrs. Rehm said, "he would beat her, smash windows, and break up the furniture. She would call me very upset and ask if she could come to stay with me and bring the children."

This had gone on for twelve years, and Natalie Rehm, despite the fact she was a Pisces, the sign of the Messianic complex, decided she had had enough. "I finally felt I couldn't do any more for her," she said, "so I sent her to Florence Davis."

This was two years ago, and Florence Davis, speaking as emphatically as she knew how, warned that if the woman didn't get out of this man's life she would be inviting tragedy.

The woman's face fell. She couldn't imagine life without the temperamental writer who had been the provider of ecstatic agony all these years.

"You mean, I shouldn't marry him?" she said.

Florence Davis was beside herself. "Would you destroy yourself and your children?"

Natalie Rehm was pleased at the way the sitting had gone, but she underrated the neurotic attraction.

As if sensing that the psychic threatened her relationship, Natalie's artist friend plunged headlong into marriage.

Natalie was crushed. "I reminded her that Florence had warned against the marriage, and she replied that now that they were finally married she was sure everything would be better."

Another psychic reading was arranged.

Florence, as a clairvoyant, was not as shocked as another counselor might have been.

But she again warned: "Marriage or no marriage, you must leave him before he destroys you."

The woman thanked Florence for the warning, but went home to the writer. He had promised to turn over a new leaf and she believed him.

One night, not long after, however, the man went into an alcoholic rage, and blindly drew a knife not only on his wife, but on her two children. There was little question now of the danger. Quickly, the mother gathered up her children and ran out into the street, without stopping to dress.

The next day she returned when the husband wasn't there, and picked up her things. She hasn't been back since.

"I think," said Natalie Rehm with a sigh, "that Florence's message finally got home to her."

As they are useful in romance and marriage, some psychics are also supremely helpful in divorce.

After twenty-eight years of marriage, Ginny could have been excused for resenting the fact that she had been displaced by a younger woman. Accordingly she wanted a better settlement than had been originally discussed.

"When he first brought up the divorce, I had no idea," she said, "that there was anybody else."

We were sitting together overlooking the sea, in her comfortable home which she had bought with a portion of her property settlement.

"How did you find out about her?" I asked.

She crossed her legs and stretched luxuriously, accenting a still youthful figure.

"Bill Corrado," she said. "I had gone to him for a general reading, and he said there was somebody else involved in the breakup of my marriage. He told me to get a private detective, as it would improve my position in any divorce proceeding."

It was not that simple. She had no income of her own, and private detectives were expensive—$160 a day with expenses.

Corrado had practically drawn a picture of the other woman.

"She was much younger, in her twenties, and highly aggressive, and she had set her cap for my husband."

She checked out Corrado's information and it tallied in every detail, including his description of the girl. She decided her husband should pay for his pleasure.

She scraped together $160, practically all the cash she had in the world, and hired a detective for one day.

"I could only afford one twenty-four-hour period, and

asked Corrado to pick out a day when they would be in a compromising state."

Corrado picked out the day.

It was a Friday.

The detective, together with a photographer, staged a raid on the girl's premises, and found the pair together, *flagrante delicto*.

Ginny shook her head at the thought of what the picture must have been like.

"Fortunately," she said, "the evidence obtained by the private detective made my husband agree to the settlement I was entitled to after all those years. Bill Corrado deserved a medal."

6

Miracles without Medicine

I could accept clairvoyance, telepathy, precognition, even if not sure how they worked. I could visualize a world of spirits on a different dimension, and the rebirth of the soul. But my mind, brainwashed from childhood by the authoritarian doctor figure, boggled at medical miracles.

"I had lost my sight," the woman was saying, "and the doctors could offer no hope of my ever seeing again. Something had gone wrong with a blood vessel feeding the optic nerve. I was despondent, depressed, bitter at this happening to me."

Now with her sight restored, Mrs. Viola Scardina had agreed reluctantly to describe the miracle out of consideration for the man who had returned her sight to her.

"Doug Johnson," she said, "deserves all the recognition in the world. People should know about him and others like him."

We were talking in the living room of her Los Angeles apartment, and as she turned occasionally to her husband, Joseph, I noticed that there were several fingers missing on one of his hands, but it didn't seem to bother him. He was as absorbed as I in what she was saying.

"I can see now as well as ever," said this fifty-year-old woman, "and it's like a blessing from the Lord."

Her husband's head bobbed, acknowledging the divine miracle, as well as Doug Johnson's gift.

"Did your sight come back all at once?" I asked.

"No, I went to Reverend Johnson five or six times. He would tell me to think positive, and pass his hands across my eyes so that after a while I felt the heat from his hands."

She had gone to him out of desperation, having no place else to turn. Dr. Richard Elander, a prominent Los Angeles eye specialist, had, she stated, said there was nothing more he could do to restore her sight. "I cried all over his office, but I didn't accept the fact that I would be blind. Originally, I lost the sight of my right eye, but soon the sight in the other eye went, too. The doctor said my sight might return within a few years or never."

Well-wishers tried to interest her in Braille, the finger language of the blind, but she refused because that would indicate acceptance of her blindness. She was determined to see again. She had heard of psychic healing, not confusing it with faith healing, which functions at a more emotional level, and she asked the Southern California affiliate of the American Society for Psychical Research to recommend a psychic. They gave her Doug Johnson's name.

She traveled to Doug Johnson's address, poking along with her husband up the steep steps to the psychic's hilltop home. "I was very bitter and thought, what have I got to lose? I wasn't thinking positive. I went because I didn't have any place else to go."

Johnson spoke to her gently, telling her that Spirit (energy forces in nature) accomplished the healing, and that he was merely an instrument. She didn't follow everything he said, but his hands passing over her sightless eyes were pleasantly warming. The first session was painless, but she noticed no improvement.

His big task was elevating her spirits, as her outlook, body, and mind were mutually involved in any recovery. "As you become more positive," he said, "it will renew the power to heal that is in you."

She was not terribly impressed, but she still had no place else to go.

He had warned that she might feel pain in the region of the eye, and told her not to get alarmed, as this would be a positive reaction to the healing. Three days later the pain was so severe that she paced the floor all night. But by morning it was gone.

She began to notice improvement after her second visit. The shadows were getting clearer, and she saw blurs where she had seen nothing before.

In the meantime she was receiving spinal adjustments from an osteopath, thinking perhaps that pressure on her spine might have impinged on a nerve.

After seeing Johnson four times, she was able to negotiate short distances in the street unaided, but she was still blind for all practical purposes, seeing only shadows. Despite moments of depression, she kept telling herself she would never give in.

The great day came unexpectedly. Like Paul on the road to Damascus, she saw a blinding light, and had a vision bringing a state of exaltation. But unlike Paul, who temporarily lost his sight, Viola Scardina was to regain hers.

It was an indescribable experience. "That day, my daughter asked how my eyes were, and, without meaning to be rude, I told her not to bother me about it. I didn't want to be questioned. Something much larger seemed to be happening inside of me."

Aware that her daughter's feelings were hurt, she made an effort to explain:

"If I were to stay blind and feel this great, I couldn't care less."

Her sight did not come back at once, but improved gradually, until she regained her normal vision—in her case 20/25.

She went back to her doctor, and then to the Jules Stein Eye Institute at UCLA. "They like unusual cases, and they put me through numerous tests."

"What came of it?" I asked.

She shrugged. "The clinic had no explanation whatsoever of my recovery."

"Did you tell them you had been to a psychic?"

She waved her hand. "Oh, no, they're scientifically oriented. They have to prove everything in their laboratories. I went through all the tests. It took six weeks. When they finally released me, they said to come back in six months. They are still not sure of what happened."

"Did they find the same thing Dr. Elander had?"

"They accepted Dr. Elander's findings because he was from UCLA and they respected him."

It was not hard to understand their confusion.

As I understood the diagnosis, the vessel to the optic nerve did not bring any blood, and there was no nerve impulse.

"The X rays showed this," Mrs. Scardina said, "but Doug Johnson kept telling me I would regain my sight, and he kept repeating, 'You have the power to heal yourself.'"

As she regained her sight, she developed a corresponding awareness of her surroundings. It was as if Johnson had induced an increased sensitivity. "I could look at people in a way I never had before, and not only realize what they were saying but what they wanted. I became newly aware of the detailed beauty of the sky and the clouds, the trees and flowers. I had never really seen them before, just passed my eyes over them."

Her mind was now involved in whatever she was looking at. She was in a state of exaltation. Her nerve ends tingled and she felt charged up. This transformation manifested itself in various ways. "My little granddaughter would sit on my lap, and suddenly twitch as from an electrical charge. When I touched her, she would stagger. Even riding in a car, I felt light and suspended."

Whatever happened in the healing had affected not only her eyes but every atom of her body. She reached a heady high without any conscious effort. "At one time I had the feeling my body became detached from my soul and disintegrated. My soul became aware of the Universe as a fluid sort of thing, I saw myself coming out of this strange sea."

Viola Scardina had synthesized into her own experience the race memory that the humanist C. G. Jung said we all had. It was like an LSD trip, except that the results were beneficial.

Johnson had apparently awakened the power of healing in her. She couldn't believe it at first, any more than she could believe that he could heal her with a few passes of his hands. She found out through touching her small granddaughter. The child had a chronic ear problem. "When she caught cold her sinuses wouldn't drain," Viola said. "The mucus would back up through the tubes in the ears. But I touched her there, and soon she had no more trouble with her ear."

She considered, then dismissed the thought that this could be coincidence.

"During my own healing strange things happened to

my hands. They seemed to have a life of their own. I touched them to my face and they didn't feel like my hands at all. They had a weird detached feel to them."

"Would you call yourself a healer?" I asked.

"I don't know about that, but I was able to help my husband."

He had been so quietly listening to everything his wife was saying that I had almost forgotten him. Now his hand again caught my eye.

He noticed my interest. "That's from an accident with a power saw seven years ago." He held up the hand with the missing fingers, and nodded towards his wife. "I would have lost the whole hand if it hadn't been for her. The surgeon was ready to take it off."

Viola gave him a look of affection.

"My husband has had nine operations on his hand and wrist. It has been a constant worry. Six months ago he still had three pins left in his wrist, and Dr. Wilson said on examining him that he had an infection around the bone from one of the pins. He said that if it didn't heal within a week he would have to take the hand off here." She pointed to the wrist.

As with her own case, there was nothing to lose. And as she had helped her grandchild, she might help him.

"As I touched his hand," she said, "I could see what was festering inside."

I couldn't help but think how ironical it was that this woman, who had been without sight, could now presumably see through skin, bone, and flesh.

"I told him the exact positions of the pins, and I could see the inflammation. I felt an electric charge going from my hand into his. Every day I would hold his hand, and the day before he was to go in for re-examination and possibly surgery, I told him he was healed. He went to Dr. Wilson the following day. They took X rays again, and they were negative. Then Dr. Wilson called his colleague in, and they checked together. They just couldn't believe it. The infection was gone."

The doctor had asked curiously, "What healed your hand?"

And Joseph Scardina had told him.

Viola Scardina was impressed by the doctor's openness.

"He didn't scoff or sneer," she said, "but acknowledged a belief in a Higher Power."

After this remarkable testimony I sought out the Reverend Johnson for some explanation of what had happened.

He remembered the case very well. "Sometimes," he said, "the healing force comes from an individual with healing ability, and if the subject has it, all the better, as you get her working, too. Some people have more of this power than others. And I believe, from observation, that there is a magnetic force that produces an instant chemical reaction on the ailing body."

"Did you actually touch Mrs. Scardina?" I asked.

"No, I just put my hand close to her."

I was naturally interested in what the doctors had to say about all this, and to determine accordingly whether Mrs. Scardina had correctly represented her case. Dr. Elander's office required an authorization from the patient for any discussion of the case, and so she promptly wrote the doctor, saying:

"As you recall when I first visited your office I was at the time losing vision of the right eye and was told that no surgery would benefit my condition and was consoled by the fact that in no case histories had this same condition occurred in the other eye. However, I was the exception, for within a few weeks I had begun experiencing the same condition in the left eye. I was seen at the Jules Stein Institute, for a period of six weeks, undergoing numerous tests there . . . no explanation for my recovery was given."

In response, Dr. Elander gave a summary, which attributed the visual problem, as Mrs. Scardina had recalled to me, to the blockage of a blood vessel. "As you recall," he stated, "I first saw you in my office in February 1969, at which time you had a visual defect of the right eye in the inferior nasal quadrant. I felt that the diagnosis was a blockage of the superior temporal arteriole and we treated you with cortico-steroids . . . I remember that you did have some similar complaints in the left eye, but, according to my records, there was never any defect of the visual fields. There was some narrowing of the vessels in the left eye, but I did not see any blockage."

Elander checked Mrs. Scardina last in September 1969 (after Mrs. Scardina had been to Johnson). It was his final examination, and he reported, "The condition improved and the last time I saw you that eye looked very good with the blocked vessel appearing to be open . . . the intraocular pressures were normal."

Dr. Elander's comment on the recovery, which Mrs. Scardina said he had not anticipated in any conversation with her, was quite interesting.

"I don't think that we can say why you got this or, on the other hand, I don't see anything particularly unusual about your spontaneous recovery, either.

"I would feel, though, that the medicine we did give you helped to a certain extent."

Dr. Elander's reaction to a claim of psychic healing reminded me of another physician's dismissal of a psychic cure as a spontaneous remission.

The healer, a less gentle man than Johnson, asked:

"Why is it that *they* don't have these spontaneous remissions?"

With Doug Johnson, Spirit is the power source for

any psychic healing, Spirit of course being a part of the Universal Mind as we are here on earth.

"We all are Spirit—as we are in tune with Spirit and have a mortal mind and also a soul consciousness. This affects us at all times, putting us in tune with the oneness of the universe. So, even when the subject apparently has no faith or is resisting a healing, he still can be helped, because his subconscious has recognized the need in his coming for help."

Oriented as I was to conventional medicine, Viola Scardina's renewed sight was nothing short of a miracle. And yet my mind couldn't grasp how her eyes could be restored unless some corrective changes had occurred.

"What," I asked Johnson, "happened to make the optic nerve function again?"

Johnson sighed. "It is hard for people on this wave length to understand, but the subconscious force—Spirit, if you like—knows what the underlying problem is, and invokes natural forces to revitalize the entire system, and this of course includes the eyes."

Not all his cases are successes. "What intrigues me are the failures," Johnson said. "Why the healing force works in some cases, and not in others."

Sometimes there is no real desire to get well, and the illness is a bid for attention or withdrawal.

He recalled a woman who came to him on the verge of suicide. She was blind—not completely—but enough to be considered legally blind. She had had a job she didn't like and despised working at it. One day she woke up and found she was going blind. So of course she had to give up the job. She couldn't work.

Some would see a form of retribution in what had befallen her, and others that her blindness had been induced through self-hypnosis, for she kept repeating to herself:

"I wish something would happen so I would never have to work again."

Without sight, more depressed than ever, not wanting to live, she turned to a psychic.

At first the transformation was remarkable. "You couldn't believe the difference in her," Johnson said. "She became cheerful, optimistic, even enthusiastic. And her sight began to respond."

Instead of being overjoyed, she told Johnson, "If I get my sight completely back, how will I be able to live with myself? I've been nothing but a failure all my life."

After this her sight began to diminish. "Deep down she didn't want to get well," Johnson said, "and so she stopped coming to me, and stayed home, waiting for blindness to take over."

It seemed odd that she would seek help and then turn away when she received it.

"You forget," Johnson said, "that she came not to get her sight back, but because she was suicidal."

Some healers feel that anybody can be healed once his subconscious is laid open to suggestion. Hypnotist Frank Hevesy of Hollywood, who reports healings in various areas—diabetes, arthritis, emphysema—says that the healing takes place instantly, but that it takes longer to prepare some for it than others. "It takes an inner subconscious conviction to be healed," he said. "Some ten to twenty-five per cent of the population are instantly susceptible, almost somnambulistic in their subconscious receptivity, accounting for the numbers that are healed instantly privately or at mass faith healing sessions."

Essentially, Hevesy's healing is accomplished through some form of hypnosis, or self-hypnosis, to get through the conscious to the all-powerful subconscious. "For this reason, the intellectual type, with their stress on the conscious mind," Hevesy said, "is the most difficult to cure.

But if we work enough to get the healing message to the subconscious that performs the healing, then we can heal."

In the difficult case of a Vietnam veteran who couldn't walk because of nerve damage, the subject's subconscious was apparently closed off to the possibility of his walking again. "A friend had brought him to me, and consciously he was willing to accept the premise he might walk again," Hevesy said, "but deep down he didn't really believe it. From the time he had been hit by shrapnel four years before, and his legs went numb, he had been programmed the other way. He had become reconciled to the wheelchair. He had no control over his legs."

To get through the subconscious barrier, Hevesy, hypnotizing the subject, gradually regressed in time the man's subconscious to the day he was wounded, and then beyond. "I started him visualizing his legs moving, walking, swimming, dancing. It was almost as though he had forgotten how to walk, like a baby learning to walk. All memory of how to walk was blocked from his mind."

When the subconscious accepted the idea of walking again, it was then ready to accept the healing suggestion, and the healing was accomplished. The disabled Los Angeles veteran could walk again. His subconscious had first expressed its new receptivity in the dream state. "First, I began to dream that I was walking again," the veteran told me, in confirming the healing.

Unlike Douglas Johnson, Hevesy approached healing almost mundanely, while recognizing spiritual belief as a point of subconscious contact. As a spiritualist, believing in the Spirit force, Johnson only gradually became aware of his power to heal. At first he manifested a spontaneous ability to tune in on bodily disorders. One night, he was at a dinner in Laguna given by a friend, Mrs. Bennona

Dieroff, a well-known socialite, who had recently returned from a trip around the world. The experience had been fun, but tiring, and she was glad to be home.

She was telling friends about the high spots of the trip—three cracked ribs from a fall during a storm and a room steward falling madly in love with her—when she noticed Doug Johnson watching her closely.

As their eyes met, he said, "You don't feel very well, do you?"

"I am tired," she admitted.

Later, he sat by her and held her hand, trying to tune into her bodily vibration.

"Promise me," he said, "that you'll see the doctor this week for a checkup."

"There's nothing wrong with me," she replied. "I'm just weary."

A few days later, a friend called, and asked if she had seen the doctor yet.

"No, I haven't," she said.

"Well," the friend said, "Doug told me you must see a doctor right away."

Now alarmed, she called to make an appointment with her physician. He was away but she got his replacement, Dr. Archie Miller of Pasadena. As the examination proceeded, the doctor's concern matched the psychic's.

"He said he couldn't afford to overlook anything. He wanted me to come back in two days with my husband."

Mrs. Dieroff now noticed a rapid deterioration in her mobility. By her next appointment, she could barely walk across the doctor's waiting room.

The verdict came quickly.

"When I walked into his office with my husband, the doctor told me I had a rare ailment known as *lupus erythematosis disseminata,* which was detected through one of the blood tests. The disease is considered incurable, destroying the connective tissues, though high dosages of cortisone could keep it under control. There are three types, the skin type, with red blotches—'Red Wolf'—that's where the *lupus* comes in. The second type is arthritic in nature, and the third, systemic, attacking the liver and spleen, and that's what I had."

Had she not undergone treatment promptly, she might have succumbed in two weeks. "The doctor ordered me into the hospital that day. I was disintegrating."

Doug Johnson visited her in the hospital, and was now encouraging. "That night at the party, he hadn't wanted to frighten me, but he saw death around me and knew I had to get help right away. But before he left the hospital, he told me I would recover, but it would be a while."

Benni Dieroff was in and out of hospitals for the next few years. The cortisone controlled the disease, but it was still dormant. "I was on cortisone for eight years, three times a day, and all those years I couldn't be in the sun without being completely covered, as it poisons the body of any lupus sufferer."

The attack came in 1960, and now eleven years later, looking at the vivacious woman before me, it was difficult to picture her as a sick woman. Though perhaps sixty at this time, she had a youthful face, unlined, and a sparkle in her eyes. She brimmed with vitality.

"You certainly don't look sick," I said.

She smiled. "It was a long haul, and without this healer I wouldn't have made it back."

The healer was not Johnson but a Tarzana, California, layman, Howard Thrasher. He worked all day at a job and did his healings in his spare time. He made only two conditions, that there must be no payment, and that the disease was medically incurable.

"He said he didn't know if he could help, but he would

come out to my home, and have one session with me, and then he would know."

She was favorably impressed with the pleasant man who walked briskly into her room. He seemed to move with an electrical charge. As she lay prone for the test, too weak to sit up, Thrasher stood some distance behind her.

"He didn't touch me or say a word. He didn't want me to think about anything in particular, but told me if I had any reactions or feelings to let him know."

She felt a tremendous heat through her body. He said it was a good reaction, and he would come the following week every day for five days, and that would do it.

She hadn't been quite sure what he was doing. Once she heard a squeaky noise. "When I turned, he was sitting on a little ottoman clear across the room and his whole body was shaking, and the ottoman was squeaking."

Actually, the presence of the healer is not always necessary. The English healer Harry Edwards prayed in London for an infant in New Orleans with a congenital eye ailment, and the cure three weeks later was confirmed by the child's parents.

Nevertheless, I had trouble trying to form a picture of what had happened to Benni Dieroff.

"He didn't touch you then?" I said.

"Oh no, he was never anywhere near me. He seldom said anything. Every once in a while he would refer to an incident in my past, a fall or an accident, with his own body reliving the symptoms."

As the sessions ended, she was ready to give a testimonial to Howard Thrasher.

"At the end of the fifth day I could walk out to the kitchen from my bedroom for the first time. I could dress myself unaided, I could even drive a car."

"Had you been taking the cortisone during this period?" I asked.

"He told me he wanted me to keep on taking it. You normally have to decrease large dosages of cortisone a little at a time. Apparently he didn't want to interfere with my doctor's treatment. And he didn't want me to tell the doctor or anybody else about our meetings."

She had an unexpected caller the next day. "The doorbell rang, and I went sailing to the door, all dressed and full of pep. It was the doctor."

"What happened?" he asked in surprise.

"I just decided not to be sick any more," she said with a smile.

She had relapses from time to time when she became overtired, or had a nerve-racking day in traffic. "After six months, I got off the cortisone, but kept going back to it intermittently. Even when I felt great, I was afraid to take the chance that lupus was entirely gone. And I was equally afraid to sit in the sun. So I never knew for sure that I was cured."

But, ironically, ten years after the global trip climaxed by lupus, another voyage around the world apparently marked the end of the disease she may have picked up on the previous journey.

"This second trip around the world took ten months," she said, "and I got so caught up in everything that I didn't have time to wonder whether I still carried lupus around with me or not. I got off the cortisone completely and I haven't gone back since. So I guess lupus and I have finally parted company."

Psychic healers don't always practice what they preach. Happening to be in the Hollywood area one evening, I called unexpectedly on healer Doug Johnson. Nobody answered, and I was turning away when a familiar face loomed in the doorway.

Johnson was sniffling audibly, into his handkerchief. "Oh, it's you," he wheezed, "come in."

He ushered me to a chair, and asked if I would like a spot of hot tea.

"You had better take it," I said.

"I intend to," he said, "with lots of lemon." He wheezed a little. "I was running quite a fever, but it's broken now, and I'll soon be myself."

He didn't seem embarrassed by the incongruity of his illness.

"Since you invoke the healing forces for other people," I said, "how did you allow this to happen to you?"

He shrugged. "I'm like the doctor who doesn't follow his own advice. I was overdoing in everything. Spirit said I was going to end up with the flu. But I wouldn't cut down. Every day they told me this for one week." He sighed. "We can't go against the laws of nature. We have to be sensible, but I guess I needed a lesson."

"Why didn't you listen?"

Doug Johnson laughed. "I'm not that different, consciously, from other people. I kept saying, 'Well, next week I'll cut down. I won't see this person or that, and I'll taper off in my work activities.' But then the flu hit me. I screamed for every spirit I knew. I wanted their help. But they told me I had to pay the price of thinking I could break the natural laws that govern our health."

The flu was well into him when his father's voice came through. Harry Glen Johnson had been close to his son in life, and now presumably in death.

"We tried to warn but you wouldn't listen," this voice said. "Then when you called for help, there was nothing anyone could do. We had to let you remain in bed to let you build up your resistance."

He still looked under the weather to me.

"I'm all right now," Johnson said, reading my thought.

"When I woke up this morning a voice said, 'You'll be able to continue with your work now.'"

He had scheduled several appointments for the next day.

"This was not only a lesson for me," he said, "but a lesson to pass on. In dealing with dramatic illnesses—cancer, heart disease, blindness—we forget that a daily regimen—proper food, rest, exercise, positive thinking—is a requisite of everyday health."

"You sound like a doctor," I said.

"There's nothing wrong with that, if it works."

Unlike the faith healers, who operate on a predominantly hypnotic level, the psychic healers don't limit the scope of their therapy. The Mexican marvel Maria Moreno, often, like Edgar Cayce, prescribes specific remedies for ailments through a mediumistic corps of medical guides.

After a whiplash injury had left my right shoulder with a painful crimp, she had picked up a calcium deposit through a Dr. Dermas, one of her spirit guides. Dr. Dermas recommended a concoction of one tablespoonful of cream of tartar and one of Epsom salts, dissolved in the remnants of two quarts of water which had been brought to a boil with the cut-up rinds of one grapefruit, orange, and lemon. Two or three ounces of the cooled mixture were to be sipped twice a day.

The potion smacked of a witch's brew, and I would never have tried it if it hadn't been for actress Lisa St. Germain, who liked to put things together in the kitchen. "What can you lose?" said she.

I kept the concoction in the refrigerator and consumed it gradually. I soon found that I was doing floor exercises I had abandoned because of the pain in the shoulder. I reported the result with gratification to Maria Moreno.

"Take more," she said. "One week not enough."

Dr. Dermas was often amazingly accurate. At a demonstration one night at the home of the Los Angeles psychologist Dr. Lorene Chase, Maria's subject was a young woman she had never seen before, twenty-five-year-old artist Kathleen Bleser.

Miss Bleser suffered from attacks of vertigo—dizziness —symptomatic of Ménière's syndrome, a middle ear disturbance. These spells at times were so severe they were incapacitating. She had twice been operated on by one of the nation's leading ear specialists, but the condition continued.

Nobody in the room but myself, and of course Miss Bleser, knew of this disorder, and, certainly, sitting there with the medium, she looked the picture of radiant health.

As was her practice, Maria Moreno went immediately into trance, calling on her guide Clarita. Clarita in turn brought in various medical guides, including Dr. Dermas. Dr. Dermas was briskly authoritative in tone. He discussed Miss Bleser's pathology from head to toe, seeming to approve of her overall constitution, before fastening on one problem.

"You have trouble with the middle ear, it bring on dizziness, not right?"

Dr. Dermas, alias Maria Moreno, waited for an answer.

"Yes," Miss Bleser said, "for fourteen years."

Maria Moreno retched as if she were about to throw up.

"Sometimes," she said, "you so dizzy, so nauseated, you have to throw up like that. Yes?"

"Yes," said Miss Bleser, "I get the dry heaves."

"We get rid of them," said Dr. Dermas' voice.

Dr. Dermas pondered. "Your problem has much to do with emotional strain, attacks of dizziness come when you are upset. But Dr. Dermas fix."

It was apparent that Miss Bleser was favorably impressed by the reading.

"What must I do?" she said.

"Take some Floratila tea every night, very good for your dizziness."

She looked around at the seven or eight people in the room, and said, "You are all here to help with the healing." The healing consisted of prayer, for Maria believes that where two or three are gathered God's work will be done.

We said some solid prayers for Kathy Bleser's recovery, interspersing, I am sure, a prayer or two for ourselves.

As Dr. Dermas receded, Clarita returned, and she, too, seemed to tune in on Kathy.

"You have a bad fall, on a stone step."

Maria Moreno indicated the base of her spine, the coccyx.

Miss Bleser nodded vigorously.

"You had some chiropractor adjustments, and still feel it, but it will go away."

Miss Bleser was sufficiently impressed to scout about for the Floratila tea, which she finally located in a Mexican herb store in downtown Los Angeles. She took it for a week or so, noticing no immediate improvement. However, the reading gave her valuable insight into her own condition. She recognized that the spells, including the nausea, did occur when she was under stress, and she tried thereafter to avoid such situations. Whatever, the prayers, herb tea, or the calmness which self-analysis induced, the attacks gradually were fewer and farther between, until months passed without her experiencing one, and then they faded out.

A third operation, for which she had been programmed, was unnecessary.

Maria's readings are doubly impressive because she

so often picks up convincing psychic information along with the medical prognosis. With Miss Bleser, she picked up the name of a friend in Hawaii, and the friend's son, and described an auto accident involving the two of them, even specifying correctly that the boy's leg had been broken.

Her diagnoses are often readily provable. Reading once for the actress-dancer Ann Miller, Maria advised that she would require eye surgery in a year or so. Miss Miller was flabbergasted. Her vision was good, and her eyes gave her no trouble. Nevertheless, as a precautionary measure, she consulted a well-known oculist in Beverly Hills. She had a thorough examination, and when it was over, the specialist with a shake of his head told the beautiful actress:

"I've never before known anyone so young who was developing a cataract condition. However, it may not be ripe for removal for a year or so."

As incredible as these things may seem to the average person, they were as nothing compared to the session that Maria Moreno had with twenty-seven-year-old Bob Dursi of Manhattan Beach, California, and Judy, his beautiful blond wife. They seemed ideally happy, except for Judy's health. She tired quickly, was anemic, suffered from low blood pressure, and was even losing some hair.

A dermatologist detected a thyroid problem and gave Judy some pills. Her own doctor confirmed the diagnosis, but said the pills weren't strong enough. The situation was confused when Bob, interested in a musical career, went to Maria Moreno for vocational guidance. Suddenly, the medium inquired:

"Who is Judy?"

"My wife," Bob replied.

Dr. Dermas came on now. "There is nothing terribly

wrong," Maria interpreted. "The hormones are out of balance. Put back in balance she will feel better."

Clarita came on now, and said, "Have Judy come to me for a reading."

As the reading progressed, Bob Dursi was impressed when Maria Moreno mentioned a twenty-nine-year-old sister with a heart condition, which Bob knew about, and said another sister, in Oklahoma, had a breast tumor and would require an operation. This he didn't know about, until he got a telephone call later that night.

Judy's reading was an unforgettable experience.

Dr. Dermas appeared in rare form. He concurred with the more conventional diagnoses of the earth doctors, saying that a faulty thyroid was the seat of her difficulty.

Judy nodded, not sure whether to be impressed or amused.

"You want Dr. Dermas to help?" said Maria Moreno.

"If he will," said Judy politely.

"All right," said Maria, apparently holding a private parley with her spirit doctor. "Dr. Dermas is going to give you a transfusion. Don't worry, it will not hurt."

This was a bit unexpected but Judy was game. "Fine," she said, "give me the transfusion."

Maria reached out for Judy's arm, held it as if indeed preparing it for a transfusion, and then grimaced as an imaginary needle presumably pricked Judy's skin.

"Where is the blood coming from?" Judy asked, feeling no pain.

"Dr. Dermas," Maria said confidentially, "say the blood is coming from your husband."

Judy could hardly restrain a smile as she good-naturedly thanked Clarita and Dr. Dermas through Maria Moreno and made her departure.

That evening, not yet aware of the "transfusion," Bob Dursi had all the symptoms of a man who had lost too much blood. He took to his bed, not suspecting what was wrong. "When I got home from work," he related, "I couldn't even stand up. I was chilled to the bone and couldn't get warm. I went to bed, and started wrapping up in blankets, and fell off to sleep at once, I was so weak."

But by the time she got home that night, Judy was feeling good. And for the next three or four days she felt progressively better. Her husband, meanwhile, had regained his strength and gone back for another sitting.

"I just didn't understand this transfusion business," he said, "not that I minded giving Judy blood if it would help her. But I thought it would be nice to know how it was happening."

Dr. Dermas made his usual appearance.

"Dr. Dermas tells me," Maria said, "that they will have to keep giving her transfusions. One won't do the job."

Bob was willing.

Several transfusions, similar to the first, followed. But this time Judy stayed at home and profited at her convenience. Maria advised her to call on Dr. Dermas once a week—mentally—for a treatment.

It was as wild a story as any I had ever heard. But meeting Judy at a small dinner, appreciating her slim, lovely—and radiantly healthful—beauty, I recognized that whatever was done had a gratifying if unaccountable result.

"So every week, Judy, you got your transfusion?" I asked.

Judy frowned. "I don't really know. She just said to have him come to me, and I put my mind to it once a week as she said. Meanwhile, in two or three weeks, I started getting energy again, and I felt great."

Before this she had made an appointment with a less

dramatic doctor, a specialist in internal medicine. Because of a busy schedule he couldn't see her for two weeks, and though she was feeling better by this time, she decided to have a complete physical, with all the tests, anyway.

"I had to wait another week for the results," she said, "and Maria meanwhile told Bob that Dr. Dermas said the tests would show I was all right."

Old Dr. Dermas was right on.

"Judy," Bob reported, "got the results back from the doctor and they were perfect. Perfect blood count, perfect blood pressure, perfect thyroid. She hadn't been so well off in years."

Her recovery came as a relief to Bob. For as in some preposterous vampire movie, the "transfusions" had apparently weakened him. "Judy was out in the yard planting flowers, fixing things around the house, and I was exhausted, hardly able to make it to bed." Maria relieved his concern by telling him that he would be all right now that Judy needed no more transfusions.

"She's taken care of," she said. "She's had several good transfusions, and when she needed iodine for the thyroid, we gave her that."

The changes in Judy were truly remarkable. Before Dr. Dermas, she slept ten hours a day, and was still tired. Now she was bouncing around so that Bob looked at her with a jaundiced eye.

As his own strength returned Bob reviewed his wife's amazing recovery. Maria had said that Judy's red blood cells had been damaged by excessive use of penicillin, given her most recently after a wisdom tooth extraction. She had also had it for numerous things of a minor nature. "They gave it to her," Bob said, "like it was candy."

While some concoctions may work in healings, the

answer appears to lie in the latent power of the mind, that subconscious intelligence which pervades each and every cell of the body.

The miracle of subconscious healing may occur in private sittings, without witnesses, or before thousands, where, as Frank Hevesy suggests, mass emotion seems to provide a hypnotic effect strong enough to impress itself on the particularly susceptible subconscious. In the camps of the evangelistic healers, I have witnessed miracles my eyes could hardly credit. The blind regain their sight, the cripples throw away their walkers, crutches, and canes, the arthritic and rheumatic stretch their joints painlessly. The cures are so radical that one could be forgiven for immediately suspecting collusion, no matter how much talk there is of Jesus. Not all are cured, and the mass-oriented psychic, the evangelist, reaches out only for those with whom he feels some electric rapport, passing over others whose need is perhaps greater but whose subconscious is not nearly as receptive.

In a Long Beach auditorium, I spoke to a boy whose sight had been restored by the Georgia evangelist Reverend Leroy Jenkins, and the boy's eyes shone with the reflected zeal which may have been instrumental in helping him. At another evangelistic revival in Downey, California, held by the Reverend Jerry Walker of Dallas, Texas, I saw an unbeliever, asthmatic businessman Marshall Chortow, step forward. He moved uncertainly, without conviction, but soon his face lighted up, and he took a deep breath. "I can hardly believe it," he said. "I can breathe easy for the first time."

Like the boy with the restored vision, this asthma sufferer apparently had an impressionable subconscious.

Testimonials to faith healings are so commonplace that they are rightfully suspect. I was somewhat reassurred by similar testimonials in *Time* magazine, which, certainly, from its track record, is highly skeptical of anything metaphysical. In October 1970, *Time* chronicled the work of the peripatetic preacher Kathryn Kuhlman, whose face and demeanor have become familiar to national audiences on television.

The magazine cited three Kuhlman miracles:

"In July, 12-year-old Venus Yates lay in Los Angeles County General Hospital under intensive care for rheumatoid arthritis, rheumatic fever and a tumor on her spine. Against the hospital's wishes, Venus's parents took her on a stretcher to one of Kuhlman's monthly services in the [Los Angeles] Shrine Auditorium. As the service neared the end, Venus's mother suddenly said, 'You're cured!' Medical tests for the ailments now prove entirely negative.

"Paul Garnreiter, the seven-year-old boy who regained his hearing at the August service in Los Angeles, had suffered a proteus infection in his left ear for four years. A mastoidectomy two years ago showed a severely deteriorated eardrum. Last week Paul's physician could find no evidence of damage.

"Judith Schipper, twenty-nine, had a calcified tendon in her left elbow when she went to a Kuhlman service in Los Angeles. Her illness had been diagnosed by X ray last summer after she had complained of pain. X rays taken last week showed that the calcification no longer existed. Her doctor admitted it could have cleared up by itself, but Mrs. Schipper contends that it pained her only days before the service."

As with so many of the mass healers, Kathryn Kuhlman's healing powers just manifested themselves one day, and she reacted to them on a spiritual level, motivated by her love for Christ to carry His message to the multitudes.

She was as surprised as anybody by her first healing. One night, a woman in the audience stood up and announced she had been cured of a tumor during a previous Kuhlman sermon.

At first Kathryn Kuhlman believed that faith dictated healing, but she saw too many nonbelievers cured, and too many believers go away lame or sick to retain this belief.

Knowing the value of dramatics on making an impact, she usually wears a shimmering white silk dress at her services and leads the choir in singing her theme hymn:

> He touched me. Oh, He touched me.
> And oh the joy that filled my soul!
> Something happened and now I know
> He touched me, and made me whole.

An atmosphere of emotionalism is close to the surface as she calls on Christ for help in curing the ill.

"There is power in the name of Jesus," she says in an ecstatic voice. "Yes, there is power in the name of Jesus."

As a hush falls over the crowd, Kathryn Kuhlman prays aloud:

"We know, Father, yes we know, that miracles are going to happen in this place today. Oh, we feel the blessed presence of thy Holy Spirit. We promise to give you all the praise, all the glory, for what is about to happen here. Pour out your power on us for Jesus' sake."

Dr. Martin Biery, a surgeon formerly of the Veterans Hospital in Long Beach, California, examines many of those who come to be helped, recording medical evidence of their infirmities, then re-examining them after the cure.

Kathryn Kuhlman cannot explain how she knows the

exact nature of the body being healed, but she does know, as Joan of Arc did, what the Holy Spirit tells her.

She picks out the people to be healed and mentions their ailments. Others in the crowd have the agreeable experience of sharing in the therapy, and perhaps contributing to it with their emotion.

When she lays hands on some they reel back under her power, and one of her assistants stands close by to catch them as they collapse.

"Wonderful as physical healing is," she says, "it's secondary to the healing of the soul. You can be transformed in a moment by the spirit of God and become a new creature in Christ. Come, come and accept Christ."

She has a final message:

"Those of you who have been healed, go to your doctor and get medical documentation. And remember, Kathryn Kuhlman had nothing to do with your healing. It is all God's doing. Give Him the glory."

7
Fate and Free Will

> Nor time, nor space, nor deep, nor high can keep my
> own away from me.
>
> —John Burroughs

"How much free will do we have?" I asked.

Dr. Andrija Puharich, author of *Beyond Telepathy* and a pioneer psychic researcher, yawned over his bowl of won ton.

"You can probably decide for yourself whether you shave in the morning or at night."

"We must have more choice than that," I protested.

The eminent doctor squinted into the light.

"At birth the major decisions are made for you—sex, color, religion, finances, home environment."

"We change things as we go along."

"Yes, but the changes are only inevitable sequels to the starting point."

It sounded like a testimonial for reincarnation.

"Not really," said the man who had investigated many psychics. "But how, day after day, week after week, can we observe psychics who accurately predict everything under the sun, and not recognize that the future must be fixed?"

"Not all things are set," I said.

He shrugged. "Knowing the event, we can prepare or adapt to it, that's about the size of it."

"Suppose a psychic, an Edgar Cayce, for instance, foresees an earthquake in Southern California at a certain time, and I, believing him, take myself out of the quake area in time to be spared? Doesn't that alter my fate?"

"How do you know that the warning, plus your receptivity to it, isn't part of your destiny pattern?"

While a person's destiny may be fixed, it seemed to me in evaluating the contributions of the psychic, there were many roads to that destiny, and it was a wise man who pursued a course that was so conveniently drawn for him.

Perhaps it isn't so much what happens but how we handle it that determines our destiny. I had once made the rounds of soothsayers with a girl in her twenties, and all had predicted that she would live into her eighties.

As I was taking her home, the cabdriver, driving at a reckless rate, came close to smashing up the car.

"Tell that idiot to drive carefully," the girl shrieked.

"What are you worried about?" I said. "You've got sixty years to go."

"Yes," she snapped, "but I want to spend them in one piece."

She had perhaps put her finger on the whole issue of fate and free will. Cutting through time and space, the psychic sees the event in its ultimate conclusion, but along the way there are many choices which make the trip pleasant or unpleasant, without changing the final destination. For example, a psychic once warned a young woman of an automobile accident, telling her to watch her head. She drove more carefully after the warning.

But one evening, she was riding with a friend, when he lost control of the car, and it left the road. As it crashed with a sickening thud, her hands went protectively to her face. She was badly hurt, but her face was spared, thanks to her listening to the psychic.

Instead of embracing the psychic as a reassuring indication of an interested Higher Power, many shrink from knowing a future that may be unpleasant or tragic.

"What good does it do," asked one woman, "to know when somebody I love will die?"

"If it were your husband," I suggested, "it might give you an opportunity to do a few extra things for him before you called Forest Lawn."

Very few psychics discuss life or death, unless there is some positive reason for it. Edgar Cayce, consulted by an anxious serviceman being sent to the front lines, was able to assure him that he would return home unscathed.

"I had so much confidence in Cayce," this man recalled, "that I acted like a blooming hero, volunteering for every mission."

On a less dramatic level, an intimate of mine, a writer in his fifties, who had achieved some success, was told by psychics that his life's work was just beginning, and that he could anticipate, illogically as it seemed, thirty years of increased productivity. Instead of succumbing to the pap about youth being served, he plunged fearlessly into the most vigorous period of his life—and in a few months was doing more, looking younger, and feeling better than he ever had in his life.

"They've never been wrong with me before," he said, "why should they be wrong now?"

Gullibility has little to do with the fulfillment of psychic predictions. I know of nobody foolish enough to marry just because some psychic has ordained it, or sufficiently impressionable to become mysteriously ill, and then as mysteriously well, because some psychic he may never have seen before predicted such a development.

In apparently perfect health, Henry Herrmann, a New York businessman, visited psychic Marie Welt at the La Veranda Restaurant in midtown Manhattan, on November 10, 1970. Marie, ever optimistic, saw a number of situations that brought smiles to the businessman's face, and then mentioned an approaching leg condition.

"It is nothing to worry about," she said. "It will blow away as suddenly as it came."

Herrmann knew from experience that Marie Welt did not speak idly. So for the next two weeks he was particularly careful, as he was planning a trip abroad and wanted to be able to travel freely.

On Thanksgiving Day, the Herrmanns were invited to the country home of friends in Middletown, Connecticut. Herrmann never appeared in finer fettle when he retired that night, promising to be up early for breakfast.

He woke unexpectedly at 1:00 A.M., with a fever. With his temperature at 103 degrees, a doctor was summoned, and he immediately ordered Herrmann to the hospital. The fever rose to 104, and then a complication developed. "Suddenly, my left foot started to swell. Doctors spoke of a blood infection of undetermined origin."

Everybody seemed concerned except the patient. He had confidence in Marie and her predictions. "I flatly stated to everyone," he said, "that I knew—knew—that I would get better soon."

His confidence was justified. "After two days my temperature disappeared. In two more days I left the hospital—my foot back to normal."

The illness was never properly diagnosed and Herrmann never gave it another thought except to ponder the uncertainties of free will. "This precise prediction, at a time when nothing was less predictable, was certainly extraordinary. It caused me to wonder whether, if one is told something similarly psychic, one can evade one's fate by staying home on a given day or fleeing from the place where something is supposed to happen to you."

But then, might not the step to avoid this fate prankishly bring one closer to it?

Where psychics map out the lives of people days, weeks, months, and years ahead, the information is invariably presented as unchangeable.

"We see the future," Bill Corrado once stressed, "because it is there waiting."

For a hopeful glimpse of this future, Sahra Nichols, a writer, of Malibu, California, consulted psychic Vera Winston in Los Angeles in February 1960. Sahra was then twenty-five, a make-up artist, living in Hollywood. She had been married and divorced, and had two sons, ages eight and four. The psychic knew absolutely nothing about her, except that she was beautiful and blonde, and apparently had enough curiosity to visit a psychic.

Vera Winston is an impressive reader, with a bearing that bespeaks the patience of Job. She always begins her consultations by readings from the Psalms. She is not interested in the appearance of her clients. Once, she identified my researcher, Ginette Lawson, as a singer, and predicted marked success for her, even when she had no reason to believe she was anything but a researcher. A few months later, Ginette, on schedule, signed her first singing contract.

For Miss Nichols, the psychic outlined the major events of the next few years, not only for herself but for her children. Though the psychic was accurate about every tangible situation, Miss Nichols was not quite sure how to react to the reading. She had been comforted and relaxed by the Bible passage, but was not quite ready for the statement that her dead father was in the room in spirit, and wanted her to listen closely so that he could help her from the other side.

More substantially, the psychic picked up Miss Nichols' recent divorce and the remarriage of her ex-husband, and said he would have two sons by his second wife—giving him four sons in all.

She tuned into Sahra's two children precisely.

"She gave a perfect physical description of my sons. She not only described how they looked as children but how they would look as young men. She said the younger, Scott, would grow even taller than the older, Dana, and be taken as the older. Ten years later, Dana at eighteen, is six feet two inches, and Scott, at fourteen, is six feet three."

Dana was eight when Vera Winston foresaw he would have artistic ability, and eventually become a teacher and writer. At eighteen, his ceramics are selling in exclusive shops and he has won several prizes for them. He is already teaching ceramics in Hawaii, and his paintings, which I have seen, already show professional ability. The psychic had seen the younger boy, then four, excelling in sports. At fourteen Scott (Hubbell) had won the Los Angeles city-wide freestyle swimming championship and awards in basketball and baseball.

The psychic had also cautioned that the older boy would have trouble with drugs, but would profit through the experience and help other boys as a result. "Now," said the mother, "we are collaborating on a screen play on his experiences with drugs, the damage they do, and how he found a better way without them."

Sahra had been closer to Scott than the older boy, but the psychic said Scott would later choose to live with his father.

A thoughtful person, Sahra Nichols did not live her life by psychics. As a matter of fact, she had been to

Mrs. Winston but three times in eleven years. Nevertheless, she couldn't help but be impressed by the way things were laid out.

"There wasn't a thing that ever happened to me and my family that she didn't foresee."

But of what good was a foreknowledge which hadn't spared her son his drug experience?

Sahra was philosophical.

"I don't know how it could have been avoided, since the schools were full of drugs and the teachers recommended it. But though a bad experience, it did bring about a realization early in life that worthwhile development comes out of one's own spiritual resources."

The psychic also got into Sahra's career, telling the lovely blonde that she saw her doing television hair commercials.

Miss Nichols had not modeled before, and was not of an age to normally begin a modeling career. But one day, driving past the Clairol hair-conditioning office in Hollywood, the impulse came to stop in and ask about modeling work.

"They loved my hair," Sahra said, "and before I knew it I was working with them on a more or less steady basis."

The prediction was striking, but hardly conclusive, as Sahra herself had initiated the action making it come true. Still, if the prediction did influence a person decisively, perhaps it was intended that such a prediction should shape one's destiny pattern.

Even more unlikely events were predicted by Vera Winston.

"I see you in the Walt Disney Studios, writing," she said, "just as I see Walt Disney's spirit in the room guiding you."

Sahra found this incredible.

"I didn't have any desire to write, nor did I feel that I had the slightest qualification."

Vera Winston had seen these incredulous looks before.

"A gray-haired man in his seventies will be your teacher, and a doctor, also an older man, will help you with both your writing career and your health."

By chance, after the reading, Sahra took to studying writing. "An actor I was friendly with came back into my life. He was studying with the Hungarian author Lajos Egri, and urged me to join the class. To qualify for Egri's class, you had to write something which showed promise."

So she wrote a story called *The Christmas Tree That Cried,* now being offered for the Christmas trade.

Egri liked it, and took her into his class.

He was in his seventies, gray-haired, and a fine teacher.

Other bits and pieces in the unfolding drama began to come together. Even as she attended writing classes, Sahra picked up a part for a movie at Columbia Studios. One day, she was having coffee at the studio commissary, when the film writer, Roger MacDougall, sat down next to her.

He asked what she did, and she told him she was a writer.

"After all," she explained, "I had done one short story."

He mentioned that his agency was looking for promising new writers, with television ideas.

She had a comedy idea about a psychiatrist who treated people's pets.

Again, as with Clairol, she initiated the action materializing the event. Thinking of the prediction, she suggested that the agency contact Walt Disney with her idea.

Roger MacDougall thought the idea too far out for Disney. But Sahra did an outline, anyway, and it was presented to the producer.

"Walt Disney liked the idea so much," Sahra said, "that he sent for me, and gave me a contract for seventy-five hundred dollars to write a screen treatment."

She met frequently with Disney at his studio, and ultimately turned in a script, which was never produced.

"Vera Winston," Sahra said ruefully, "never said anything about the play being produced."

Sahra, too, had thought about the prediction and the way in which it came true.

"Everybody," said she, "is an instrument one way or the other, so why shouldn't a psychic, such as Vera Winston, be as instrumental in her way as Roger Mac-Dougall was in his?"

I wasn't sure of her point.

"My meeting with Vera Winston was apparently as much a part of my destiny pattern as any other consequential meeting."

Not all of the psychic's predictions were pleasant, since they mirrored the vicissitudes of life. But Sahra understood she was being prepared.

"Vera Winston said that I would experience much sadness, but it would be necessary to give me the understanding for the work I was to do later on. She saw a gulf between my mother and myself, but said this breach would be healed due to the death of someone we both loved. This gulf did develop through misunderstandings. And then last August [1970] my sister, who was only nineteen, was killed in an auto accident, and the tragedy brought my mother and me back together."

Her stepfather had died of cancer shortly before, and the psychic had foretold this, too. "She said my mother would remarry and outlive her next husband."

The remarriage had not yet taken place, but Mrs. Winston had said, as illogically as it seemed, that Sahra's mother would go into real estate, handling home rentals.

"My mother," said Sahra, "has been in real estate now for six years, handling rental properties."

One prediction impressed Sahra Nichols enormously because with all the warning she received, she was still powerless to prevent it, even though it almost took her life.

"Back in February 1960," Sahra said, "Mrs. Winston told me to make sure that I had spiritual protection around me when driving. As long as I was the one driving, she said, I would never be in an accident, but to be careful with people I let drive my car."

Three years after the reading, August 31, 1963, Sahra had been visiting with friends in Los Angeles. She was suffering from a migraine headache. And so when it came time to drive back to her home in San Bernardino, some sixty miles away, she asked a young friend, who had come down with her for the evening, if he would drive her back.

"If I had remembered the prediction, I might not have turned the car over to him. As it was, he began driving so fast that I tried to take the wheel away from him. He promised to slow down. Then, for some reason, he picked up speed again as we neared the exit ramp. The car skidded out of control on an S curve that had a forty-five-mile speed limit and crashed into a palm tree at eighty-five miles an hour."

She was pulled out of the wreckage more dead than alive, with head and internal injuries. One elbow was shattered, an arm broken, both knees smashed. She was hospitalized for a year.

When she got herself together, Sahra Nichols decided to go back to Vera Winston for another reading. This was in July 1965, and many of the predictions, including the accident had come true. Her sons were now thirteen and nine, and the younger boy had already gone to live with his father, who by now, as forecast, had two sons by his second marriage.

Sahra had new cause for amazement as she walked into the room where the psychic gave her readings. Though she hadn't seen her for five years, the psychic recalled her at once, and said reprovingly:

"You had an auto accident, even though I warned you about it."

She frowned.

"Did you let somebody else drive the car?"

Sahra nodded grimly.

The psychic sighed. "Well, it's over with, and you learned a great deal out of it."

Mrs. Winston was now primarily concerned with Sahra's health. She picked up a vibration of liver damage from the accident, damage which had escaped medical detection up to now, told her that it could bring severe weight problems. She advised Sahra to be extremely careful with her diet. At this time, Sahra, at five feet six, weighed about 120 pounds, and a weight problem was nowhere in sight.

"She said I would have a writing career, and reminded me of her prediction that I would meet a doctor who would not only help with my health but with my career."

For the next two years, Sahra was busy modeling, acting, writing. And then, early in 1968, three years after the psychic's warning, her body began to swell. The weight piled up but the doctors couldn't help. She took pills to reduce the excess fluid until she became ill. She felt sluggish and listless, and could hardly move around. She had gained more than sixty pounds, and most of it was on her body. Her face remained as smooth and pretty as before.

"I thought I was going to die," she recalled. "I had dreams of my skin bursting—I retained so much water."

She was gloomy and depressed. On the hottest days, she wore a wrap to conceal her figure. One thing alone encouraged her: Vera Winston had said she would find a doctor who would help her.

In February of 1970, a friend made an appointment for her with Dr. Henry Bieler, the famed nutritionist, of San Juan Capistrano. Up in his eighties, he was a healthy example of his own medicine—proper food. His book *Food Is Your Best Medicine* had sold over 300,000 copies.

Dr. Bieler looked at her, and shook his head. He could give her immediate help, but the ultimate cure would take years. His examination showed liver damage, presumably from the drugs given in the hospital to numb the pain. He prescribed a diet featuring zucchini to help her reduce. She weighed 176 pounds.

That first week, she lost sixteen pounds, and the drop continued until one year later, she weighed 140 pounds, headed for her old weight of 120 pounds or so.

Meanwhile, another prediction began to materialize.

After his successful book, Dr. Bieler had been approached by publishers for a second book on nutrition. Liking what he saw of Sahra Nichols' writing, he asked her to collaborate on a book about food and sex. She signed a contract with a publisher, and began the job Vera Winston had predicted a doctor would get for her.

Her most recent session with Vera Winston took place in April of 1971. The reading occurred at a time when Miss Nichols and her son Dana were moving into a house overlooking the Pacific.

"Mrs. Winston said the house would be close to a cliff in the Santa Monica area, with flowers and trees all around it." Her house, in Malibu, fits this description.

The psychic was quite optimistic, and Sahra breathed easy as she left.

"She said I would never lack for money again. I would have some problems with the book I was writing, partly because of the doctor. And this was so, since Dr. Bieler had trouble finding the time to work with me. She saw me making a lot of money, and saw me inheriting a lot. Both things are possible."

She gave her hope on her weight. "She said my weight problem would be resolved by the end of 1972, and would never recur."

Vera Winston was again explicit about her children.

"She saw both of them married, the younger one twice. She said the older would have a very beautiful marriage, and the younger would have two children, a boy and a girl. The older would become a great writer and teacher."

This was Dana, and he was already showing interest in the written word, when not sculpting, glazing, or painting.

Now that the children were—prophetically—comfortably married off, how about the mother?

Sahra smiled.

"She said it would be years before I would be ready to get married again. The man I married would be involved in writing and would be about six feet tall. He would be fair, with blue eyes. The marriage would be based on companionship, not sex, and it would last."

Off the past record, it looked like a happy ending for a deserving lady who had grown through adversity, and was ready now to reap the rewards of growth.

There is something very comforting I suppose, about the feeling that we can change our lives at will, but it is apparent, in studying the psychic, that the changes often take a direction the individual never intended. Filled with zeal, ambition, and enthusiasm, it is particularly hard for young people to feel their efforts can't achieve whatever it is they want to achieve. Gradually, as she

was exposed to the concept of inevitability, a new outlook took hold of my assistant, twenty-two-year-old
Ginette Lawson, who had all the bumptious assurance
of youth. She became thoughtful and contemplative, con-
fronted with the notion that the future somehow shaped
the present, rather than the reverse, as time after time
incidents and events tumbled unexpectedly into place to
bring about a predicted result.

As a searcher herself, Ginette was interested in the
psychic before she got into psychic research. Several
predictions made for her had remarkably come true, including a forecast that a woman she was to meet through
a friend would launch her singing career.

She had accepted these predictions on their face value,
without considering the philosophical implications. But
before long she was wondering aloud how it was that
psychics could be so accurate if the individual really
managed his own life.

In the matter of the Corso family, of Hollywood, she
finally acknowledged that she was thoroughly flabbergasted.

"How," she asked, "could Bill Corrado predict all those
deaths, divorces, and accidents, without the Corsos being
able to do something about it?"

Never had a psychic been more specific. And the readings, together with the consequent events, sounded like a
Greek drama.

Grace Corso, unmarried at fifty, had consulted Corrado in the summer of 1965 because she was concerned
about the declining health of her father, octogenarian
Pasquale Corso.

"Bill Corrado told me," Grace Corso recalled for
Ginette, "that my dad would be ill for the next three
years, and that he would pass away, not from illness,
but from a fall in the house. On June 30, 1968, Dad

tripped in the dining room, and broke his hip. He was
taken to the hospital, then sent home, and died of
complications from the fracture."

Even the timing was precise.

"Bill said he would suffer the injury just before his
birthday, July fifteen, and that he would pass away in
August. He died at the age of ninety on August ten."

With Grace Corso there had been health problems.

In 1969, after her father's death, she had pains in the
back and neck, and was put in traction for weeks. Corrado, visiting her, told her there would have to be surgery. In November of that year, with no improvement
noted, the doctors ordered her into a hospital, X rays
showed a ruptured disc, and surgery was performed.

But the pain continued after her discharge from the
hospital.

"It got so bad," she said, "I was having trouble holding
on to things."

In August 1970, she had another reading with Corrado.
"He said I would have to go back to the hospital because
another disc was involved."

With new X rays and tests, two more ruptured discs
were found. A second operation, again as predicted, was
performed on December 14, 1970.

Grace Corso is sure everything will be all right now.
"Two days after the operation, Bill said things would
finally straighten out."

Ginette was even more impressed by what Corrado
foresaw for Patricia Corso, forty, Grace's sister-in-law. He
saw somebody close laid up with a stomach operation,
and it turned out to be her husband, Tony. Corrado,
reading for Pat late in 1969, also said that she would
be working away from home at the beginning of 1971.

"I laughed about it," Pat said, "because I have a young

daughter at home and there was no possibility of my going into business. I hadn't worked in ten years. But then my husband got sick and I ended up going to work early in January as Bill said."

He also told her that she would be coming into a little money soon. She didn't see how.

"My grandmother passed away soon after, and the estate sent me a check for seven hundred and fifty dollars. It was from the sale of a house."

There was another Grace Corso in the family, married to Grace and Tony's brother John, sixty-two. She had been in discomfort, though no acute pain, from swollen ankles. Corrado had urged she change doctors and get a thorough checkup, as he felt she was sicker than she realized.

"If she doesn't get to the base of the trouble soon," he warned the family, "it will be too late. She has a number of tumors."

The "diagnosis" wasn't passed on to Mrs. Grace Corso, lest it frighten her. But when she reported passing blood, her sister-in-law Patricia urged her to see another doctor immediately. Grace consulted a specialist the next day, and he got her into the hospital at once, and performed a colostomy. She went home, and seemed to be holding her own, until six months later she had a kidney problem and was again rushed to the hospital.

A Catholic priest administered the last rites, for it looked as if she was going to die that night. But Bill Corrado thought otherwise.

"Bill said she would not die then," Pat recalled. "He said she would linger on for another six months and would die in another hospital." She was transferred to Mt. Sinai Hospital in Los Angeles and surgery was performed on her kidneys and stomach. "She came home,"

Pat said, "then went back and passed away, six months after her first trip to the hospital, just as Bill Corrado had said."

Corrado only foresees, he doesn't manufacture. But had Mrs. Grace Corso listened to him, and gone to a specialist right away, could she have been spared? Ginette wasn't too sure now. "He already saw the cancer," said she, "so it was a question of time. And besides, he saw her dying in the hospital, just when she did, so how could he have accurately predicted that, with the priest there and all, if it wasn't meant to be?"

What Corrado foresaw for Grace Corso's husband, John, was equally provocative. Corrado, reading for his sister-in-law, Pat, said that John, who worked in an automobile service station, would have an accident there. John was told to be extra careful. And in spite of that, it happened anyway.

Could it have been avoided?

Perhaps if John Corso had stayed at home, put his head under the blankets, and never stepped outside his door.

"But then," Ginette pointed out, "he couldn't have supported his family, and would probably have gone mad from not doing anything."

His disposition, aptitudes and circumstances, part of the built-in destiny pattern earlier outlined by Dr. Puharich, put him where he was, doing what he was, as a prelude to the accident.

"On this particular night," Pat Corso recalled, "John was checking a man's car and the man turned on the ignition while John was examining the air conditioner back of the fan belt. His hand got caught, and he lost part of one finger."

Obviously, Pat Corso was an unusual catalyst. But as correct as Corrado had been, Pat was still dubious when he saw her brother Ken getting a divorce after fifteen years of marriage and four children.

"He will have several children with this other woman," Corrado said.

"Impossible," she said. "He's got a very good marriage, they're highly compatible, and have no difficulties we know of."

In a few months her tune changed.

"Bill had made his prediction early in nineteen sixty-seven," Pat recalled. "Toward the end of that year, the family learned that my brother had been seeing another woman and had filed for divorce. In May nineteen sixty-eight, he married the other woman, and he automatically acquired more children, since she had four children by her previous marriage."

Nobody had any inkling of the breakup.

"Not even his wife," Pat said. "Nobody knew, but since then she has remarried and has a baby boy herself."

Was the family sorry, considering the plethora of bad news, that they had consulted Corrado?

"Heavens no," said Miss Grace Corso. "He's helped us a lot."

Sister-in-law Pat explained how he had helped.

"When things happened as he predicted, we were not at a complete loss. We now had the thought in our minds, and it braced us for the reality. We were prepared, and so we handled it better, since our subconscious minds had probably already taken us through the entire experience. Also, since there seems little we can do about these things, it made us more ready to accept whatever happened as God's will."

In timing, difficult even for the best psychics, Corrado seemed to excel. Sometimes, uncannily, he saw the precise date. In November of 1970, reading for Pete Condoli, a trumpet player and musical scorer, Corrado told the silver-haired musician he would be doing a regular stint on a television show beginning that December 20. He couldn't quite get the whole name of the man he would be working for, but it was "Griff," or something like that. Pete had a hunch who it was, a hunch realized three weeks later.

I got a call from the orchestra leader of the Merv Griffin Show on CBS telling me they wanted me. That was if I could start on December twenty, and I said yes, for it was the very date that Bill had said I would start."

Later on the Merv Griffin Show, someone mentioned to Griffin that Condoli knew he was coming to work with the band before Griffin knew it.

Merv laughed and said that he knew something that Condoli didn't—when Condoli was going off the show.

But Pete only smiled. He had better information, from the psychic he trusted. "Corrado said it would be a long run for me." And so it was.

Corrado had to be right about the show because he was so right about other things. It all ran together.

"He told me," Condoli said, "that I would require an operation within the year, for a hernia, and that I should go ahead and have it and it would be all right."

In eight months, at a doctor's suggestion, the surgery was performed, and Pete has had no trouble in that area since.

Then there was that wild thing about the car.

"Corrado told me there was something wrong with the front of my car and to have it checked because it could get worse. He said it was in the wheels, and my brakes were shot as well. So I had the car checked the next day, and the service station guy said I could have lost a wheel at any time."

Through Pete, Corrado realized there was something wrong with Pete's brother.

"My brother at that time had a problem with his neck, but Bill said the real problem was in the spine, a pinched nerve. He said that if he would go to a chiropractor four or five times it would relieve the pain in his neck."

Pete had not known about his brother's problem until Corrado mentioned it. However, when he passed on the information, his brother confirmed the stiffness in the neck.

Impressed, the brother went to a chiropractor, who agreed that the source of the complaint lay in the back.

"He went four times," Pete said, "and the problem never recurred."

Here were instances, it seems, where free will had a role in helping the informed individual to avail himself of help before it was too late.

"Successful living is all in the way we react," said Victor Dobryn, the Hollywood trial lawyer, who was convinced by Corrado's predictions that all we can do is respond to the program laid out by the Master Planner. "We can either smile and go along with an event," said this exponent of the evidential, "or weep and make ourselves generally unhappy, without improving the situation."

In the area of timing, the psychic sometimes seems amiss. When he is right about time, as Corrado so often is, it is invariably because he has a definite mental picture of a specific time. Generally, though, the impression is one of imminence or distance.

To serve the client, so often concerned about timing, psychics will move out of their subconscious into their conscious mind for an interpretation of what they feel. And for this reason, even when they are right about the incident itself, frequently err in this area of timing.

Sensitive Maude Robinson of Norfolk, Virginia, a truly

spiritual metaphysician, cannot always judge time to suit a client. But she will try.

She told a discontented brunette who came for marital guidance:

"I see a divorce for you, not too far away."

"How far away?" the disgruntled girl demanded.

"Oh, maybe a year or two," Maude replied.

"Couldn't you make it sooner?" the girl said unhappily.

"I see a two as plain as the nose on your face," Maude said. "And it will happen without any initiative on your part."

"Couldn't it be two months?" the girl cried. "I want my freedom now."

Maude shrugged. "I suppose it could be. But two years isn't too long to wait for a change as important as that."

Two months came and went, of course, without the semblance of a move from an unobliging husband.

After six months, the wife, thoroughly disgusted, told friends, "Maude was wrong with me."

But Maude wasn't wrong. In two years, the divorce occurred, and just as Maude said. The husband suddenly initiated it, and it came without the wife doing anything about it.

When she does pick up the image of a specific time period, Maude Robinson is invariably right.

On one occasion, I was on the phone with her from New York, inquiring about a young lady I had not seen for some time.

"Do you think I will hear from her again?" I asked.

"Hear from her?" she said. "You won't be able to keep her away."

Since the girl was presumably planning to marry somebody else, I could hardly agree.

"Nonsense," said Maude. "Even as we're talking on the telephone, she is trying to reach you from California.

And the moment we hang up, the phone will ring, and it will be she."

"I can hardly believe it," I said.

"All right, just hang up."

I rang off as directed.

I don't think fifteen seconds elapsed before the telephone jangled. It was the light, airy voice that I knew so well, the girl that should have been married by then, calling from California.

Many psychics believe that events are foreshadowed as the Bible suggests. Where an event is of a powerful nature, affecting the lives of multitudes, it seems to touch off a current which many psychics tune in to with remarkable precision.

Before the "unsinkable" *Titanic* sank on her maiden voyage in 1912, with a heavy loss of life, there were so many predictions of this implausible event that some wag suggested more people had predicted the tragedy than there were lives lost in it.

Lincoln's assassination was pretty well foretold. Even the victim had a premonitory dream of his body lying in a casket, a dream discussed with his Cabinet only a few days before he was shot at Ford's Theater.

Vibrations of John F. Kennedy's approaching assassination appeared to hang electrically in the air, charging the atmosphere with foreboding. In her Edgewater, New Jersey, home, the late Florence Sternfels, known as Florence Psychic to thousands, pleaded to everyone who called:

"Tell the FBI not to let the President go to Texas; he is going to be shot."

In New York, Helen Stalls, who later predicted Bobby Kennedy's death in the same manner, cried that the President would be shot in a few days.

There are times when an event is so surely destined

that the vibration of that event almost overwhelms the psychic with its intensity.

In this way, psychic Doug Johnson had seen a number of things over the years for his friend, Ruth Adams: death, marriage, a new home, accidents, the whole record of a life. He saw Ruth's mother in a casket, and shortly thereafter her stepmother was killed by a car. He saw her son Bob, then five years old, falling down a staircase and splitting his head, and a week later the boy was in the hospital having his head stitched. He saw Ruth moving into a big brick house, with a huge Christmas tree in the living room, where she was comfortably ensconced in a home she loved, and had no thought of moving. "But the day we moved into this house, it hit me—this was a brick house, and that's what Doug had told me."

In one case, Doug Johnson saw a marriage with an old friend Rose —— hadn't seen in years—a man she had run into at the theater only the night before.

As she mentioned the meeting, an almost overpowering vibration shook Johnson.

"Who is that man, Rose?" he asked. "Whoever he is, you are going to marry him."

Johnson has his problems with timing. But this time the vibration was so strong that he felt he could almost reach out and touch the wedding bells.

"In June," he said, "you will be married to this man."

June came and went, and there was no marriage, not even the hint of a proposal. But Doug wasn't discouraged.

"It will happen in September then," he said. "Buy your trousseau."

Rose brought him the material for her marriage gown and psychometrist Johnson held the fabric for a moment.

"You are absolutely going to marry this man, I see it as plain as day."

Two years passed, then three, four, with no marriage. Rose had begun to look at him reproachfully.

One day she came to him almost in tears.

"Harper has met somebody else," she said, "and I haven't seen him for months."

He had telephoned the night before, to say that he was getting engaged to the other woman.

Rose may have been discouraged, but not Doug. The vibration was as strong as ever.

"Even as she was standing there before me," he said, "I could hear a voice in me saying—'Harper will marry nobody but Rose.'"

He saw it now as plain as the calendar on the wall.

"I told her," he said, "that in two weeks Harper would be back with her. Two weeks later, Harper called and told her that he could never love anybody but her."

Now reinstated as a prophet, Johnson predicted the marriage for September of that year.

And so, five years after his first prediction, they were finally married, and Rose fulfilled the destiny he had seen for her.

Wondering what could have delayed Rose's marriage, I recalled Bill Corrado having said once that destiny could be delayed but not thwarted.

"Where," I asked Johnson, "did the prediction go wrong?"

Johnson had given it considerable thought, and had even tried to find out, on a conscious level, what had been passing through the mind of the other person—Harper.

"I learned," Johnson said, "that he was several times on the verge of asking her to marry him, and so it may have confused my own thinking somewhat. I saw the event at its conclusion, and then picking up her vibration, together with his vibration when it was inclined toward marriage, assumed it would occur at a time when they were both thinking about it."

Johnson felt somehow the flaw was in him, for *thinking* it out, but viewing the episode from the sidelines, it appeared to me that he had a considerable part in the eventual consummation of the relationship.

"Yours was a necessary role," I said.

"How was that?"

"Did you ever think you would be wrong?"

"Not for a moment," he said. "I didn't understand the delay, but I just knew it would happen."

"And that confidence," I said, "from a psychic she believed in, was enough to give her the courage to go on for five years."

Johnson smiled. "Perhaps, but don't forget those vibrations—that's what eventually told the story."

8
The Psychic Watchers

The American parapsychologists visiting the research laboratories at Leningrad University in the summer of 1971 came home with great tales of a psychic holding her hand near an object and making it hop across the table without touching it.

"As clear-cut a case of psychokinesis as ever I saw," enthused one of the returning parapsychologists.

His wife, listening with a frown, said finally, "But dear, couldn't you have picked up the object and moved it just as well?"

Like the parapsychologist's wife, I have never been impressed by what psychic buffs call physical phenomena. I wouldn't cross the street to watch somebody levitate, as I see nothing to be gained by somebody suspending their body in midair, when it is considerably more restful and practical to stretch out comfortably on a mattress. For the same reason, I have been unimpressed, as was clairvoyant Edgar Cayce, by the efforts to restrict psychics to a laboratory, regardless of the auspices.

I recognized the contributions of Dr. Joseph Rhine, who with his laboratory card tricks at Duke University helped give the psychic field some cloak of respectability, and I cheered the work of the two lady reporters Sheila Ostrander and Lynn Schroeder, who delved into the *Psychic Discoveries behind the Iron Curtain.*

However, it is my feeling, as an observer, that the critique or yardstick for psychic phenomena lies not in isolated experience, in or out of the laboratory, but in the measure of help psychics bring to mankind.

Many great psychics—the Cayces, the Arthur Fords, the Maude Robinsons, the Bill Corrados—have shunned the parapsychologists and their tests like the plague, even as they performed metaphysical miracles for the troubled who beat a path to their modest studios.

"Why should I go down to Duke," the Dutch psychic Peter Hurkos once asked, "and have Dr. Rhine put me through a lot of card tests with a machine on my head, when I could be helping a police department solve a major crime?"

Not all parapsychologists, fortunately, are armchair generals, but meet the psychic on his own testing ground, the laboratory of human need. When a three-year-old Los Angeles boy had been reported missing, Marjorie Kern and Louise Ludwig of the Southern California affiliate of the American Society for Psychical Research, were brought into the case. They in turn called on psychic Doug Johnson. Johnson was not given any cards, no machines were thrust on his head, he was not given any directions on how to proceed. He performed in his own way, motivated only by a desire to help. As a psychometrist who often tunes in through holding objects belonging to the subject, he was given a pair of blue jeans belonging to the boy.

"I see a little blond boy," he said.

Louise Ludwig nodded. "Yes, he is blond."

Johnson sighed. "Then I am in tune."

He closed his eyes again and the information from the Universal Mind which he calls Spirit flowed through him.

A frown darkened his features.

"I hate to tell you this," he said, "but the little boy is dead."

He put down the blue jeans.

"Do they have a swimming pool in the back of their home?"

The parapsychologist nodded.

"Well, the body is floating in the swimming pool in the backyard."

"Impossible," Louise Ludwig said, "the police have been all over the place."

Even as she spoke, the vision of the boy in the swimming pool grew. But since Mrs. Ludwig was so sure that he couldn't be right, Johnson, as he recalled it, began thinking about other possibilities, in the process reverting from the subconscious to the conscious.

He wondered aloud whether there might be another swimming pool nearby or a lake.

"There's a reservoir a mile away, but there's a fence around it."

As Mrs. Ludwig mentioned the fence, Johnson, slipping back into the subconscious, knew the boy wasn't there, but in the area of a swimming pool.

Still, how could it be the family's pool, without the family or the police knowing it?

For the next hour nothing came through but a body floating in a swimming pool. Johnson asked if he could keep the blue jeans overnight.

That night, holding the blue jeans, Johnson allowed his mind to drift. Suddenly, he saw a little boy lying in a ravine, with blood on his face.

Startled, he called Louise Ludwig. "The boy was killed," he said. "I don't know why I ever saw him floating in the pool. I must have been wrong."

By now the problem seemed well confused.

Seeking another opinion, parapsychologist Ludwig returned to the boy's home with still another psychic. Sensitive Lottie Von Strahl, like Johnson, felt that the boy was dead, by accident or foul play.

And there the case stood for three weeks.

Then one day, the boy's father walked out into his backyard, and found his son's body floating in the swimming pool. Nobody could understand how it could have been there for three weeks unnoticed. One theory was that the boy had been at the bottom of the pool all this time, and that the water was so dirty that the bottom couldn't be seen. It seemed unlikely.

The results were inconclusive; Johnson had seen the ultimate conclusion, the floating body. But if one accepts that it had been underwater in a small, relatively shallow pool for three weeks, then his vision of the body in the ravine was off the mark.

Johnson himself still feels he was right in both respects, and that the body must have been moved. "I've never seen a home pool you couldn't see the bottom of," he observed.

Johnson is forever ready to contribute, in the interest of research, or for the good of humanity.

Once Marjorie Kern, founder of the Southern California affiliate of the American Society for Psychical Research, conducted an impromptu experiment of her own with Johnson. One New Year's Eve, December 31, 1963, she happened to be at a small gathering Johnson was at, and while they were talking she handed him a letter from a friend, singer Christine Murphy, who was appearing professionally in Europe.

She asked if he could describe the singer.

"He had never met her," she recalled later, "and knew nothing about her except that I had told him she was singing in Europe."

The party stopped while Johnson went into his delineation. In all, he registered fifty-one different impressions, some of which were predictions unverifiable until the day they came true. Nevertheless, his accuracy was remarkably significant.

"We found on checking," Mrs. Kern said, "that twelve items were true, as known by me at the time. In another four months, fourteen more items had materialized out of the future or been otherwise verified, making a total of twenty-six, or better than half, verified at this point." Of the remaining items, only the future could tell whether most of these would prove correct. But he was still not provably wrong on any count.

Many of the things Johnson had seen were important only to the singer herself. At this time, he said she was having trouble with her throat and was using a spray. This of course is true of many singers. But in any event, in her next letter, Christine Murphy mentioned her throat problem and using a spray. "Johnson said the trouble would recur," Marjorie Kern added, "and this was true, too."

Johnson had mentioned that Christine was in opera and would travel from Germany, where she had been performing, to Italy, where she would work regularly. He singled out a number of things that happened very soon —a recording contract, an older man (an agent) who would help her, a contract with an opera association, visualizing correctly the very room in which the signing took place.

He saw things in no particular chronology or importance. A pink frilly dress—the only dress Christine had ever owned of this description—was lost in transit, apparently bringing it to the psychic's attention. He saw Christine telephoning Marjorie Kern from Europe to give her a bit of good news, and this soon happened.

He even picked up a friendly spirit, an old-time singer, who expressed interest in Christine's career and said she would help her whenever she could.

Oddly, this information dovetailed with a Ouija board experience Marjorie Kern had shared with Christine. "It so happened," Mrs. Kern recalled, "that we had picked up on the board one of the very famous old singers, who had been dead many years and had the same type of voice and other characteristics of Christine's. It was a standing joke with us that she had come through to help Christine."

Johnson worked best in response to human need. One day, the American Society for Psychical Research called the psychic because of an SOS from relatives concerned about an inmate who had wandered off from a mental institution. They were concerned not only because of her condition, but that she had no adequate clothing or money.

"Have you any idea," an ASPR secretary asked, "where this poor woman might be?"

Still on the phone, Johnson went into his subconscious.

"I see her in Griffith Park," he said, mentioning a large park near the Silver Lake area of Los Angeles.

"Can we send over an object of hers for you to hold?"

Johnson checked his watch; it was shortly before two in the afternoon.

"It won't be necessary," he said, "she should be back by four o'clock."

At five o'clock the secretary called to say the mental patient had not turned up, and she would be at Johnson's house at eight with an article of hers for him to psychometrize.

An hour later, the ASPR called again, apologetically. The woman had arrived sometime before at the home of a daughter, but the parapsychologists had only now been told. Arrival time—four o'clock.

The parapsychologist's job was concluded, but the task of the psychic consultant had only begun. Because of Johnson's success the family thought he might help the patient, a schoolteacher, through counseling. She was hopelessly despondent, disinterested in bettering her own condition, unable to cope with the reality of everyday living, completely without confidence.

Johnson saw the woman perhaps six or seven times, trying to give her a positive attitude. She was about fifty or so, and she felt that she had come to the twilight of her life without any prospect of finding anybody to ease her loneliness and restore a sense of purpose.

Johnson's therapy was basic. "We have to make them realize there's hope for everyone, provided they look first within themselves. I get them to ask themselves, what am I doing that isn't right? So many people just complain and don't do anything about changing destructive attitudes."

Johnson elaborated.

"When the mental attitude changes, the life plan changes accordingly. Just eliminating destructive thinking is a starter."

"Where," I asked, "does your handling of a situation differ from that of a psychiatrist?"

"I turn it over to Spirit, asking for guidance, and ask the individual to do the same."

"Does Spirit represent God to you?"

"Yes, God force, it works through all of us. Spirit tells us where to look for help. Sometimes a certain doctor is needed. What difference where people receive help, as long as they receive it?"

We had come a long way from a parapsychologist's province, as I was to realize when I spoke to the teacher.

She was willing to talk about Johnson's help, provided her name wasn't used.

"I'm teaching again," she said, "and I don't think the school would like that sort of publicity."

I sympathized with her wish.

"How do you think he helped you?" I asked.

She didn't hesitate. "He restored my faith in a God interested in me."

I was struck by the fact that she had gone back to teaching.

"Doug realized that my problem was feeling useful, and he showed me that we all serve God in our own way."

Again I wondered aloud why a psychic should have been more effective than an institution of psychiatrists.

"When he saw where I had gone to that day, and when I would be back, I knew then he had a pipeline to God. How else could it be explained?"

Although psychics are becoming increasingly popular as consultants, the psychic field would have far more recognition if all who used psychics gave them their due. One millionaire of some prestige constantly checked his affairs by phone from New York with psychic Maya Perez in Balboa, California. Yet, from a wish not to appear ridiculous to associates, he insisted she not divulge he was a client.

Still others, while being helped, have disclaimed help from this source as a reflection on their ability to manage their own lives.

In one instance, a young writer, shattered by the experience of surprising his wife with another man, sought counsel from friends, acquaintances, and psychiatrists before he turned to psychic Bill Corrado.

Two or three days after his session with Corrado, he telephoned to say that Corrado was a miracle man. "He picked up the situation immediately," he told me, "and tuned into a number of things that were true. He was very encouraging, and told me to get off by myself and plunge into my work."

I saw the writer occasionally, and he seemed duly appreciative of whatever it was that Corrado had done for him, to the point of inviting the psychic down to his new home for a weekend.

And so it was that in preparing to examine Corrado's work, I thought of talking to the writer who had seemed so grateful to the psychic at the time.

I had my first misgivings, however, almost as soon as I came through his door.

"I certainly can't allow you to use my name," he said. "It's all too personal."

"The names won't be necessary," I said.

"How evidential can it be without names?"

"I'll manage," I said, "but of course if you don't care to talk about it, that's perfectly all right."

He turned to my assistant, Ginette Lawson, who had brought along a tape recorder.

"What do you do?" he said.

"She'll be handling the interview," I said.

"What prompted you to see Bill Corrado?" Ginette promptly asked.

He gave her an almost pitying look.

"One goes to a psychic because one has an area of uncertainty. You are emotionally upset. You are seeking reassurance. You go for the same reason that people go to witch doctors—they are twentieth-century witch doctors. That's what I told Bill Corrado he was."

Ginette looked at him doubtfully. "What did Bill tell you that reassured you?"

"I'm not saying he did. I went looking for reassurance. I wasn't particularly reassured."

My jaw must have dropped, for he added quickly, "I was reassured a year after the fact."

Ginette interposed, "But what made you reassured then?"

He showed signs of impatience.

"When you seek reassurance, you are sensitive not just to what you see or hear or taste and smell." His voice held a trace of hauteur. "And I must say the initial contact was less than reassuring. The suburban aspect of Corrado's house, the particular decor, the clutter of animals, all of them were alien to me. I'd never had a psychic reading before and I expected a crystal ball with all the trimmings, piped-in music, and all that. His house and the particular room in which the reading took place had anything but atmosphere. It smelled like somebody was cooking lunch or a late breakfast, or the animals were particularly unruly the night before."

Considering his expressions of gratitude at the time, I could hardly believe what I was hearing.

"He was like any other person, then?" Ginette asked.

"You might say that."

He described the session. "I didn't ask him anything, I just said I came for a reading. He was expecting me. First of all, I had never seen the cards he uses before. They fascinated me. I was highly aware of the surroundings. Writers are schizophrenic. They never participate, they only go through the motions. They make an inventory of events and experience life without ever living it."

He brushed aside my protest.

"Here I was, nevertheless, in desperate emotional need, sitting at a card table in a closet, projecting my aura of me and making an inventory of us both sitting at the table. Obviously I was skeptical."

"But you were still there," I put in.

"Of course. Just as if I were a Catholic I might have gone to confession. The central point of the whole thing is that I had been to my analyst, and a hypnotist, and if I had been a churchgoer, I would have gone to confession. Corrado just happened to be another way station on my voyage of self-punishment. When you have any kind of ego deflation, a certain amount of flagellation takes place. You have failed yourself, so you reach out for verification of who you are. Who is it you failed? What you are doing in this emotional exploration is like having to pinch yourself. You don't eat, you don't sleep, you drink too much, you will do anything you can to cause self-destruction."

Despite myself, I was impressed with his eloquent dramatization of his own inadequacies.

Ginette, however, seemed baffled. "But going to Bill," she protested, "wasn't in itself a punishment of yourself as an individual."

"How do you know I wasn't looking for humiliation? Does a nymphomaniac go to a man looking for reassurance or humiliation?"

"You were looking for help," I said, "you didn't know if he could be helpful or not, but it was a chance. You were just grabbing anything for support because of your shattered ego."

I suppose this is why most people consult psychics. They are looking for miracles, and who but a psychic can perform them?

The interview seemed to have wandered from its original objective of checking Corrado's validity as a psychic.

"Why did you check back with Corrado?" I asked.

"Only to verify that what he had said had happened."

This was suddenly a new turn of affairs.

"What had he told you?"

"On March twelve of nineteen-seventy, when I went to him, he said I would begin a new cycle in April nineteen seventy-one. He said that in the beginning of April I would receive good news about money. On April first, I received a call from New York, advising that instead of losing quite a bit of money in a business deal, I had made money, contrary to all logic."

He was now being factual instead of philosophical.

"Corrado correctly foresaw the date of the divorce from my wife, and the date I left. He also said that she would eventually want to come back to me and"—he smiled thinly—"she recently suggested something like that."

Corrado had also gone into his career.

"I was quite worried about a book I had contracted to do, because I was already two years overdue and the publishers had given me until May of nineteen-seventy to produce the manuscript or give back the fifty-thousand-dollar advance. Bill said I would deliver the manuscript late, but the contract would not be canceled. That was accurate."

There had been one more question.

"I asked if in nineteen seventy-one (wondering if there would be a nineteen seventy-one) things would begin to add up."

And what had Corrado held out?

"He just said to hang on until then, and things would turn dramatically for the better."

And so they had.

I don't know why he had suddenly changed his tune, but the interview had told me more about him than it did about Corrado.

"As a matter of fact," he said, as we were leaving, "Corrado wasn't at all bad, if you believe in psychics."

Many people are psychic hoppers, jumping from one psychic to another, in the hope of hearing what they want to hear. When her married boyfriend went back to his wife, one Beverly Hills designer consulted three different psychics. All told her the relationship was finished, but she wouldn't accept it.

"But he must come back to me," she said, "I love him."

When Bill Corrado couldn't give her what she was looking for, she went to George Dareos of San Bernardino, California, and though he also hit her situation, she went on to psychic Nellie Sanders of Los Angeles.

She saw nothing strange about her behavior.

"I needed more assurance," she said. "I was so upset that first week that Jeffrey left me that I consulted both Corrado and Dareos. They both told me the same things, that the affair was over, and I would soon be laughing where I was now crying. But it didn't help, because I wanted to be told that Jeffrey was coming back."

Nevertheless, talking about her problem seemed to help, and she weathered the emotional storm. Since the two psychics had said the same thing, and both were right, she got to thinking that maybe clairvoyants were the answer to all her problems, business as well as personal.

And then she met Nellie Sanders, and realized, she said, that the greatest boon the psychic could give one was a sense of spiritual awareness.

"At first," she said, "I just wanted to know what they could see. Now I believe in a universal concept that permits me to use this psychic power in my own behalf."

Nellie Sanders' studio is rich with American Indian lore, and Nellie Sanders herself, though totally Caucasian in background, seems to draw on the mystic tradition of the noble red man.

"You walk into a room that is completely Indian," the designer said. "There is a big round table in the middle of the room where she used to give seances. But she has given this up, saying that evil spirits lurk there and she is afraid."

Nellie Sanders put on a good show.

"She washes her hands and then comes into the reading room with a cup of coffee. She produces some Indian-backed cards, shuffles them, and tells you to concentrate. She lights a candle, and then you pick a card, and hold it above the candle, and make a wish."

The designer's wish, now that she had gotten over Jeffrey, was always the same, that she be extremely successful in her fashion field.

She had seen Nellie Sanders three times, and each time she felt she had come away with greater understanding.

"I see now that I have to make it happen, nobody else can do it for me. I don't even think of making money any more like I used to. I just go away feeling a higher vibration, knowing that the inspiration produced within me will automatically bring money."

It seemed obvious that Nellie Sanders had given her faith where the others had offered hope.

"Through her," said the designer, "I have become in tune with the universe."

Many messages had come through in the Indian room before the designer was convinced of her own symphonic accord with the universe.

"She said I would be dealing with various countries, and my dresses are now all over. She told me there was money in the mail from a contract—and the next day the postman delivered it. She said my clothes would set a trend, and this is already happening in fashion circles.

She said I would be invited to parties where film people would be, and they would admire my designs, and this, too, has occurred."

I didn't see anything suggestive of universal truths about all this.

She clucked her tongue impatiently.

"True, these are all material things, but the concept which makes them happen is the important thing. I am doing it now, not the psychic."

"How do you figure that?" I asked.

"When I used to go to a psychic," she said, "I just wanted to know what they could see. Now I understand why they can see what they do—tuning into the Universal Mind as they do. And so I do the same thing myself, with Nellie Sanders' help of course."

While Nellie was concentrating over the candle and cards, she concentrated with her, and actually felt the same vibration, she said, that the psychic felt.

"I can make things happen for myself," she said.

"Why then," I asked, "go to a psychic?"

She laughed. "Because they make me feel so good."

9
Enter the Spirit

> I believe, even to the point of positive conviction, that
> the Power that gave me existence is able to continue it in
> any form or manner He pleases.
>
> —Thomas Paine

To Hollywood's Douglas Johnson, Spirit is a universal
force that not only communicates through him, but is
capable of invoking universal laws that help people with
their practical problems.

I have often wondered why Spirit should be so concerned about the mundane affairs of a dreary life experience they had left, when they are now presumably a part
of a much richer experience, rubbing elbows, so to speak,
with all the great and wonderful people of history who
have passed on to this new dimension of living.

Many times, in discussions with mediums, I have questioned whether they were getting their extrasensory information in a special pipeline from the great beyond, as
they thought, or as a dramatic exercise of their own subconscious.

The most celebrated of American mediums, the late
Arthur Ford, who claimed spirit contact with thousands,
including the magician Harry Houdini and young Jim
Pike, the bishop's son, was not quite as sure toward the

twilight of his career of the authenticity of his spirit guide as he had once been.

Like other guides, Fletcher was a friendly entity or spirit which presumably attached itself to the medium's subconscious, but which the medium considered a force outside himself through which the spirit world conveniently communicated, being on the same wavelength.

"Wouldn't it be amusing," Ford said once with a wry smile, "if what I thought was Fletcher all these years was actually my own subconscious dramatizing a purely clairvoyant experience?"

However, before his own death, the medium's faith in Fletcher was reinforced by a reassuring message from young Jim Pike for his father.

In the case of Bishop Pike's son, the transition to the spirit world was reported by several mediums, who served as a communication medium for the other side.

As a churchman dedicated to Christ's teaching, Pike professed belief in everlasting life, but he had not equated this concept with spirits reaching back into this life from the ethereal world. Yet there was no question in Bishop Pike's mind that he was communicating with his dead son. "I realized of course," this iconoclast told me, "that there is a danger of believing what I want to believe, but the messages that came through three different mediums dealt with so many things that only Jim and I knew that it was impossible to escape the conclusion that Jim was truly communicating."

Pike had consulted London medium Ena Twigg, Arthur Ford, and British-born George Daisley in Santa Barbara—and thought that he would feel in closer contact with his son in the Holy Land. They had visited there together, sharing deeply religious experiences, just before Jim ended his life in New York City.

In Southern California, this controversial crusader for Christ had told me:

"I am planning to visit the places in the Holy Land where Jim and I were together, and I know that I will feel a unity of spirit with him there."

I was to think of this conversation when word came later that Pike had lost his life while roaming Israel's bleak desert land.

But death held no fears for the bishop. "Life after death," Pike said just before his own death, "is not supernatural but natural." And, paraphrasing St. Paul: "If there is no resurrection of the dead, then Christ is not risen. And if Christ is not risen then is our preaching vain, and your faith is also vain. For if Christ was resurrected, we are all resurrected."

In the search for evidence of survival, any subjective experience is suspect on the grounds of wishful thinking. With my imagination I can visualize anyone I know who has passed on, and by sinking into the subconscious invoke conversations that are clearly offshoots of this imagination.

What assurance did I have that the psychics weren't doing pretty much the same thing?

Recognizing this problem of distinguishing reality from fantasy, Douglas Johnson felt the test lay not only in the vividness of a presumed communication, but in the nature of the information, information that could have come from only the other side.

And so it was at Johnson's suggestion that I phoned the Harry Halversons in Altadena, California, to inquire about an apparent communication with their son.

Halverson said rather shortly, "I don't know why Doug Johnson should have mentioned him to you—or why you would be interested."

"What greater mission could one be on," I said, "than to learn whether there is life after death?"

"Ours is a personal matter," Halverson said.

"How reassuring it would be to so many to feel there is evidence of life after death."

There was a strained pause.

"I am familiar with your books," Halverson said finally, "and I will talk it over with my wife and let you know."

As Halverson rang off, I felt a definite sense of disappointment. He was a practical man, a successful business executive, and his reaction to whatever it was that Johnson had picked up might have been enlightening.

As I understood it, the Halversons had consulted Doug Johnson three or four weeks after their son's tragic death in the spring of 1969. Peter had been only sixteen when he died, and his death had seemed as inexplicable as it was hard to bear. He had died, apparently by his own hand, by asphyxiation.

Two years had passed, but the Halverson household was not the same, even though there were four other children, two brothers and two sisters.

I could understand the family grief, and fully sympathized with their wish to draw a curtain over the tragedy. And so I was pleasantly surprised a week or two later when Halverson called back to say that he would discuss the Johnson sitting with me.

The Halversons lived in a big house in a middle-class neighborhood. They were solid people, with nothing in their backgrounds to suggest the occult or esoteric. Born Mormons, they already believed in survival, as it was one of the credos of the Church of Jesus Christ of Latter-Day Saints that a family is rejoined in death.

"We went to Johnson," Halverson explained, after making me comfortable, "not because we questioned survival, but because we wanted to know whether Peter had really intended to kill himself, or had just dramatized the act of suicide, and then been overcome by fumes before he could escape."

The boy, a keen chemistry student, had hooked up an elaborate contraption to a wall jet, creating his own gas chamber out of plastic, when he could just as easily have sealed the doors and windows, with nobody at home, and lowered his head over the open jets.

He was a volatile, sensitive youth, given to alternate high and low moods, as so many adolescents are. On the morning of his death, he had wanted to borrow the family car. "It had been raining that day," Mrs. Halverson said, "and I had refused him permission to use the car, not only because the streets were slippery, but because I had an errand to do myself."

Other things seemed to have annoyed him more. He had been upset about a teacher he couldn't seem to satisfy, and increasingly concerned by the war in Vietnam. But none of this seemed a prelude to suicide.

"As I look back," Halverson said, a catch in his voice, "I realize I didn't know him as well as I did my other sons."

Mrs. Halverson brought out a snapshot, showing Peter as a clean-cut looking boy with wavy hair and an engaging smile. It seemed a pity that his young life should have been snuffed out almost before it had begun.

The death had been a double shock, compounded by the uncertainty as to how Peter had died, and why. There were so many questions in their minds that only he could answer, and so, finally, at the suggestion of a friend, they consulted Johnson.

The meeting with Johnson was easy. He had asked them to bring a couple of articles belonging to Peter, as by psychometrizing them—holding them in his hand—he seemed better able to tune into the electrical vibration or frequency that keyed him into the miraculous world of the subconscious.

The Halversons had brought Peter's billfold.

As he held the wallet, the psychic seemed to latch onto Peter right away. Peter's features appeared to him almost as they had in the snapshot I had seen. And Johnson had a distinct impression of his personality, of an unusual sensitivity and love of beauty.

Johnson said to the parents, "He is a Libra, is he not?"

This Venus-ruled Sun sign is often, astrologically, the harbinger of a delicate imbalance, as well as a sense of beauty.

They nodded. "Yes, his birthday was in October."

Johnson had a vivid impression of a spirit voice. It was not an audible voice, such as the late medium Sophia Williams, of Glendale, California, seemed to invoke at will, for it was heard only by Johnson. The voice had no association with any body form, and was received in a separate image from the one in which Johnson had recognized Peter's handsome, regular features, his wavy brown hair, and mercurial smile.

As he tuned in, still holding the wallet, the boy's past seemed to move through Johnson's subconscious, in a series of kaleidoscopic impressions.

Finally he picked up a breathing difficulty that he associated with Peter and felt an oppressiveness in his own chest. He looked questioningly at the Halversons.

"He found it very hard to breathe," he said, laboring a little himself.

"Yes," Halverson said, "he was overcome by gas."

So far the Halversons didn't know what to make of the sitting. They had come hoping not only to learn how their son had died, but also, if his spirit force did materialize, whether he had anything to tell them, reassuring or otherwise.

"One can believe in survival," Halverson said, "and still find comfort in whatever evidence there is this side of eternity."

In Johnson he had found an unusual medium, a person as analytical as himself. As had Arthur Ford, Johnson had learned to question the spirits that spoke to him, realizing he might only be dramatizing a clairvoyant experience.

Silently now, he asked the universal consciousness through which he worked for proof that he was really in communication with Peter's spirit.

The answer was soon forthcoming. Almost at once he saw a couple standing together; they seemed anxious to identify themselves. He had the distinct impression they were the boy's grandparents.

He turned to Mrs. Halverson. "Aren't your mother and father in spirit?"

She nodded.

The elderly couple stood a few moments, talking together, then they stepped aside, and Johnson saw the son standing where they had been.

Peter—the voice, spirit—began to communicate. He mentioned things that only the family would have known about, including a cabin in the mountains damaged by the California floods of January and February of 1969.

As Johnson listened to the flow of conversation, he passed it directly on to the Halversons.

"You know," he said, "Peter is very keen on wanting you to repair the damage to the cabin. He loved the place so."

The Halversons were startled in spite of themselves.

Only they knew of the boy's preoccupation with the cabin, and the way he had been after them to get the mountain retreat fixed up after the floods.

Voice and substance now merged in Johnson's sub-conscious. He saw a radiant Peter holding up a large fish at the end of a line, and speaking of the fun he had had fishing with his family before his death.

The Halversons reacted at once to this latest communication.

"Our last summer together," Mrs. Halverson said, "we took a trip to Oregon, and Peter wanted to fish every stream—he was so taken with the fishing."

Peter seemed to be reliving that period.

"Tell my parents," the voice said, "that it is just as beautiful here where I am as it was where I caught this fish."

Peter discussed one sister who was especially dear to him, a grandmother who had a family reputation for being psychic, and a relative's farm in Utah where he had gone bareback riding. All this was true.

He then spoke of the cat they had, which they had raised from a kitten, and expressed some concern for its welfare.

None of this was very exciting, and Johnson pointed out there was no reason for the spirit force, until it had developed fully, to be any more extraordinary in death than in life.

The Halversons were very impressed even though they realized some of this could have been telepathically revealed, as the facts touched upon were stored in their subconscious minds.

"Is there anything else?" they asked.

New impressions flashed across Johnson's vision.

"Peter is talking about a car. He wanted to drive it on the day he died, but it was raining and his mother thought it best that he did not drive that day."

At last, the crucial day!

The Halversons leaned forward.

"I was annoyed at the time," Peter's voice said, "but not any more. I understand better now."

The conversation abruptly turned away to Peter's teacher in mathematics, at the local high school. The Halversons' interest quickened, as they recalled how troubled Peter had been by what he considered undeserved criticism from this teacher.

They had thought that his exaggerated reaction to this criticism might have contributed to a momentary instability tragic in its consequence.

They regarded Johnson solemnly.

"Yes," they said, "he was having trouble with this particular teacher."

Johnson looked up with a smile.

"He wants you to know that while he had difficulties with her at the time he does like her now, and realizes that he had exaggerated the problem."

Johnson told them that Peter was speaking calmly and rationally, very differently from the lad who thought himself an object of persecution.

"He wants you to know," said Johnson, "that he is happy and in congenial surroundings, and that he and his friends are working for world peace, in Vietnam and elsewhere, and want you to work for peace as well."

The time had come for the Halversons to ask the question that had brought them to Johnson.

Halverson hesitated for a moment, the words caught in his throat.

"Would you ask," he said finally, "if my son committed suicide?"

The answer came back strong and clear—from Johnson.

"No, it was an accident.

"He was only toying with the idea," Johnson said, "experimenting, seeing how far he could go, and still pull back. Before he was aware of his danger, it was too late. He was overcome by the fumes."

This, he said, was what Peter had told him.

There was not much more, and the Halversons left with mingled emotions. They were still not satisfied, they told me, that anything had come through of an evidential nature, or that the doubt gnawing away at them had been resolved.

I looked at them in some surprise.

"Wasn't this the response you were looking for?"

Halverson shook his head doubtfully.

"Everything else, the cabin, the fishing, the teacher, had apparently come from Peter, but I got the impression from the almost perfunctory way Johnson answered our question that this answer came directly from him."

"The answer may have come through before, and was in Johnson's subconscious mind, only waiting to be invoked by the proper question."

"That may be," Halverson said, "except everything else seemed to have the flow of spontaneity, and this seemed to emerge deliberately as an almost expected response."

I made a mental note to take this up with Johnson. Meanwhile, the discussion had left me with no clearcut impression. I have an open mind on ghosts, spirits, entities, and whatever energy force it is that is supposed to materialize on a different frequency after death. However, aside from a few subjective impressions of dead friends and relatives, and one biblical figure, I have never had any feeling that I was tuned into anything but imagination.

Now, though, as we were concluding our talk, I felt a distinct presence in the room.

I turned to a young friend who had served as my chauffeur for the day.

"Do you feel anything in this room?" I asked.

He nodded gravely. "Very much so."

I turned back to the Halversons.

"Have you ever felt Peter's presence in this house?" Halverson shook his head.

"No, I haven't," he frowned, "that is, not until now. It almost seemed for a moment as if he were here, listening."

I smiled, encouraged now to speak. "That was the impression I suddenly had, of Peter being here, and saying, as plainly as I am speaking, that it *was* an accident, and that he had not intended to go through with the suicide. He was only playing with the idea, and childishly trying to draw attention to the injustices that he felt had been thrust upon him."

"You may be right," Halverson said, "I do know for a moment I thought he was in the room, and I had never thought that before."

As I left, there was no doubt in my mind that Peter Halverson's death had been accidentally induced. But my impression of course could very well have been clairvoyantly conceived—or imagination.

A day or two later I checked back with Doug Johnson.

"How," I asked, "do you separate a purely clairvoyant impression from spirit communication?"

"Sometimes I can just reach out and touch Spirit, he is so close, as was the case with a relative of mine, Joe Walmsley, back in Minneapolis. As he was leaving his body miles away, I got the impression of a smoky substance about him that some might call ectoplasm. I knew then that death was near, and he was merging into Spirit."

Johnson sees changes in the human aura very clearly.

"When we die," said Johnson, "we take on our spiritual body, which is no different than our physical body right now. I believe that our spiritual body is attached to our physical body at all times."

I didn't quite comprehend.

"When somebody dies at ninety, when they first appear as a spiritual being, they look ninety," he explained. "Gradually, as they take more and more spiritual form, having left the body, they begin to take on a more desirable age."

Without really accepting any of this, I asked, "Are these spirits invisible?"

"Sometimes. They become visible when they learn to tune in and we—at least those of us who are mediumistic —learn to tune in on them."

"Are these spirits in heaven?"

Johnson laughed good-naturedly. "No, they're right here on earth. They're just on a different vibration than we are. All life is on a rate of vibration. Now, our problem is recognizing how many levels of vibration there are. Just because, say, we are tuning into Channel Two on television, doesn't mean that other channels aren't functioning. We're just not tuned into their frequency. And so it is with Spirit; we've got to get onto their vibration."

I looked at Johnson doubtfully, even though I knew him to be a remarkable psychic whose healing gifts had miraculously helped many people. "How do you know when you're on the right vibration?"

He smiled. "By the result."

Several years ago he had been giving services in a small spiritualist church in Minneapolis, when a woman he had never seen before came forward for a clairvoyant reading, offering her wristwatch as a psychometric clue.

As he handled her watch, Johnson said casually, "I see you are soon to be leaving Minneapolis."

The woman nodded. "I'm just here on a trip, and I'm leaving tomorrow."

Johnson closed his eyes, concentrating deeply.

"Don't you have a husband in spirit?"

The woman started in some surprise.

"Yes," she said.

Almost as she spoke, Johnson became conscious of a spirit force in the room. "I don't know whether you will accept this or not," he said, "but at this moment your husband is standing right in front of me. He is wearing a white coat, and he is saying, 'Tell my wife this is the same white uniform I used when I lived on earth and that I wore it regularly at work.'"

The woman stood transfixed.

"He was a druggist," she said. "He owned his own drugstore, and he constantly wore this white coat in his shop."

The druggist had something important to say to his widow, and he didn't mince words. The voice, said Johnson, clearly expressed a righteous indignation.

"Tell my wife," it said, "that I am absolutely furious with her. All my life I worked hard and saved for her to have an income after I died, and she has taken every cent I left her and invested it with a man who is a common criminal."

As the message flowed through Johnson, the woman began sobbing hysterically.

"It's true," she said, "the man's a fraud. I just found out yesterday that another widow who had invested with him has lost everything."

Johnson advised her to go to the police before it was too late.

She nodded tearful assent, and left.

He never saw the woman again. She had apparently been guided to that church that day, just to receive this communication.

It was all very clear to Johnson.

"Her husband directed her to that church," he said.

"He knew that I would be there and he could communicate through me in time to help her."

It was too bad, I observed, that he hadn't warned her before she turned the money over to the crook.

Johnson shrugged. "She might not have accepted it then, or perhaps she had a lesson to learn from this experience."

I was still puzzled by the mechanics of communication.

"Were you able to see the husband's face?"

"Yes, I could see everything about him."

"Did you describe him to her?"

"No, I just mentioned the white garb, that was enough to identify him, that and the circumstance he described."

Why couldn't the explanation have been that Johnson saw the widow's predicament, psychically, and knew what any dead husband's attitude would have been?

"It just didn't happen that way," said Johnson. "It began with the husband. I saw him first."

"But why," I asked, "should the husband have appeared at this time?"

"Because it was important to him. He had devoted his whole life to providing for her after he was gone, and here she was throwing it away."

He explained how spiritualism works.

"The first few days or weeks after we have lost a loved one we are in mourning. Five years later, how often do we think of them? It's the same way with spirits. The first few days and months they can't release you. But later, they must go on living their lives, communicating with other spirits, the same as we on the mortal plane do on earth. But, suddenly, when something important is taking place, something they are interested in on earth, they are so affected that the rate of vibration changes. They pick up on what is happening and they break through all barriers to get through to us. That's true here in life, too, to some extent. We have people who send thought waves to each other thousands of miles away. It's no different in Spirit. This is why tragedies and emergencies come through so powerfully. There's a higher rate of intensity. That's why so many people were able to predict Lincoln's, and then Kennedy's assassination. Spirit had tuned into the charged-up atmosphere, and was letting clairvoyants and other people with this gift know what was on the way."

It was all very interesting, but why should Spirit know more about what was happening than the people it was happening to?

"In life, when we take on a mortal body," Johnson said, "we have a subconscious that records everything we've ever seen or done in this life. With death, this transfers into a soul consciousness that remembers and records everything since creation. And this soul consciousness keeps developing to fit the needs of the situation. And then expresses itself as the situation warrants."

In time, through positive thinking, through faith, he thinks instant communication with the dead possible for everyone, thus ending the prevalent concept of death as the end-all, with the people on the earth raising their vibration and the spirit world lowering its vibration for constant attunement on the same frequency.

Johnson is very demanding of himself—and his spirits.

"We psychics and spiritualists must constantly make sure that we are not fooling ourselves as to where the information is coming from. That's why I always try to demand proof of Spirit."

Proof could come unexpectedly. One day Johnson was sitting at the counter of a Pasadena restaurant, reading a book over his coffee, when his attention was caught by a woman who had just walked in with a boy who was about twelve. He assumed it was her son, they seemed so close.

As they took seats at a table, he sensed another presence, a man's, and he knew that he had just died and they were grieving for him.

"Tears almost came to my eyes, they were suffering so. I became so emotional over it, picking up their feelings, that I started to get up from the counter and go over and ask the woman if her husband had just died. And then I decided I had better not, because of how she might react in her present state.

"But then I asked Spirit how I would ever know whether I had properly tuned in. How could anything appear so real to my subconscious, and then not be so?"

As Johnson sent out his questioning thought, the woman and boy got up from the table and came over to the counter. She was evidently an old customer, for the waitress came up to her and asked pleasantly why she hadn't seen her all week.

At this the woman's lips trembled, and she said in a faltering voice.

"Haven't you heard, my husband dropped dead of a heart attack a week ago?"

In the work of so-called physical mediums, Johnson also sees evidence of spirit survival, sometimes more evidential than his own silent communications. The late Sophia Williams, for instance, would apparently attract a voice directly from the ether, audible not only to her but to anybody present at her sittings.

Johnson's own experience with Sophia in her lifetime supported his belief in these voices. In 1963, shortly after the death of an aunt and uncle who had raised him after his mother's death, he arranged for an appointment with Sophia Williams, hoping she could contact them.

As it turned out, he got more than he hoped for.

"All of a sudden," he recalled, "I began to hear this little voice over Sophia's head: 'Doug, this is your mother.'"

Johnson stiffened to attention.

"Doug, please don't leave your father," the voice continued.

Johnson, living then with his father and stepmother, inquired, "Why shouldn't I leave?"

"Your father isn't well," the voice went on. "He is in great pain with arthritis, particularly in the left leg, which he broke before we were married."

Johnson remembered that his father had a bump on his leg, and only that evening he was in such terrible pain that he could not get out of bed.

After Johnson promised to stay with his father, his Aunt Mabel came through and, speaking very casually, described her own death.

She had died unexpectedly of a heart attack, while watching television in her living room in Minneapolis.

Johnson asked what time she had died, and the voice replied, 2:38 P.M.

"We knew this was right," Johnson said, "because she had been talking to a friend on the telephone at two-thirty. She told that friend that she had to hang up because she wanted to watch a television show. Her husband came home from work at three P.M. and found her dead, so she had died in this period."

She—the voice over Sophia Williams' head—said she had attended her own funeral. She listed who was at the funeral and when Johnson asked if anybody had seen her, she said only one person, her mother-in-law, Karen Bushbaum.

This tied it all together for Johnson. "Karen Bushbaum and I rode to the cemetery together, and Karen had told me at the time that she had seen a misty materialization of Mabel standing before the casket."

Technically, Doug Johnson is not a medium. He sees Spirit, but has no spirit guide or control. The information comes directly through him as it does other clairvoyants, and so he is, I suppose, mediumistic without being a medium, as he is never in trance.

On the other hand, others who claim to communicate with the dead have many spirit guides. Medium Maria Moreno's principal guide is the gypsy Clarita, and when she goes into trance, ostensibly getting into the world of spirit, her voice changes to that of her presumed guide and her face becomes transfigured with Clarita's emotions.

With all the observing I had done, it was in the end a visit to this simple Mexican medium's studio in Hollywood that came as close as anything to convincing me that professional psychics provide the best clue to survival.

I settled myself for a reading, and had just turned on a tape recorder when Clarita's voice somberly announced, "I see a beautiful girl with blue eyes and long blond hair. Her name is ———."

She mentioned an unusual name, belonging to a family prominent in Southern California financial and social circles. I had known the girl quite well before the suicide that untimely took her life.

"She wants you to know," the voice continued, "that she is sorry for what she did. She was on drugs."

I came up with a start, almost imagining the girl was in the room, and I recalled a friend telling me that she probably had taken her life while her mind was affected by LSD.

"Is there anything you would like to ask her?" the voice inquired.

I was so startled by the situation that had unexpectedly presented itself that I was speechless.

"No," I said finally. "Just wish her well."

In a way, as I mulled over it later, Clarita actually hadn't told me anything I didn't know. I was aware of the girl's name, of her resort to hallucinogenic drugs, of her suicide. Unfortunately, I had not taken the opportunity to explore whatever it was that she had come to say. On two or three occasions, I sought to re-establish communication through Maria Moreno, and all I could turn up were warnings for one of the dead girl's brothers, who was mentioned by name.

Often the quest for the secret of survival seems more concerned with the needs of the survivors than with the search for a universal principle that will justify the concept of different frequencies postulated by Doug Johnson.

And yet this quest, self-oriented as it is, appears to hold forth the best available evidence of life after death. Many have loved ones they would like to contact on the other side, if there is another side. And many people, particularly those who have lost intimate friends or relatives under tragic circumstances, find a special need for this type of communication. Where a parent loses an only child prematurely, altering the natural pattern of the family, so much is so often left unsaid or undone, so much unfinished, that the need for further communication is sometimes compulsive. Even when the receiver believes true spirit contact has been established, as did Bishop Pike, the sense of premature loss still lingers.

With some who are left behind, the quest for reassurance never ends. For almost fifty years opera singer Nanette Flack had concentrated on trying to contact her only son, who died in a freak accident at sixteen. At one point in her grief, she had welcomed death, thinking in her despair that she might in this way rejoin him on the other side.

Had it not been for a message received through a psychic, Nanette might not have had the courage to keep going. Well on in years, teaching voice in Hollywood, she was convinced that her son was waiting for her.

"After my son died I was absolutely crazy," this grand old lady told me quite calmly. "I just couldn't seem to put myself together. I kept running around to psychics, hoping in this way, I suppose, to keep him alive."

The death had been a double shock, it had been so senseless. The boy had been skating on a New York City rink, when a skater in front of him tripped, and the back of his skate was driven into the boy's head, wounding him fatally.

As Nanette hopped from psychic to psychic, common sense told her she was often the dupe of frauds and charlatans who weren't communicating with anything but her pocketbook. Only one message seemed authentic, and this came during a spiritualist meeting.

"I got one message that seemed valid from a woman who had a group of students. She said, 'I see a boy standing back of you, he is five feet ten inches tall (which was exactly his height) and he says his life was cut down, when it didn't have to be, but that you must go on.'"

As we sat together in her high-ceilinged apartment, redolent with memories of a bygone era, the curtain of time was pulled away and the years laid bare. Nanette hadn't been able to go on with her singing. She was restless, nervous, unable to concentrate or sit still. She gave up a promising career because there seemed no reason to sing now. She didn't know what to do with herself— her marriage had long ago foundered—so she traveled and visited friends. She had given up on psychic-hopping, it had been so unproductive, except for that one brief message.

And then one day she found herself in her hometown, Cincinnati, Ohio, visiting with a friend from long ago. The friend, knowing Nanette's great loss, had made an appointment for her with the celebrated local medium Laura Pruden, who has since passed on.

Nanette received the news listlessly.

"By this time," she recalled, "I was thoroughly bored with the whole psychic bit, but since my friend had been thoughtful enough to make the date, I felt I should go through with it."

She was pleasantly surprised by Mrs. Pruden's quality.

"The medium had a nice house on Cincinnati's Price Hill. She was about fifty-five, and a very charming woman, not at all the spooky type you might have expected. But I still wasn't the least interested. She sat me down opposite her, brought out a small old-fashioned slate, with parallel tables, and put a pencil between the two sections. She motioned me to hold one side of the slate and she held the other. I was thinking what a waste of time it was when the pencil began to move, and some writing formed on the slate."

The medium withdrew the pencil, and read what was apparently a message from Nanette Flack's mother, who had died sometime before.

"Don't grieve so much about Adrien," it said, "because I met him when he came over and we've been such good companions since. He's all right, and you must calm yourself or you will be very ill."

As Nanette Flack recalled that scene of long ago, her eyes shone and color came to her cheeks.

"Did she have any way of knowing his name?" I asked.

She shook her head. "It was even spelled Adrien, with an *e*, when logic would have made it an *a*."

Nanette seemed to relish the story.

"The medium then wiped the slate clean, and the pencil started moving again. Soon the slate advised that she return to the theater—she had been one of the stars of the old Hippodrome in New York—but she wanted only to hear about her son. No message had yet come in directly from Adrien.

Finally, Laura Pruden decided she would make a special effort to contact Adrien.

"I'm going to try something I can't guarantee," said she. "I'll give you a slip of paper. On the top you write a brief message to Adrien, but leave the rest blank."

Nanette Flack was so flustered that all she could write was, "If you can give me any kind of message it would be wonderful."

The slip of paper was then placed under a small table with a lead pencil on the paper.

After a while, the medium's fingers began to move. "I think we have something," she said.

She held up the paper, and Nanette almost fainted as she looked at it.

The handwriting was clearly her son's, there could have been no mistaking that, and the salutation could only have had meaning for the two of them.

When he was quite young Adrien had called his mother Nanny, and she had corrected him and told him to call her Momma.

The next day, when they were alone, he called her Momma Nanny. And this had become a private joke between them. And this is how the message began—Momma Nanny.

But there was more to the message, and she read on avidly.

"Momma Nanny," it said, "I am still your darling boy and progressing fine here. I'm happy and want you to be."

The message was signed with the initials, ABB, and this to her was the clincher.

Nanette's married name was Bellevue, and Adrien, of course, was Adrien Bellevue.

"What's that extra B for?" the medium asked.

Bradford was a family name, and it had been given the boy as a middle name.

Nanette was overjoyed. She clasped the medium to her and cried, "You must never get out of my life. I won't let you get out of my life."

This was in 1929, three years after her son's death, and she was to see Laura Pruden once more in New York. There were no more messages from Adrien, though. Apparently, there was nothing more to be said at this time.

Nanette withdrew from public appearances. She had no more heart for the stage. But she didn't vegetate.

She eventually settled in Southern California, where psychism is popular. But she resisted any inclinations in this direction. She found life interesting, becoming a voice coach and sublimating herself in her students.

Finally, after a forty-year hiatus, now closer to the other side, she decided it was time to see another medium. Accordingly, she arranged a sitting in June of 1970 with the English-born medium Brenda Crenshaw, wife of Los Angeles journalist James Crenshaw.

She approached the session calmly but expectantly. A friend, Leila Sherman, accompanied her to the sitting, and was permitted to stay in the room and take notes. It was all very down-to-earth. There was no hocus-pocus. no mumbo-jumbo, no hidden voices or trumpets. Clairvoyantly, mediumistically, or whatever, medium Crenshaw tuned in quickly to the vibrations of another plane, the vision of another, spirit world passing through her subconscious.

"I see a large bunch of red roses," she began. "They are connected with a death. I see this person giving you the red roses." She paused. "I get the name Adie . . ."

A thrill ran through the mother at her son's nickname. She listened raptly.

"I get the name Adie, who was so much loved. He tells me he is now grown up and has his dog still."

Out of the misty past, Nanette recalled the German shepherd that had been so dear to her son.

She was too enthralled to consider the startling implication that animals too were joined in spirit in this Kingdom of Heaven.

The medium continued with her message from Adie.

"He loved freedom here on earth as a young boy and says he now has it where he is. He is a very advanced soul and was very philosophical for a boy. He would have been a fine doctor, as he loved people. He would have tried to serve humanity. He had a marvelous head on his shoulders."

The mother could hardly restrain a sigh for all those lost years. But perhaps there had been a higher purpose to which young Adrien had been called.

Brenda Crenshaw's voice went on unemotionally. "He is doing an ever greater work in the higher life and does not regret that he did not continue here in a world filled with so much confusion and chaos."

As the mother sat fascinated, the medium picked up Adrien's death and the transition that followed. "He was sixteen and he died of an accident. He was in great pain but that has passed and you must not think of it again." He had been well protected. "Someone else close to you passed on a short time before your son did and others there, too, loved and looked after him so that he did not feel strange or confused in his passing. There is a Charlie who knew your son and loved him. They are frequent pals in the spirit world."

Nanette nodded. "I was once engaged to Charlie. Our friendship continued after my marriage, and he loved Adrien as his own son. The dog was one he had bought for him. He once said that if he was ever a father, Adrien was the boy he would pick."

The sitting had been so successful that Nanette left the medium's chambers on a cloud, puzzled by only one injunction.

"You are anxious to cross the border," Brenda Crenshaw had said, "but there is still a chapter for you to write before you leave this world. When you do cross, the passage will be a very easy one and your son will greet you."

Our interview had obviously taxed Nanette's strength. She was in good spirits, but her frail body seemed hardly able to hold itself together.

Why, I wondered, when she wanted so badly to pass on, feeling that she would be united with her beloved Adie, why did she linger on with all the aches and pains old age is heir to?

This thought ran through my mind as I stood at the door saying good-by to this gracious lady and her charming companion, Leila Sherman. And it was Leila then who, inadvertently perhaps, suggested the answer.

"Who knows," she said, "but what Nanette may yet help another Caruso or a Sutherland in the time allotted to her?"

And that time came all too soon, just before Christmas 1971, when this grand old lady finally realized her supreme ambition, passing on to the promised land of an oft-dreamed reunion.

10
Reincarnation Comes to Life

Dust thou art, to dust returnest, was not spoken of thy
soul.

—Longfellow

Proof of reincarnation is everywhere, the reincarnationists say. Some see it in remembrance of things past, others
in natural aptitudes or talents developed in previous lives.
To some it explains instant love or hate, illnesses, emotional upheavals, and even the course of destiny, as one
works out his karma—the debit and credit ledger—carried over from an earlier life experience.

As the interest in reincarnation mounts, sparked by an
increasing need to feel some purpose in an all too brief life-
span, the interest in life readings, such as those given by
Edgar Cayce, has grown apace. Not satisfied with hypnotic regressions, which turn up a completely subjective
past life, more and more people are turning to psychic
readers, who appear to be able to tune into individual
destiny patterns in this life and in previous life experiences.

In some instances, these life readings have been effective in explaining the individual's often inexplicable be-

havior to his own satisfaction, and have prepared him for events foreshadowed by his karma.

To some, reincarnation explains everything that we otherwise have no explanation of—the inspired verse of the immortal Shakespeare, genetically a peasant; Beethoven and his childhood sonatas, the genius of an Edison, the wisdom of the unlettered Lincoln, or a Christ who asked who men thought He had been before.

If not for reincarnation, why then, the reincarnationists ask, are some talented musicians and writers, others skilled dancers and painters, some seeming bred to fortune, others, through no apparent fault of their own, to misfortune?

Is all life an accident? Does the bullet take one and not the other by chance? And, if accident, what purpose then to plan or contrive, to study and learn, if every conceivable event can be moved out of context at any moment for no apparent reason?

With reincarnation, everything happens in orderly fashion. For reincarnation, despite the fatalism of the East, does not demand a destiny over which the individual has no control, but allows options and choices by which he works out his karma, hence his own destiny.

"It is such a plausible way of explaining our lives," observed Hugh Lynn Cayce, the son of the clairvoyant, "that it is almost too plausible to be true."

In his life readings, in which he picked up previous lives in Atlantis, ancient Greece, and Egypt, Edgar Cayce related the current life to the past in cause and effect, but stressed that the life that one lived in the present was the only one that counted.

"Live not in the past," said he.

Unfortunately, many of his followers, vainly stressing these pasts, dwell on themselves as kings and queens and princes and princesses, in a glaring misapplication of the spiritual message the Sleeping Prophet was spelling out for them.

It has always seemed odd to me that there should be so many more chiefs than Indians in the past, but reincarnation itself cannot be blamed for the frailties of psychics appealing to human vanity or for the pretensions of a few cultists.

Characteristically, I have been told by life readers that in a previous life I was the English writer Robert Browning, and the lesser writer Branwell Brontë, brother of Charlotte and Emily Brontë, and I found this rather confusing, as both lived at the same time in Victorian England.

I find these glamorous connections of the past rather suspect, unless there is some definite tie-in with the present and future. And, of course, if the life reader can foresee the future from the past, this is not only useful to the subject but evidentially interesting.

I was not impressed when clairvoyant Maya Perez, who frequently gets into past lives, told a young Orange County housewife that she liked long flowing gowns because she had been a princess in a previous life. That housewife, Nancy Hively, of Cypress, California, looked more like a princess in this life, and that was good enough for me.

Had Maya Perez stopped there, there would have been nothing to write about. However, there were other lives, other experiences, which apparently had some bearing on this one.

Nancy Hively had consulted the clairvoyant because she was dissatisfied with her lot in this life, having strong stirrings of ambition which she couldn't otherwise identify or relate to.

"I wanted to do something," she told me, "but didn't know what it was."

She had quite a checkered past—reincarnation-wise.

"I worked with priests in the temples and also was a moon maiden at one time and did black magic and had my powers taken from me. In many lifetimes I was a slave (a welcome respite), and that's why (said the psychic) I now have this feeling that I want to get out and do something more."

I didn't see how being a slave in the past affected one's freedom in this life.

"Maya told me this past experience was subconsciously holding me back, since I had no confidence, and was used to being confined. But she told me I would break out of these fetters, and would do lecture work, which I am now doing." She had started lecturing on the metaphysical, receiving groups into her home.

The life reading went into every aspect of Nancy Hively's life—marriage, children, hobbies, and work.

"She told me I had lost several children in this lifetime and told me when, and what sex they were. They were male children, and she said that they were masters who only came here for a short time and were now developing on the other side."

Nancy was prepared to accept this explanation of the deaths, since the psychic had correctly seen the deaths themselves in every instance.

Her marriage was not as fulfilling as she would have liked it and she wondered about it. Maya said that it was a karmic carryover, a lesson that had to be learned. She had been married ten years, and had one child, and the marriage would putter along until this lesson had been learned. Then she was to have another marriage and another child, but this would be adopted, as she would no longer be able to have any of her own.

Nancy had thought of adopting another child, so this,

too, along with her feelings about her marriage, fell into place.

But even with another marriage coming, subsequent to a divorce which soon took place, she still had to look outside herself for fulfillment, to satisfy that strong lack of purpose within her. From a skeptic's standpoint, the reading didn't prove much about reincarnation. Yet there was little doubt that Nancy believed she had been helped to better understanding of her function in this life by the reading.

The impression it had made on her was truly remarkable.

"How was it," I asked, "that a psychic could boost your spirits with a discussion of reincarnation when a minister or a doctor couldn't affect you?"

Nancy's dark brown eyes lighted up.

"I went to all those people, and they didn't begin to understand what I was talking about when I spoke of a gap in my life. I knew I was put on earth to do a job, but I didn't know what it was." She was suffering from suburban ennui. "I was married, but my husband traveled on his job, and was gone most of the time. I worked as a dental assistant for ten years, but tired of it, and needed something to fulfill me."

And so, how was she being fulfilled?

"From the reading I learned that I had a teaching role in this life. When Maya told me I was put here to help others by guiding them, it seemed to click off something inside me."

Although alien to the workaday world, reincarnation by no means is an unfamiliar concept. Many notables have reported subjective impressions of past lives—Emerson, Thoreau, Mark Twain, General Patton, Benjamin Franklin. Thoreau said he walked with Christ, and that his friend Hawthorne lived at that time, too, but didn't know the Savior; Mark Twain dreamed of many lives with the same love-mate, always in a different land and different guise; Patton not only remembered previous experiences as a warrior but unerringly pointed to ancient military encampments and battlefields he had no conscious knowledge of. Ben Franklin planned to come back, the same soul, in different garb.

Many, many more, like actress Susan Strasberg, have from childhood had deep but vague likes and dislikes whose origin baffled them.

Brought up in the Jewish faith, Susan as a child felt an inexplicable surge of emotion when she passed a Christian church, and had an overwhelming desire to enter and pray.

"It was an overpowering thing," she observed, "stronger even than the feeling I had when I visited the German concentration camps, where, logically, I should have had more of a reaction, since people of my faith were persecuted there."

She also had feelings about the Elizabethan era in England, and read every book she could about this period: Elizabeth and Essex, Mary, Queen of Scots, Shakespeare, the Spanish Armada, Henry the Eighth.

It had never occurred to her that she may have lived before, and she dismissed her feelings as mere idiosyncrasies.

But one day, the psychic Patricia McLain of the San Fernando Valley, tuning into various facets of Miss Strasberg's life, including her broken marriage, said unexpectedly:

"You know, you had a previous life as a Christian, at the time of Christ, and hid out in the catacombs of Rome to escape persecution."

This almost startled the actress out of her skin.

If true, it not only explained her compulsion to prayer when she passed a church, but resolved a curious antip- athy that had gone unexplained for years.

"I lived in Rome for four years," she said, "and in all that time, I never visited the number one tourist attrac- tion, which was the catacombs. Whenever friends sug- gested a visit, I brushed it nervously aside without know- ing why, not dreaming for an instant it may have had some terrible association with the Roman persecution of the early Christians."

To some psychics, there is no present-day human ac- tivity without relevance to a past life, and consequently to a future life, which it helps shape. To this purpose, the Reverend Violet Gilbert of Roseburg, Oregon, tries to show the people consulting her a way to avoid the errors of the past, and to understand from the destiny patterns of the past their own actions and the actions of others close to them.

There is nothing mystical about the way she operates. The people who beat a path to her studio find her as comfortable as an old shoe. She does not look at all esoteric, for she is middle-aged, of medium height, on the plump side, and as frequently as not wears pink curlers in her hair, and pink slippers. She works methodically, with a style peculiarly her own. She takes the birth date of the client, and of five or six people he or she is con- cerned with, and jots them down in a boxlike pattern on a piece of paper.

In her readings, she wanders around the universe, talking about Atlantis as if it were her backyard. But she is still specific about conditions in this life, the past, and the future, making many converts to the concept of rein- carnation, and influencing many lives.

One of those she influenced was Audrey Jampol, a businesswoman, of Redondo Beach, California, who was perplexed by the unevenness of her own life and her inexplicable relationships with friends and relatives. With a friend, Bob Dursi, who is something of a psychic buff, she drove one day to Santa Barbara, where Violet Gilbert once lived before moving on to Oregon.

On the road, they stopped off for lunch, and Dursi throughout the meal kept rubbing his bare arms until Audrey began to itch herself.

"Whatever is bothering you?" she finally asked.

"It's the dust," he said, his eyes watering. "The dust in this restaurant is driving me crazy. It gets into my nose and sinus, and gives me terrible headaches."

She didn't notice any dust herself, and was glad to get back into the car, and on the way.

After a while, they arrived in Santa Barbara, and Bob sat down first for his life reading.

Audrey was permitted to sit in, but even though she was sold on reincarnation, with its karmic law of cause and effect, she was hardly prepared for the psychic's first words to Dursi.

"You are highly allergic to dust," Violet Gilbert said, "and even imagine it when there isn't any." She closed her eyes. "In your last life, you were trapped in a mine cave-in, and smothered to death from the dust and fumes. That is the reason for your allergy; your subconscious still remembers."

The terrible headaches between the eyes had no relation to the allergy. But it was again a matter of subconscious remembrance, carried over from a previous life, this time in the rough-and-tumble era of the wild, wild West.

"In the brawling days of the American frontier," she said, "you were shot between the eyes."

Apparently, memory of the pain lingered on.

Though this was not the entire scope of the reading, I

still didn't see that it was particularly pertinent to this life.

"How," I asked Audrey, "did it help Dursi to know how he had died in those previous lives?"

I had known Audrey casually for some time, as a practical business woman, and had only learned a short time before of her interest in life readings.

At my question, Audrey's dark eyes twinkled. "I only brought it up to show her accuracy potential. Basically, she went into the kind of lives that induced these tragic deaths, stressing the tendencies to repeat the pattern in this life, and warning of self-indulgence."

One of the puzzling things about reincarnation is the mathematical improbability of familiar souls refinding one another among the billions of souls on the earth. But the reincarnationist explains these reunions as part of a grand design which makes it possible for the same people to advance their relationships from one life to another, even to winding up in the same family.

According to Violet Gilbert, Audrey's own daughter, Katherine, twenty-three, had been a rival of hers in a previous life, and this accounted for the fact that she was very competitive with her mother as she grew older.

For Audrey this was quite an eye-opener.

"I just didn't know how to cope with this competitiveness," Audrey said, "especially since there didn't seem to be any reason for it."

Violet was tuned into Audrey's daughter. "She picked up that Kathy would have a divorce and a child, and would then marry again. She had the divorce and does have the child."

I didn't see the connection to a previous life, but Audrey thought Violet Gilbert had worked it in quite plausibly.

"The Reverend Gilbert based the divorce on the belief

that Kathy, subconsciously, was looking for a lover she had in a previous life, who had promised to come back to her in this one."

Apparently, the husband wasn't the man. And the search, influenced by the strong subconscious desire, moved restlessly ahead.

As Audrey told me all this, there was little doubt that she for one felt that Violet Gilbert had clarified many of her relationships, including her own mismatches in the past, and her own search, like her daughter's, for a soul mate in this life.

Guided by Violet Gilbert's words, Audrey had apparently found this soul mate, for she had recently married the man she felt she had a karmic destiny with.

Violet Gilbert had said there would be apparent discrepancies, and these seemed obvious as the three of us —Audrey, her husband, and myself—sat together calmly discussing what Violet Gilbert had said of life, death, and marriage.

Audrey's new husband, her soul mate by Violet Gilbert's definition, was a young man named Jim Bohan. He was darkly handsome and rugged, looking every inch the Texan he is, and, like Audrey, he was interested in the metaphysical. The big discrepancy was in age, for Jim was about twenty-five years younger than Audrey, who was in her early fifties. But they still seemed very happy together. For even as she discussed her visits with Violet Gilbert, Audrey turned constantly for assurance to her new husband. It was apparent that they were in love.

From the first, Violet held forth this beacon of a great new love for the searching Audrey.

"Three different times I went to Violet," Audrey related, "and she told me each time that in spite of all the stormy relationships in my life I would meet my soul mate, and any other relationship before was just a trial-

and-error process. The first time she said I had a great deal of trouble to go through yet—financial, emotional, and business problems—but if I handled these correctly I would meet my soul mate."

On the second occasion, Audrey was told the time for the great meeting was drawing closer. On the third, the psychic sensed the time was closer than Audrey thought. However, the road to happiness was fraught with pitfalls. "Violet said I should be very careful because my soul mate would be one who had the same spiritual values I did, but not the same material values. He would not come in the form I would be looking for, and I would not recognize him at first."

Looking at the pair, as they held hands, I wondered if the terms lovebirds and soul mates were synonymous.

"What she meant by soul mate," Audrey explained, "was someone you have lived many lives with. As Edgar Cayce said, no relationship is very deep unless it has this carryover from previous lives—someone whom your soul recognizes as the completing half."

I found myself wondering how and when the pair had met, and suddenly recalled with a start that I was at the meeting, which had taken place in July of 1970, six months after Audrey's third session with Violet Gilbert.

Audrey was the proprietress of a Venice song palace, and Jim and I had been separately invited by a friend of Audrey's to a performance there of country music. The initial meeting hadn't seemed to touch off a spark.

"You two hardly looked at each other," I recalled.

Audrey smiled. "That's right, it was very casual, and as Violet said, no recognition at first."

Chance, fate, karma, what you will, soon got them off on a different footing. What with Venice being an explosive community, somebody threatened Audrey, and Jim Bohan, in the neighborhood, heard of the threat. He promptly marched over to her place, plunked himself in the doorway, and stood ready to defend her. Until the threat passed, he was a daily visitor.

"It seemed almost," Audrey said, "as if he had been protecting me all his life."

A feeling of togetherness, the familiarity and ease which only a lifetime could produce, existed between them for months unspoken. Then one day, simultaneously, they started to tell one another they felt they had been through eternity together.

Two weeks later they were married.

As I looked at them, I could only hope that Audrey had correctly singled out the right man from the psychic's description.

"I had been married before, and knew other men," Audrey said, "but I never before felt a part of another person, and he a part of me. We pick up the same thoughts, and send messages to each other when we are apart."

They were obviously mentally in tune, but what of the material values that Violet Gilbert had said would be so different?

Audrey laughed. "They were obvious. Here I was a bourgeois Jewish girl hung up on a velvet sofa in the living room, and there was Jim, a free soul from Texas, not caring a tinker's damn for a stick of furniture."

Some vague recollection of Violet Gilbert's reading stuck in my mind.

"Oh, yes," I said, "how about your soul mate not appearing in the form you would be looking for?"

Audrey and Jim smiled as if sharing some secret.

"I certainly wasn't thinking in terms of somebody all that much younger than myself."

She gave him a fond look.

"But we have found that age doesn't make the slightest difference—not when you are soul mates."

One does not always find his soul mate in this life, as the divorce records attest, and may have to endure several lives before the paragon turns up. A lovely brunette of thirty, previously married, was warned by the Reverend Gilbert:

"You are at the crossroads, along one path there is a man with black hair beckoning, and since you are searching for a soul mate, you have a feeling this is he, because in your dream you saw him as dark and with similar features. However, your soul mate is not in body at this time and you will never meet him in this life."

Knowing the young woman had already made up her mind, the Reverend Gilbert admonished, "Do not marry this man, it will be disaster."

The brunette had to decide whether she would listen to a clairvoyant she had never seen before or her own antennae.

And so she went to the altar. A few months later, when I met her, the marriage had already broken up and she was suing for divorce.

"I should have listened to Violet Gilbert," she said.

In the long run, nothing was lost, I suppose, as she was either working out karma, or building it for the next time around, when, hopefully, she would encounter her true soul mate.

Although she sees sundry past lives, Violet Gilbert deals only with those which have some karmic attachment to the present life. In this perspective, she analyzes the personalities of her clients, clarifying qualities which sometimes puzzle them and the psychiatrist.

In reading for pretty Marlene Dantzer, a twenty-four-year-old artist of Hermosa Beach, California, Violet Gilbert saw her standing in a great hall filled with paintings,

in the England of the early 1700s. She was the wife of a
noted artist, and had dabbled in painting herself.

Consciously knowing nothing about the young woman
sitting across from her, the Reverend Gilbert said that she
had come into this life on a cosmic ray channeled into
metaphysical growth and artistic development. Everybody
at birth was under the influence of some ray in this
perspective.

"You don't like inharmonious things," Violet advised.
"You must produce things of beauty to be at harmony
with yourself."

There were many other things, and, all in all, Marlene
thought the life reading a great help.

"She said my purpose was to free myself of all karmic
debts and prepare myself for the new Aquarian Age. By
entering this life on a certain cosmic ray, a yellow ray, in
my case, it enabled me to put my previous training to
use in this life."

But there were also difficulties. "Violet said my past
experience makes it hard for me to understand the ul-
terior motives of people who may maneuver me to their
liking."

She appeared quite independent to me.

"Oh no, I do tend to let people dominate me against
my better judgment."

She had another hangup, a common one. "She told me
that anytime I go against what I think right, I will meet
with difficulty, and have throat problems."

"And how have you done, knowing your weakness?"
Marlene smiled. "I have constant sore throats."

This life for Marlene was an opportunity to assert herself. "I'm here not only to fight for freedom from domination by those who control me but for freedom from my
own vanity as well."

Violet Gilbert couldn't emphasize this enough.

"This," she said, "is the song of your soul, to free yourself of ego, to strive for emotional balance, to go forth in the service of God."

"In the service of God," I said, "what does that mean?"

"Getting involved in the spiritual revolution the young people are in today."

I found nothing substantial in the reading.

"Shouldn't the English life have had some relation to this one if she found it worthy of mention?"

"Oh, yes, she told me I was to meet my artist husband again in this life. She said my husband did outstanding paintings, but was very difficult to get along with. He would still be difficult, but I would know better how to handle the situation."

"How were you to recognize him?" I asked.

"Through a process of recall."

But she was first to meet somebody from another past life, a French experience, when she led the glamorous life that seems to inevitably turn up in these readings.

"I was a dancer or stripper at this time," Marlene said, "and I apparently had a good time of it."

Brought up a strict Catholic in sedate Santa Barbara, Marlene listened avidly to her uninhibited past.

"You were one of the most fabulous ladies of the time," the Reverend Gilbert said. "You did some singing in this life, wearing a hat that was large and floppy and had a feather on it that trailed to the floor. This was all that you wore."

I shot a covert glance at the pretty girl with the conventional background.

"Did you believe all this?" I asked.

She laughed. "Judge for yourself, it's all connected."

Violet Gilbert seemed to particularly relish Marlene's scandalous past life.

"People would have paid anything to see you in that

hat," she said. "You had an absolute ball." But there was always something to spoil things. "Your downfall was a Frenchman, thin and short, a queer, unfortunate, down-trodden type, and your heart went out to him."

She had taken him in, then had trouble getting rid of him, and worse luck, was to encounter him again in this life.

"In this life," the psychic said, "he has a bad ankle and leg, and a different look. But he will still have black hair, and you will recognize the eyes. You will resist him, because you have already subconsciously made up your mind to have nothing more to do with him, since you burned your fingers so badly before."

With this description, how could she miss him?

And she didn't.

One night she went to a party, and looking across the room, at once saw a dark-haired man standing off by him-self. She averted her head, trying to avoid his eyes. The hackles rose on her neck, yet she was curiously drawn to him.

"For the whole evening," she said, "I looked past him, never once catching his eye." But his eyes followed her like a hawk.

She tried to get away from him. "I finally got up and went into the kitchen, but he followed and backed me into a corner and asked why I wouldn't look at him."

"I just told him I didn't know why, but I was afraid."

He took her by the hand and spoke earnestly. The con-versation was typical of people who had known one an-other a very, very long time.

"We spent the whole night walking on the beach and talking," Marlene said. "I was hopelessly infatuated, and it was no use fighting it."

They dated for two months. He was a young sculptor with talent, charming, intelligent, witty, but not very good for her, and she had the strength, finally, to get out from under his domination.

But until her next visit to Violet Gilbert, she was still not sure the Frenchman and the sculptor were the same.

"Didn't I warn you," the psychic said, "not to get involved with him? You fell into a habit trap."

Marlene was philosophical.

"At least I got rid of some karma."

The Reverend Gilbert snorted. "You just incurred more karma, and you can now plan on more of him in lives to come."

When she saw the sculptor again, casually, she said jokingly, "Even if we don't see anything more of each other in this life, we have a few other lifetimes in which to get together."

A thought suddenly occurred to her, as he was walking away.

"By the way," she said, "do you have any problems with your legs?"

He turned, and gave her a startled look.

"I certainly do. One ankle constantly goes out of joint, and I get a cramp in the calf and knee of the same leg."

Marlene blinked.

"Was it from an accident?"

He shrugged. "I've always had it, without knowing where it came from."

The meeting with the sculptor prepared Marlene mentally for the renewal of another relationship, the artist husband who was so difficult in her English experience.

It was hard for me to understand why anybody would want to go back to anybody who was unpleasant.

Marlene threw up her hands. "It's karma; we have to finish things off, learn our lessons, and go on to something better."

"As soon as the one is out of the way," Violet Gilbert

had said, "you will meet the man you will marry—the artist who was your husband in the English experience."

Marlene was thoroughly confused.

"How will I know him?" she asked.

"Shortly after you meet him in an unexpected way, he will tell you he wants to move to Washington state."

Marlene smiled as she thought about it.

"Have you already met this man?" I asked.

"Yes, two years ago."

"And you're still together?"

She nodded.

"Why aren't you married, if this is the right man?"

"George," she said, "has divorce problems. He's trying to get custody of his children."

"Was there anything unusual about your meeting?"

"As Violet Gilbert said, it happened unexpectedly. I was walking by this house, and I saw him standing by the stoop. Our eyes met, and I felt somehow that I knew him."

The stranger was an artist, of course.

"He smiled, and asked if I would like to come into the studio and see his paintings."

I couldn't help myself. "In other words, he wanted you to come up and see his etchings."

"Something like that, but the odd thing is that I went. I had never spoken to anybody in the street like that before, not to mention accepting an invitation into a strange house."

"Well, you were certainly set up for it, psychologically."

"All right, listen to this. I'm not in his studio five minutes, looking at his paintings, when he says to me, 'How do you like California?'

"I said, 'I like it fine, why?' And he said, 'I would like to move to the state of Washington.'"

"How does it all tie in with the English experience?" I asked.

She smiled. "He picked that up himself. I had never mentioned my feelings about our English past life together, but he was quite psychic, and frequently read for people on past lives. So one day, I said, 'You're always telling everybody else about their past lives, so why don't you tell me about mine?'"

He immediately launched into a description of their life together in England in the eighteenth century. "He saw me being driven off in a coach in front of a huge home, such as Violet Gilbert had described, living the type of life she had outlined. It was really exciting."

"You had never discussed any of this with him?"

"I had deliberately kept it from him."

"And how about Violet Gilbert, could he have gotten it from her?"

"All he knew about her was what I told him."

If I understood reincarnation correctly, the important thing was how one managed one's life in relating it to the experience one had before.

"Even if you knew each other before," I said, "how do you associate the two lives in any beneficial way?"

"I have to work on our relationship."

"Why is that?"

"Because in this life, he is a very difficult man to get along with, and for the same reason as before."

"And why is that?"

"He is extremely possessive, and if I'm not home when I'm supposed to be, or don't call, he's furious."

"That's the way he was previously?"

"That was how Violet Gilbert saw it, and now I am beginning to remember it through the hazy past. This is our only problem. And I keep telling him, now that we

both understand the past, that we are here together to
work this out between us."

She was truly an attractive girl, beautiful, witty, artistic. She could have had almost anybody, and yet she was
hung up on a divorced man tied by his children to a previous marriage.

"Why keep up a relationship that isn't pleasant?" I
asked.

She smiled.

"That is what reincarnation is all about. I have known
George before, and I am now trying to apply what I
learned before to our present relationship."

"And what did you learn?" I asked.

"Love and patience. They go together."

Unlike Marlene Dantzer and Audrey Jampol Bohan,
most people who go to psychics have only a passing interest in reincarnation, and are concerned chiefly with this
life and the immediate future.

However, spiritually oriented psychics believe in some
form of survival, including reincarnation, and so, more
often than not, in the midst of a "fortunetelling," the
client may inadvertently find his present problems or
future prospects related to a past life.

And so it was for Gene Mitchell, an engineer for a
casualty insurance company in Los Angeles, when the
Mexican-born medium Maria Moreno took him from one
life to the next. He still wouldn't have listened seriously
had she not correctly mentioned the names of his wife,
son, and daughter, and accurately described intimate
family situations.

Maria's ubiquitous guide, Dr. Dermas, reported that
Gene Mitchell, a middle-aged man with a penchant for
hunting and flying, was building up bad karma for himself by shooting birds.

"Don't kill the birds," the doctor's voice said through her.

Mitchell was a bit taken aback, as Maria in trance had picked up on a favorite pastime of his. "It was very true that I especially loved hunting game birds," he said, "but I always ate what I shot." At least he wasn't killing wantonly, but this made no difference to Dr. Dermas.

"Stop killing," the good doctor said.

Only a hunter knew what eliminating blood sports would do to Mitchell's present incarnation. "I look forward so much to hunting that it was a hard decision to make, but oddly enough, it had been plaguing my conscience lately."

He couldn't help but wonder whether the decision was being made for him. "I had been trying for the last six or seven months to get a new hunting dog, a German shorthaired pointer. I got one at Christmas and he died of distemper. I had another chance in March, just before the session with Maria Moreno, but when I went to pick up the dog, he was the wrong kind and I refused to take him."

At this point, Gene Mitchell was hoping that Maria would tune in on his back, which had been bothering him for some time, but instead she advanced further into reincarnation, moving out of future karma to past lives.

"You were a Cossack in a past life," she told the insurance man. "And as a boy, you used the Russian language."

In spite of a completely non-Russian background, Mitchell had always been interested in things connected with that country. "At the age of eighteen or nineteen, when the Korean war broke out," he related, "I was going to college and did a thesis on Russia, and had checked over a number of books on the Russian vocabulary."

As intriguing as all this was, it is hardly likely that

Gene Mitchell would have thought twice about it, had Maria Moreno not been so specific about the rest of his life.

He was admittedly impressed when she picked up the name Carol—for his wife, Carolyn—and Larry for his son Larry. She persisted in calling her Carol.

"I see Carol," said she, "with a man in a carriage with a tall hat."

In trance, she seemed to be ranging back over the centuries, conjuring up the images which shot through her subconscious like so many motion picture frames.

"Larry, is he okay?" she asked.

"Yes, he is all right now."

The medium spoke with conviction.

"He is the boy I saw in the carriage, and the carriage rolled over him and killed him." She paused for a moment, apparently making a transition from one life to another. "Larry had trouble with his arms and legs—is that okay now?"

Mitchell tried to connect two incidents, the past life accident with the carriage, and his son's own car accident at the age of twelve, almost ten years before.

"We were in a car accident," he explained, "and Larry suffered a whiplash; three days later he was paralyzed from the elbows and knees down. He was out of school for two months and couldn't walk correctly for a year."

Maria Moreno attributed it to karma. "Larry was your son in your previous life and you went away from him, so you were paying for it in this life."

It seemed to me that if anybody was paying, it was Larry, and then I remembered what Dr. Casey Jones, head of an institution for retarded children, had said about the parents of afflicted children suffering more than the children.

Maria continued to tune into the son.

"Larry," she said, "has had trouble with his throat."

At one time Larry had such serious throat problems that his doctors thought he would come down with rheumatic fever. His health improved after his tonsils were removed.

Mitchell was still not getting what he wanted. But Maria Moreno operated in her own way.

"You have three girls," she said.

"Only two," Mitchell replied.

"You had three," she said, "and one went away. She is standing behind you now and is very beautiful."

A chill ran down Mitchell's spine.

"Our first child died a few hours after birth, because of a deformity in her spine. The doctors told us she was a very beautiful little girl."

Maria's eyes seemed glazed and distant.

"She came to help you and your wife, and then passed on. She was not meant to stay at this time."

The medium did not say what this mission was, but looking back on those trying days, Mitchell realized that he had learned a lot from the tragedy, becoming less self-centered, for one thing, a change which brought him and his wife closer together.

Maria stayed with the children for a few moments longer. She picked up the name of Linda, Mitchell's older daughter, and asked what she wanted to specialize in in school.

"She doesn't know now what she wants to do."

Maria's guides were reassuring.

"She will be a teacher."

She again rummaged around in Mitchell's family life.

"You and Carol argue too much about money."

Mitchell agreed.

"Don't worry about money, but don't ask for more right now." She picked a time a few weeks forward. "Wait

until after April fifteen before you ask for a raise. You will
get what you want at that time."

Mitchell had to laugh to himself at this, as he had been
gradually building up nerve to ask his employers for a
sizable increase.

She also saw a change of career, almost diametrically
opposed to engineering and insurance, but one, remarkably, which had been very much on his mind.

"You will eventually become a writer," she said, "but
first work at it on the side. Understand?"

He nodded, and she went on.

"Start writing small articles at first, and follow your
hunches in writing because your hunches will be the masters telling you what to do."

Mitchell finally got to the thing he came for.

"Now," he said, "I have a problem with my back which
the medical doctors say is arthritis of the spine. But I
think it is something else."

Maria's principal guide, Clarita, came through, snap-
ping her fingers in front of Mitchell with a show of confidence.

"We are going to cut all the strings," Maria said, "and
you are going to get well."

After the reading, Mitchell's health improved steadily.
However, he is inclined to credit continuing chiropractic
treatments. Nonetheless, the session did activate his inner
resolve to get on with his writing.

"I always wanted to combine writing with flying and
sports," he said. "Since I saw Maria I have had a hunch
about an article, and have been carrying it around like a
seed. I think it is time to let it sprout."

As skeptical as Mitchell, his wife listened to a taped
recording of Maria Moreno's reading, and was flabbergasted. Maria had said Carol should take vitamin A because of her eyes, otherwise she would have serious visual

problems. His wife's eyes were weak, and Mitchell was after her constantly to take vitamin A.

But Carol did nothing about it. The whole affair was a little spooky for her. But one good thing did come out of the reading, as she readily acknowledged. There have been no more family arguments about money. As Maria Moreno advised, Mitchell waited until after April 15 to ask his superiors for a raise. And just as she had predicted, he got what he asked for.

His employers were properly "psyched" out.

11
Public Service and Predictions

We had been discussing the psychic's ability to look into the future when Merv Griffin, the television personality, said:

"Wouldn't it be terrible if we had somebody in the White House who could see what lies ahead?"

This discussion, on the Mike Douglas television show in the summer of 1963, would probably have been forgotten, had not President Kennedy been assassinated that fall, fulfilling the direst predictions of many psychics.

Had Jack Kennedy foreseen the event himself, or taken notice of the many warnings, the chances are that the event would have occurred anyway. But knowing that it was going to happen, might he not have arranged a smoother transition of government, and better prepared the country for the changeover?

Abraham Lincoln, having his dream of death a few days before his assassination, was so vividly impressed by it that he not only discussed the dream with his Cabinet but summoned Vice-President Andrew Johnson to explain his program for peace between the North and South. Unfortunately, death overtook him first.

Would the country not have been better off had Franklin D. Roosevelt, in anticipation of his own death, given a rundown of secret wartime commitments to his successor Harry S. Truman, who was not even aware of the A-bomb before he dramatically took office in World War II?

How different things might have been if President Kennedy could have foretold that his withdrawal from the Bay of Pigs would assure the Communists a Cuban foothold near our shores, with missiles aimed at our heads? How different if Presidents Eisenhower and Kennedy had foreseen how their intrusion into Vietnam would violently rack their own country? And what if President Nixon had heeded the psychic predictions that his election would bring a recession? Could this recession not have been alleviated with the same foresight that the Pharaoh of Egypt revealed after Joseph interpreted his dream as meaning there would be first seven fat years, then seven lean?

Would it not be better to know what is ahead in public affairs, if for no other reason than to prepare the public mind for the event, whatever it is?

When President Nixon made his overtures to Red China, the majority of Americans, including myself, acclaimed the move. But the psychics were not as optimistic, muttering about a bloody showdown with the Yellow Race. Still others saw the move as happily postponing the inevitable, providing at least one generation of peace.

To the rational Western mind, as Merv Griffin pointed out, the use of psychics in predicting important events is folly and superstition. Yet the Romans, dominating the ancient world, seldom made a move without their augurs. Those supreme pragmatists used whatever worked for them. Julius Caesar, on the other hand, ignored the prophecy to beware the Ides of March, and was promptly assassinated.

In the current period, psychics have foreseen the windup of the war in Vietnam in 1972, with the nerve center of political danger shifting to Germany. They foresee a massive spiritual revival around the world, leading to a modern Pax Romana, with the wonders of space travel directing man to a recognition of life in other planets. Just as psychics foresaw the successful flights to the moon long before they happened, they visualize planet hopping, and the ultimate realization that there are no time or space dimensions as we know them.

Meanwhile, the little things of life continue to concern and vex man, and the knowledgeable psychic can provide an incomparable everyday service. Like other psychics, Clara Schuff, a German guru, most recently stationed in San Diego, California, has her insights into a strangely timeless world. Of French-German parentage, born in Munich seventy-six years ago, she has, without ever having studied these tongues, chanted in old Arabic, Hindustani, Sumerian, and Homeric Greek. In Germany she was known as the living radio, because of her propensity for tuning into the world around her. Sometimes she sees large events, sometimes small ones. She feels she was guided to these shores to be a witness to the paramount role this nation will take in fulfilling the divine plan. In March of 1969, she scoffed at predictions by Jeane Dixon, Peter Hurkos, and others that there would be a major earthquake in California in April 1969. She agreed with Edgar Cayce that great destruction around the world, including California, New York, and Connecticut, would not occur until the end of the century.

"But after that," says she, "there will be the dawn of a

new Aquarian Age, led by the remnants of the world population which have survived the holocaust."

Clara Schuff has a good track record. In 1965, after the northeastern power blackout, seeress Jeane Dixon darkly hinted at a sinister enemy plot. Clara Schuff said the blackout resulted from a mistake made by a couple of engineers. Two weeks later, a Washington report blamed Canadian engineers for incorrectly adjusting automatic power equipment.

Like the march of civilization, this elderly psychic-medium has gradually moved westward. In Vienna, she publicly declared a man imprisoned for a heinous murder was innocent. Subsequently, according to newspaper accounts, she was proven right when the real criminal fled the country.

She also performed many services for a Viennese art writer named Angelina Kuhn. "I had lost my eyeglasses," said Angelina, "but where, I didn't know."

Clara Schuff moved psychically through the Kuhn home, searching out every little nook and cranny with her uncanny subconscious. "When you enter through the door of your house," she said finally, "there is on the chest, on the left of the door, a singular vase. You must look there for your glasses, and not outside the house."

Angelina Kuhn did as directed.

"I went home and in the first room on the left-hand side there was a chest with a Chinese vase on it. I believed this to be the particular vase Clara Schuff had indicated. But the glasses were nowhere to be seen, and I returned to her full of indignation."

Clara Schuff shook her old gray head.

"Go and look again as I told you, just as you enter the door."

The search resumed. In the front hall, there was a chest which Angelina had passed unthinkingly. This time she examined it, and there, lo and behold, were her precious glasses, lying innocuously on the floor behind the chest.

And the singular vase Clara Schuff had mentioned? "There was a little holy water font just above the chest on the wall. It was indeed a singular vase."

In the field of art, Clara Schuff was also helpful. For four years, Angelina Kuhn had researched the existence of a little-known Madonna by Rafael, and was about to publish her findings when the picture disappeared during World War II.

"I asked Frau Schuff if she could tell me anything about the picture. She told me that the picture had not been destroyed, and would be found preserved in a sort of cellar in a mountain."

There was no way of immediately ascertaining Clara's accuracy. "But two years later," Angelina Kuhn reported, "the owner wrote that the painting had been found just as the medium said."

Moving out of Austria, into Germany, and then Switzerland, Frau Schuff continued to perform her little services. In Switzerland she was consulted by parents whose son was missing. She told them their boy was in Hamburg and quite safe. Two weeks later he returned home unharmed—from Hamburg.

Not everything turned out happily. Clara Schuff told another Swiss woman that it was imperative that she immediately write to her daughter in England. The advice was not heeded. But three days later, the woman learned that her daughter had died tragically in a fall from a roof.

In 1961, she moved West, stopping for a while in Panama. She was promptly interviewed by a skeptical reporter. He could have inquired about Mars, Venus, or the moon, but he chose to ask her about his car, then being repaired.

"Your car," she responded, "has something missing from the engine and a blockage in the fuel system." The missing something was a filter reposing in the car trunk. He then asked her to give him the numbers on his license plate, and she got them all, though not in order.

In 1963, well before the first moon shot, she announced that there were advanced intelligences on Venus, Mars, Neptune, and other distant planets. She said that the United States and Russia would work together to reach the moon (there have been friendly exchanges of information, surprisingly), that there would be no war between Russia and China, and the free world would have to watch Red China, or it would no longer be free.

Eventually, she settled in Santa Barbara, and read for whoever sought her out. The principal points of interest were money, romance, and health. "You were right again," testified a Santa Barbara woman whose misplaced purse she had located, "just as you were right when you told me my inheritance would come through in three months."

In 1969, Clara Schuff was at the Yoga camp in Tecati, Mexico, maintained by Yogi Indra Devi. "This woman," Indra Devi told me, "is out of this world."

Clara had predicted a small thing for Indra, but it had impressed her because it seemed so implausible at the time. She had been planning an extensive tour of South America, but Frau Schuff said otherwise. "You will be leaving for India early next year," she told Indra Devi.

"South America," the Yogi said.

"India," Frau Schuff repeated.

And India it was, Indra Devi's plans changing unexpectedly, because of external pressures.

Frau Schuff kindly offered to give me a reading, and she told me of all the great books I would write, which seemed more flattering than objective. In my personal life, she came up with the initials of a young lady I knew.

"Can you describe her?" I said.

She reached for a pencil and scribbled two words on a scrap of paper.

I blinked as I read. For phonetically, with just a letter or two at variance, she had correctly put down the name of the young lady.

For some reason, some psychics feature bad news just as newspapers do. But, as psychics point out, they don't make anything happen, but only reveal what is already there waiting to happen. Like Cayce thirty years before, many psychics have warned of civil war at home, with violence in the streets. "This is one of the major problems, really the most important of our times," cautions Chicago's Irene Hughes, "and it is my psychic impression that our government will begin to watch ever more closely the actions of dissident groups, because it will be discovered that an agreement between certain such groups and enemy nations is in effect and it will be shocking."

This prediction is almost too vague to be of value, but other predictions, more specific, were made by Mrs. Hughes in a newspaper column in January of 1970.

"My previous psychic impression of allowing Red China in the U.N. will come about, together with other deals made with China by U.S. to bring an end to the Viet Nam war.

"In 1970s and 1980s it will be China in the headlines as it was Germany and Hitler in the 1930s—in acts of aggression; unusual atomic weapons, greater air and ground transportation methods."

The preview continued:

"Germany will also be a source of much news with economic difficulties of a serious nature in 1972; she will become a unified Germany between 1974–1978.

"Russia will go ahead of U.S. in space programs in the 1970s."

Irene Hughes also discussed coming events of a lighter nature, for the ladies, to be sure. And in retrospect she was very, very right:

"Fashions will be exciting, with the short mini out and the longer mini and long dresses and those that touch two inches above and two inches below the knees being very popular."

As styles traditionally change back and forth, Irene Hughes might have been more perceptive than psychic in her fashion forecast. But her next prediction is psychic enough for the man with the receding hairline.

"Baldness will be a thing of the past by 1976," she predicted, "with scientific breakthroughs in the seeding of hair. Man will be bald only because he desires to be."

There was also hope for the population explosion:

"Hypnosis and autosuggestion will be used so much in birth control they will become common practice. And of course there is that spray atomizer I've already predicted for birth control."

In her own column in a community newspaper serving the Chicago area, Irene Hughes featured a letter-from-the-reader section, a metaphysical version of Dear Abby. She heard from the lonely and the lovelorn, widows, orphans, the confused, and the errant. She answered, "ESPecially Irene."

Mrs. CH, of the Chicago South Side, asked:

"I have a son who has spent ten years in prison. He was released in 1966, but has never come home. I am heartbroken and have no idea where to find him—will he ever get in touch?"

The reply:

"ESP indicates he would get in touch if you'd change your phone number (list it) so he could locate you."

At her best, Dear Abby couldn't have handled the next one:

"I put my house up for sale and want to buy a home in Florida—also, will my granddaughter marry the fellow she is going out with?—MG, West Side."

But Irene had no trouble with it.

"It's my psychic impression that you will move—no marriage by your granddaughter to that present man."

Sometimes Irene's advice seemed so sound I wondered whether she was in the "thinking business."

MMP of Chicago's North Side had thrown caution to the winds:

"I am a widow in my sixties and have been going with a widower the same age for three months. I have known this man for about thirty years. Do you see marriage for me to this man?"

Irene Hughes responded:

"Through my abilities of ESP, sorry, no marriage—not to this man, nor to any other man. Enjoy life by taking trips and keeping active in creative work—that's what I see."

Irene Hughes had a number of testimonials indicating she was helping. One of these was from Jerome Watson, a graduate student, formerly of Chicago:

"Your prediction, two years before, that I would move to another part of the country in August 1970, proved remarkably accurate. I received a fellowship and moved to Cambridge, Massachusetts, September 1.

"You made another prediction concerning my relations with one of my bosses. You said I would have little more to do with him after the fall of 1968, and that was unexpectedly correct."

While her answers are frequently general, they nevertheless seem to satisfy Irene's "Dear Abby" clientele. On December 5, 1970, Marilyn Lee, wife of a Rockford, Illinois, businessman, asked if a trip to a convention in Dallas, Texas, that December 19 and 20, would be profitable, and if her husband would change jobs.

Irene Hughes' answer at the time appeared contradictory. She said the convention trip would be highly profitable, but the husband wouldn't take the job, an apparent advancement.

But the conflicting parts of the prediction unexpectedly materialized.

"The last night of the convention there was a drawing, and my husband's name and number was called. The grand prize was a car, a Japanese Subaru wagon, and he won it. He also won a trip to Las Vegas, Nevada, on a 747 jet."

That took care of the profit, now for the job:

"My husband did not take the position because the company's Rockford branch will not open until 1972, at which time the job will be his."

Some psychics double as performers, more at ease on the stage or nightclub floor than in the sitting room. The Reverend Richard Ireland, founder of the University of Life Church in Phoenix, Arizona, appears to do psychically what a magician does with legerdemain. He stands up on a public floor, before gaping audiences, has himself blindfolded, and then he picks out names and initials of people in the audience, and discusses their health, job, and marital problems, just as if he were giving a private reading.

The actress Mae West, who has an interest in psychic matters, particularly when they apply to the prudent management of her own affairs, considers him the greatest of living psychics.

"Unless they can read from billets (slips of paper) with their eyes blindfolded, I don't think they're truly great psychics," the actress said once with dubious authority.

I had watched billets featuring individual questions read with 100 per cent accuracy by many mediums, and knew from experience that they were subject to fraud and deception. But Ireland is obviously of a different order. He has a spiritual orientation, and he does help many people, even from the stage. In Las Vegas, at the Aladdin nightclub, he told a woman in the audience that she was pregnant, after her doctor had repeatedly assured her she wasn't. It developed that she did have a tubular pregnancy. Radical surgery was performed in time to avoid a hazardous situation. On another occasion, he advised a club-goer that she had cancer, and should be operated on at once. She was promptly examined, a fistula was discovered in time, and she recovered.

I first watched Ireland perform at Mae West's rambling beach house in Santa Monica. There were perhaps a hundred in the audience when I arrived. I would have picked him out instantly even if he hadn't been blindfolded. He was a short, sandy-haired man, with nervous, quick mannerisms. He stood in the center of a large room, and asked anybody who desired to check his blindfolds, and the tapes under them, to verify that he couldn't see through them.

Miss West had gathered together a fairly representative cross section of the population—all ages and types. I particularly noticed two young giants standing near Ireland. They had turned in billets, laughing as they did so. They were professional football players, one with the Chicago Bears, the other from the Los Angeles Rams.

As the session got started, the psychic read for several whose billets he had selected at random. There were a number of scattered "oohs" and "aahs" as he seemed to strike home, getting initials of the individual and his friends and tuning into their problems. Finally, he held up a billet which belonged to one of the football players.

He sifted the paper through his fingers for a moment, then plunged in.

"At the present time," he said, "you are having trouble with your father over a young lady. There has been so much bad feeling over this that you and your father, whom you are devoted to, are not even speaking."

As Ireland spoke in that quick staccato voice of his, I looked at the man whose billet he was reading. The football player made no effort to hide his surprise. His jaw had dropped and he was speechless. And then embarrassment took over.

"How will it be resolved?" he asked meekly.

"The misunderstanding with your father will be cleared up, and the other situation will take care of itself."

He turned, still blindfolded, to the other football player.

"Have you got a ten-dollar bill?"

The player nodded.

"Can I get to keep it," he said, "if I tell you the serial number?"

"You mean, all the numbers?" the player asked.

"Yes, and the letters, too, in order."

The player handed over a bill, which Ireland promptly crunched in his hand without looking at it.

Without hesitating, the psychic read off the numbers, handing the bill back to its owner so he could check it.

Again as I watched, the player's jaw fell and his eyes bulged.

Ireland had read the eight digits and two letters of the serial number perfectly. I was not terribly impressed by this exploit, which, true as it was, I considered a psychic trick, little different from Peter Hurkos' feat in telling me once how much change I had in my trousers pocket (65 cents).

No useful service, I felt, had been performed by this information. The player could read the serial number for himself, just as I could dig into my pocket and tell how much money I had. But afterwards, I ran into the two players outside the house, and had cause to ponder my hasty judgment.

"What did you think of the demonstration?" I asked.

The player whose relationship with his father had been discussed smiled rather uneasily.

"When you see something like that," he said, "you realize there is more to life than meets the eye." He hesitated uncertainly. "It makes you feel there must be a Higher Power, a Divine Intelligence, a God, for how else could he do what he did unless he had a God-given power?"

And so a service was performed after all, psychic trick or no. The Reverend Richard Ireland obviously has a contribution to make, and as we all do, he makes it in his own way.

As a newspaperman, I had often speculated on the possible use of psychics in solving crimes, gauging the stock market, or forecasting elections.

After the sensational Tate murder case in California, I had asked several psychics for their opinion, and all had agreed that the murders were the work of several people (some accurately specified five killers) who had scattered following the mass murders of the beautiful actress and her friends. All said that the killers had been under the influence of drugs, and that they would be apprehended before long, brought to trial, and convicted. There were several interesting details about the killers which seemed to tally with the Manson gang when they were finally brought to justice, but there was nothing in the way of a clue that could have led to a solution of the case. And yet I knew that psychics had broken murder cases. The late Florence Psychic of Edgewater, New Jersey, supplied information to police that solved more than one murder case. Psychic Josephine Pittman of Stone Mountain, Georgia, led police to the scene of a crime near Atlanta, exposing the murder and murderer. Psychic sleuth Peter Hurkos gave Miami police the name —Smitty—of an unknown who had committed two murders, along with a description that led to his arrest. And spiritualist Anne Gehman had made the front pages of the Central Florida papers with at least one solution.

Yet I would have hesitated to pin a murder on anybody because of something some psychic said.

In Virginia, several years ago, Hurkos, though he impressed police with his intimate knowledge of a case, still tuned into two different men as killers, both having left a similar spoor on the murder scene. It is a hit-and-miss proposition.

The stock market seemed a better risk. Any number of psychics predicted the recession that followed President Nixon's 1968 election. Marie Blieckers of New York urged clients to get out of the market before the spring of 1969, as did Doug Johnson and Bill Corrado. With astrology, David Williams of Bayside, Long Island, had foreshadowed the Nixon election by a hairline margin, coupling it with a stock market slump the following spring. His prediction was in print the Sunday before Nixon's victory.

In political forecasting, where neither life nor fortune is at stake, and the political reporters usually have it wrong anyway, it seems that a psychic can venture safely and profitably. In New York, I once worked for a newspaper that prided itself on the accuracy of its straw polls. Regardless of the political convictions of the paper, these canvasses were handled impartially by reporters having the assignment. Yet, with all of their diligence, they were critically off on several occasions.

Long after I left this newspaper, I became exposed to the bitter Los Angeles mayoralty battle between the incumbent Sam Yorty and his challenger, City Councilman Tom Bradley, and wondered if a psychic could foresee the outcome. The election commanded the national spotlight because it appeared likely that Bradley, a black, would be elected to run the affairs of the nation's third largest city. With several men on the ballot, neither candidate had managed a majority of the first vote, so a runoff between the two top men was necessary. Bradley was clearly the betting favorite in this showdown, having received about forty-two per cent of the first vote, against Yorty's approximately twenty-six per cent. It looked like a shoo-in with the two meeting head on in the runoff.

Nevertheless, I decided, as a matter of research, to conduct my own one-man psychic pool. It would be simple, convenient, and inexpensive.

"Who," I asked psychic Bill Corrado over coffee, "is going to win the mayoralty election?"

"Yorty," he said quickly.

"How do you figure that?" I asked.

"It just came to me."

"Could it come to you," I said, "that you might be wrong?"

He smiled confidently.

"Bradley will get about the same percentage as before, with Yorty picking up the votes from the other defeated candidates."

It didn't seem possible to me that there could be such a quick reversal in form, since the issue was largely the same, and Yorty had to make up a lot of percentage points.

"How sure are you?" I asked.

"Very sure," he said. "I saw Yorty's name as soon as you put your question. Bradley hasn't got a chance. You can bet on it."

It was a hotly fought campaign, with charges of "racism" loosely bandied about, but everywhere I seemed to encounter solid Bradley support. On the radio and television that was almost all you heard in the closing days of the campaign. Of all the Hollywood celebrities who had injected themselves into the race, only John Wayne had come out for Sam Yorty. Wiseacres jestingly asked who Wayne was, and the reply was, "That man on the radio for Yorty."

And then came the final coupe de grace. On the day before the election, the Los Angeles *Times,* billed as the most influential newspaper in the West, front-paged a poll which still showed Bradley leading Yorty by sixteen percentage points—a veritable landslide.

I called Corrado almost reproachfully.

"Bill," I said, "did you see the poll in the newspaper?"

"What newspaper?" he said. "They're always wrong."

"They say it was a very carefully made, unbiased poll."

"Nothing has happened to change what I saw, except . . ."

"Except what?" I asked, looking for a slight hedge.

"Except now that it's close, I see a percentage figure, too."

"And what is that?"

"Fifty-five per cent Yorty, forty-five per cent Bradley."

"That's not quite what you saw before," I pointed out. "You had Bradley holding forty-two per cent."

"Well, that was my impression at the time, and my prediction still holds; Bradley still isn't picking up enough to change the result."

"So you stick to your original prediction?"

"Yes, but with the fifty-five—forty-five percentage. I didn't see any figure in the beginning, just Yorty winning."

As is now well known, Sam Yorty, confounding the political pollsters, scored a clear-cut upset triumph. And the percentage? Why, it was fifty-five per cent of the vote for Yorty and forty-five for Tom Bradley.

Corrado clearly deserved a dinner.

Without compensation, many psychics dedicate themselves to the public service. Anne Gehman, founder of the Spiritual Research Society of Orlando, Florida, has solved murders, tracked down runaways, located missing people, all without charging for her trouble. In one slaying, that of Mrs. June Ritter of Leesburg, Florida, she told of the victim's being abducted before police knew anything about it, located the car in which the victim (a legal secretary) had been abducted, described where the body would be found, and indicated the killer.

Her information helped in apprehending a woman named Marie Arrington, who had been embittered at Mrs. Ritter's employer, a public defender, as a result of a criminal case successfully brought against her son. Mrs. Arrington, found guilty of murder, was imprisoned, and then, to the horror of Anne's friends, escaped from the state prison where she had been confined. They feared that the escapee's first thought would be of revenge. But the psychic was not concerned. And months later, when the convicted killer was still at large, Anne said there was one very excellent reason for forgetting the whole subject.

Mrs. Arrington was recaptured shortly thereafter.

In still another instance of public confidence, after a Florida schoolgirl, Camellia Jo Hand of Ocoee, had disappeared, searchers appealed to Anne.

The psychic closed her eyes to meditate, then opened them and drew a map showing three lakes near where the child's body would be found. She was found at this spot, near a conjunction of Crooked Lake, Lake Genie, and Lake Sanchez—the three lakes she had visualized after touching an examination paper Camellia Jo had recently turned in to her teacher.

In another case, featured in Central Florida newspapers, Anne was asked to locate two fourteen-year-old Florida schoolgirls, Debbie Teufel and Karen Wichman, who had run away from Jefferson Junior High School on Merritt Island.

After five days, with the girls still missing, two of the parents turned to Anne. The spiritualist, doubling as a psychometrist, ran her hands over the pieces of cosmetic jewelry, the handbags, and handwriting samples the parents had hopefully brought for her to tune in with.

As she looked up at the anxious faces, Anne was able to smile, for she saw nothing but good news. As if tracing their course, she said the girls had been helped on their way by a young man in a blue car, that they had hitchhiked south toward Fort Lauderdale, had split up on the road, and—best of all—would be back safe and sorry within two days.

Karen Wichman, traveling alone, arrived home the following morning, announcing that she and Debbie had parted the day before, that one boy who helped them en route had a blue car. Debbie, walking along a Florida highway, was picked up by police and returned home later that same day. The girls, as Anne suggested, had run away because of a school problem. By the time they turned up, they had a home problem, too.

No sphere is alien to the professional psychic. A skeptical Florida sportswriter, hearing of her predictions, wondered if Anne might predict the outcome in 1970 of the

Sunshine State's big football game—Florida *vs.* Florida State.

Anne didn't follow football nor did she read the sports pages. But, as always, she responded positively. "I really am very stupid about the whole subject," said she, "but I will try, and will only make a prediction if I feel something very strongly."

And then she not only made her prediction, but discussed the course of the game—correctly—for two hours.

It was curious how she saw the teams in symbols. "The Gators," she suddenly blurted out to sports editor Bill Clark of the Orlando *Sentinel*, "are they from Gainesville? Is that correct? And that is the University of Florida?"

Clark confirmed that the Gators came from Gainesville. "All right, then," the psychic decided, "Florida will win. Florida State will be defeated."

As a friend explained later, "Anne saw alligators all over the place."

What impressed Clark even more than the prediction, which had a 50 per cent chance of working out, was the panoramic view she had of the contest.

"Somehow," she told Clark, "I do not see this as such a close game. I feel it will start off close, but I see maybe two touchdowns by the same team very close together.

"The middle part of the game will be very rough. I see a couple of players being removed although the injuries won't be critical.

"An auburn-haired player who is not too tall, but very broad-shouldered, will be very outstanding."

As it turned out Anne Gehman was right in nearly every detail. The Gators of Gainesville, the University of Florida, beat Florida State handily, 21 to 6, with a flurry of two quick touchdowns in the fourth quarter, and an unknown sophomore, broad-shouldered Bob Harrell, played Florida's outstanding game on defense, and was named Southeast Lineman of the Week.

The psychic was wrong about only one prediction, and this turned out to be the most provocative of all. She had predicted that the team that scored first would lose, and Florida State drove from its own twenty yard line to the Gators' one yard line in a sustained march, and then stalled. Many of the Florida State players had read Anne's prediction in the Orlando newspaper, their coach said, and had perhaps subconsciously stalled their drive. "Coach Peterson was to say later," sports editor Bill Clark reported, "that he didn't particularly appreciate Anne Geham's prediction story, since many of his kids had read it, and it may have got them thinking that scoring first was 'a kiss of death.'"

Unlike better-known psychics, who open their mouths every time a microphone yawns, Anne seldom stages her predictions for publicity purposes, but merely makes them as they come to her. She was in St. Catharines, Ontario, a couple of years ago when a reporter asked what she saw for Canada's bachelor Prime Minister, Pierre Elliott Trudeau.

She smiled.

"Well, he's not going to remain a bachelor long. He will be married to a much younger woman. It will be a successful marriage with children."

Tom Nevens, the reporter, thought so little of the prediction that he buried it at the end of the interview. But the copy editors corrected this oversight with an eight-column headline: "She Claims Trudeau to Wed Young Woman, Father Family."

Not long afterward, the Prime Minister made his own headlines, taking as his bride a twenty-two-year-old girl, less than half his age.

Anne Gehman's predictions are as broad as the universe, and many have come true. In the public press, before the event, she forecast the assassinations of John and Robert Kennedy, the sudden eclipse of Senator Edward Kennedy, the withdrawal of Lyndon Johnson from a second term, the hairline victory of President Nixon over Hubert Humphrey, with Humphrey getting back into public life in two years with his election as senator. She also foresaw the wind-down of the war in Vietnam, the successful flight to the moon, with space travel eventually helping to unify many of the nations of the world, and bringing world peace.

Her predictions for the future, politically, are even more provocative than those that have materialized. She foresees President Nixon's election in 1972, with the likelihood of a new and surprising running mate. "I feel as though Ronald Reagan (California's Republican governor) will be in the White House also. He could be Vice-President. There may be a conflict between Agnew and Nixon and this could possibly break up this team."

Like many psychics, she seems drawn psychically to the destiny pattern of that remarkably politically oriented family, the Kennedys.

"All the truths have not been revealed about the incident at Chappaquiddick (in which a young girl was mysteriously drowned), and when the truths are finally known they will reveal a great insight into Ted Kennedy's personal life and morals. He's finished as far as being President."

Having previously picked out the correct date of Jackie Kennedy's marriage to billionaire Aristotle Onassis, the Florida seer ventured a look into the course of the marriage:

"Jackie Kennedy Onassis will be widowed before five years and will remarry. Onassis will die from a chest disorder, a lung or heart ailment."

In 1969, she had foreseen a difficult two years for Nixon, with his assuming a stronger rein on the government in his third year—1971—a prediction apparently materializing with his overtures to Red China and Russia, his strong stand against school bussing for integration, and his dramatic order freezing wages and prices.

Nixon, too, would put an increasing damper on college riots, which, she said, were a reflection of greater youth problems started many years ago by an outside power. "Nixon will have positive influence on this problem, which is definitely linked with an underground political movement."

She foresaw a tremendous change in the churches. "The younger generation (as is already apparent) will scrap the old ritualistic emphasis on religion, and contemplate religions that are consistent with the natural laws of the universe."

Her forecasts range around the globe and into space, touching every facet of life:

"I foresee that some form of life will eventually be found on the moon. It will be a single-cell type of life, or a double-cell, unlike anything we have seen before. It is in the early stages of development, nothing resembling mankind, and (intriguingly) without color or shape.

"Two other planets in our solar system will be discovered before the year 2000.

"In a few short years, we will see the end of Communism. The greatest geopolitical problem will then be the smaller countries which have succumbed to it.

"As we reach into outer space, we will also undertake greater underwater explorations of the oceans of the world.

"A complete new mode of travel will be used on our highways. As a result of scientific breakthrough established through our space program, there will be a revolution in earth transport. Automobile accidents will become a thing of the past because the automobiles of the future will repel one another through a principle of reverse magnetic force."

Considering President Nixon the right man at the right time, she said that in contrast to the Kennedys he would be protected by a strong destiny pattern that would see the country through some rough spots. "Speaking generally, there is always need for being cautious, where our Presidents are concerned. But, for the good of the country, President Nixon bears a charmed life."

Like most psychics, Anne was born that way. The mystical influenced her from childhood. As a child, she foresaw a neighbor's house burning down, and was scolded by her mother for wicked thoughts. When the house did burn down, her mother in alarm asked where the information had come from. Anne explained that it was from Emma, a little old lady in a wheelchair. But nobody in Anne's family knew anybody like this, and her story was discounted as a childish fancy. Later, the family whose house had burned down moved in briefly with the Gehmans. The woman of the house, reminiscing about her family, mentioned that her mother, prior to her death, was confined to a wheelchair. Her name was Emma.

Young Anne was confused by her gift. But at seventeen she received direction. "Alone in my bedroom one night," she recalled, "I saw a bright light materialize in a corner of the room. As I watched, fascinated, it took the form of a woman. When this vision spoke, her voice instantly comforted me. I was diffused with joy, I felt calm and at great peace. It was only an instant's materialization, but it gave direction to my life from that point on."

For a voice said clearly:

"If you follow me I will lead you to a new life."

She woke the next morning with a feeling of being reborn. The depression that had been weighing her down had vanished. She got into her car, not sure where she was going, but knowing she would wind up where the voice directed.

"I drove from my home the eight or ten miles to Cassadaga, Florida, not having ever been there before, or even knowing it was a community of spiritualists."

She had the feeling of being directed.

"As I drove slowly around the village, my car would stop—actually stall—every time I passed one particular house. The fourth or fifth time it happened, I got out and went up to the door and knocked on it."

The medium Wilbur Hall answered. She had never seen him before, or heard his name, but he said:

"We've been expecting you."

And so began her introduction to spiritualism, until one day, having served her apprenticeship, she was ready to minister to people on her own.

In the years that have followed she has learned to trust her intuitive insight, even when it applied intimately to her own life. In fact, one impression led to her marriage to investment counselor Robert Robeson.

"Bob had come to me for a reading because of problems caused by his broken engagement. One didn't have to be psychic to see that he was upset."

As they sat facing one another, she got a distinct impression of a future in which she was involved.

"I wanted to say, 'Don't worry about your broken romance, because you're going to marry me.' But of course I just had to let things take their course."

Robeson kept coming back, until, as she knew he would, he proposed. Anne accepted, and now she is not only a wife, but a mother.

Theirs is a marriage in which they have been mutually

involved, with Robeson, the investment broker, also turning his hand to faith healing.

And as he delves into her field, Anne has delved into his. When asked whether she advises her husband psychically on the market, she smiles and points to her Spiritualist Research Center in Orlando.

"The center was built," she said, "with the money earned from these investments. God has been good to us."

12
The Aquarian Age

Anxiety is an affront to God.

—Ken Brock

The Reverend Douglas Johnson was not sure how much a person can shape his life, and how much is destined. He had helped many without knowing for sure whether the help he gave was part of the individual's destiny pattern, or whether he had actually changed things. He was certain, though, from his own observations, that man's happiness lay in the way he handles things, whether he calmly accepts the inevitable as God's will or rages against his fate.

The world, Johnson pointed out, begins with ourselves, but it does not end there.

"How much better," said he, "for people to look away from themselves, to recognize that in God's universe, amid the billions of galaxies, there is no beginning and no end, only infinity, and that we are part of this infinity."

If life is not ordered, then death itself has no order, and both, with everything between, are merely accidental. The great Einstein, dubbed an atheist, was once asked by an adolescent, "Why is it, Dr. Einstein, that you do not believe in God?" This great scientist replied with a smile, "I believe in an orderly process, and if you choose to call this God, I will not argue."

As we understand this process, and so fit into it, so do we seem to find the inner tranquillity that passes for happiness. In the dawn of the Aquarian Age, a time not only for outer but inner space, there is a growing feeling that we are on the verge of great happenings.

As foreshadowed in Scripture, Christ may return, not in one body perhaps, but in a Christ consciousness reaching the minds of many. In this new consciousness, with a new gospel of psychic awareness, the psychics, intuitively knowing the nature of man, become the new disciples. They stress, by the very nature of their gift, that life does not end on this plane any more than it began here. The healer, the reincarnationist, the spiritualist all call on an infinite source. And just as Christ "read" for the woman at the well, so that she would know who He was and who sent Him, so do they have a message that is greater than their work.

To the average man not holding with reincarnation, or survival in any form, life's tenure is as much a mystery as life's purpose. Why is one life long and hearty, another cut short almost before it begins? The reincarnationist, believing in an endless cycle of life, speaks of the karma carrying over from one life to the next.

"The child who dies in infancy," one reincarnationist explains, "could have accomplished no more in this life, but his spirit will return in another body one day at a better time for him."

So why was he born at all?

"For his affect on others, for the trial and test they must go through in this life experience."

As a spiritualist who believes in some form of rebirth, Doug Johnson thought of all this as he placidly surveyed the angry woman sitting across from him. He had never seen her before, nor did he have any idea why she was there. But she was so full of hate and rancor that it flooded over into his subconscious.

Johnson reached out to her.

"You are married, are you not?" he said.

"Yes," she said, not giving him any clue.

"Isn't there some trouble in your marriage, some friction?" he asked.

She shook her head. "We couldn't be closer."

He saw no point in arguing, and decided to go ahead with his reading, finding what he could. As usual, he asked Spirit for help, closing his eyes to better concentrate.

He visualized a small boy standing behind the woman, just back of her shoulder.

"There's a little boy standing here in spirit," he said, opening his eyes. "He is about nine years old."

He saw her eyes open, and the guarded look fleetingly leave her face.

"He would be ten now," she said.

Instantly, Johnson realized that she had come to him because of this boy.

"He is your son, is he not?"

"Yes, he was my son, but he's dead now. He never harmed anybody in his life, and he had to die." Her voice was bitter. "What sense does it make?"

Johnson saw, suddenly, that the boy had been killed in an auto accident.

"There is a reason for everything," he said, "even if we do not know the reason. Sometimes only God knows, and we must put our faith in Him."

"Don't talk to me about God," she said. "How can you convince me there is a God who would take my son from me?"

"I don't pretend to speak for the Almighty," Johnson said, "but I do know that he lives in us in the way we live."

"And how," the woman asked, "did my son live that was so wrong? He was an innocent child."

"It may have had nothing to do with him," Doug Johnson said.

She looked up sharply. "What do you mean by that?"

"It may have been a test, a lesson, that others had to learn."

He gave her a level look. "Right now, you are blaming somebody for the boy's death, when that other person is as blameless as yourself."

She looked at him in surprise. "You mean my husband?"

"Your husband is as broken up as you over this, and yet you show no concern for him, or for your other children."

"I have three other children," she acknowledged.

"They, too, feel the loss, and they can't understand it either."

"All my life," she said, "I went to church, and believed in God, and now I don't know what to believe in."

Johnson shook his head.

"We have no guarantee from the moment we take our first breath as to how long it will be before we take our last."

Knowing the value of catharsis, Johnson got her to talk about that tragic day. It was almost as if fate itself had intervened to set the stage for the fatality. She had taken a trip, and was flying back that morning. It was a weekend, and her husband was home taking care of the children. The telephone rang, and it was his wife's sister.

"Why don't you send the children over to me?" she said. "I'll take them to a movie."

Later, she got to thinking that her sister might be disappointed if the children weren't there to greet her. She called again to suggest the father surprise his wife by taking the whole family out to the airport.

The four children piled eagerly into the back of the car, and then as the father climbed into the front, the nine-year-old boy jumped in next to him. On the way to the airport there was a collision. The others were shaken up badly, but the boy in front was killed.

And so the mother came home to a dead son.

Johnson felt this was a case of destiny.

"His death couldn't be helped," he told the woman. "It was nobody's fault, not your husband's, nor yours, nor your sister's. Now that it has happened, you must release it, letting him go."

She looked at him doubtfully.

"Are you saying he is alive?"

"On a different dimension."

She seemed unimpressed. "Do you mean I can come to you and communicate with him?"

He shook his head. "Christ said that life belongs to the living."

"But if he isn't dead?"

"His spirit is alive, but you do not live in a spirit world, neither do your other children. Give them the love you are holding for somebody that no longer needs it. Otherwise, you will ruin not only your life but theirs."

"But why did it have to happen?" she cried.

"Perhaps," he said, "to test your faith and love. All your life you practiced your religion, and it was meaningless. When the first test came, you turned away from God. Have faith, and that faith shall set you free."

It sounded like that old-fashioned religion to me, but what was wrong with that if it worked? And there is no question, looking at the psychics and their wonders, that without the spiritual the psychic is as nothing. Even the parapsychologists, rooted as they are in the intellect, are beginning to sense there is a missing ingredient in their research. "Parapsychologists," said Dr. Bernard Grad of the psychology department of McGill University, "may find a greater success in their testing when they adopt a more spiritual approach."

In Russia, where government-sponsored scientists have been checking out the psychic in the laboratory, they do not permit a God. So even when precognition reveals an orderly pattern of events, they conveniently ignore the spiritual. "There is neither religion nor philosophy, neither atheism nor materialism nor spirituality here; it is just a question of facts and facts alone," says one Russian scientist.

With it all, the Russians have added a realistic aspect to extrasensory perception, and Soviet parapsychologists are keeping a vigilant eye out for something that may be useful in peace (espionage) and in war (thought control).

"The real struggle between the free-thinking democratic countries and the Communist countries," says psychic Richard Ireland, "is not the race for supremacy in outer space. It is the race for the control of the mind. And this race is vitally linked to extrasensory perception."

The possibilities have not been lost on Russian political leaders. The Russians, for instance, are particularly interested in suggestion at a distance, a longtime project of Professor Leonid Leonidovich Vasilyev of the Soviet Academy of Medical Sciences. "Thought-suggestion," said the Russian, "may cause in the subject a series of reactions which are not under the control of his conscious mind—it may cause him to make unconscious automatic movements, for instance, or bring about change in the activity of his brain, heart, circulation system and the like."

Vasilyev conducted suggestion-at-distance tests for years with two distinguished members of the renowned Bekhterev's Brain Institute. And it became obvious that telepathic communication could be induced in certain circumstances. Parapsychologists with no regard for the soul would be delighted with the scientific controls that the Russian rigged around his experiments. A hypnotist, separated from a subject by intervening rooms, first put the subject to sleep, and then awakened him. When commands reflected mental images or emotions, they invariably worked. But in word form, the results were invariably negative, illustrating that telepathy is effective only when channeled through the subconscious.

"It is important to note," said Professor K. I. Platonov, "that whenever I tried to hypnotize the subject, Miss M, into sleep by means of a (conscious) mental order, 'Go to sleep,' the result was invariably nil. But when I summoned in my imagination the face and figure of the sleeping Miss M (or of the awakening Miss M) I always achieved a positive result."

In addition to transmitting thought, the Russians also experimented with psychic receptors who could pick up unexpressed thought, or more realistically perhaps, the thought expressed in conversations.

Obviously, this ability could be extremely useful in espionage situations. "Just think what an advantage an enemy nation would have," said one observer, "if they could clairvoyantly tune into a high-level conference between the President of the United States and his advisers. They could get rid of their entire espionage system, and still outmaneuver us at every point."

In this country, the Air Force command toyed with the prospect of telepathizing messages to the planets, but the program died from lack of government support. More recently, some astronauts conducted telepathic experi-

ments in space with psychics—Olof Jonsson of Chicago,
for one—with assertedly positive results.

In the search for a common psychic denominator, once
the objective of Air Force researchers, the searchers might
have turned any corner and found what they were looking
for. Every day, professional psychics, more in tune with
the psychic centers than others, recognize people with a
special potential.

"Many people are unconsciously psychic, receiving psychic information most of the time," says psychic Ireland.
"What some feel to be business genius can be traced to
the subconscious psychic stream. People often go through
with deals not so much because they look good on paper,
but because they 'feel' right about them."

Ireland discovered, as I had, that innumerable people
had psychic experiences which they suppressed for fear
of being thought ridiculous. Yet, when a person appeared
interested, they would describe the experience in intimate detail.

Paradoxically, the most vulnerable present the most
skeptical facade, and the iconoclastic approach of professional commentators is often only a coverup. After doing
a book on reincarnation, *The Search for the Girl with the
Blue Eyes*, I was being interviewed on television in Atlanta, Georgia. The interviewer took the position of the
devil's advocate, questioning subjective evidence such as
remembrance as being irrelevant to the concept of a past
life. When the show was over, and the TV cameramen
had disappeared, the interviewer said he had a story to
tell me. He had been traveling with his family through
Southern Illinois, a region he had never visited before,
when, suddenly, as he approached the crest of a hill, he
knew—knew with a flutter of the stomach—that a certain
farmhouse lay on the other side. He described the farmhouse to his astounded wife and children, its size and

architecture, pictured the immediate terrain. At the same time he had a curious sensation of foreboding. As they reached the top of the hill, there, as he had depicted it, was the farmhouse before their eyes.

The uneasiness which marked his experience troubled him for some time. He now wondered whether I could offer some explanation for it.

"Why didn't you mention your experience?" I asked.

He shrugged. "People would only laugh at me."

His experience might or might not have been connected with reincarnation. There are alternative explanations. He might have had a precognitive dream, which was still slumbering in the subconscious, a dream previewing the trip he was to make sometime later. Or it could have been an example of déjà vu, the strange feeling that we've been somewhere, or heard somebody say something before, without quite knowing where this feeling of eerie familiarity was coming from.

I could give the commentator no definitive word. "All I know is that the life that counts most is the one we live now," I said. "And you could have made yours count a little more by publicly telling your story."

I have had some psychic experiences myself, of a different nature, and so I am keenly aware that Ireland is on good ground in assigning the psychic potential to the general population.

In one instance, a Santa Monica, California, housewife had telephoned me in a quandary over still another prediction that a husband would die soon.

I told her that it was not only unethical for the psychic to have made such a forecast, but that the psychic was undoubtedly wrong.

My caller was not convinced. "She said I would hear from my missing daughter in a few days, and she was right."

"You can't live your life by psychics," I said.

"But my husband could very well die," the woman replied. "He is under constant medical care, and my other child, a son, is mentally retarded, so I have to make some preparations for the future." She paused, then blurted out—"What I want to know is, should I take out insurance?"

Insurance seemed hardly unreasonable where dependent children were involved. However, she was panicky, almost hysterical, and I made an effort to allay her anxiety.

"I am sure," I said, "that nothing will happen to him within that period."

"How can you say that," she said, "unless you're psychic yourself?"

"I'm as psychic as the psychic you went to."

She mulled this over for a moment.

"If you're so psychic," she said, "what astrological sign am I?"

It hardly seemed a pertinent question, but she had certainly given me ample insight into her character. She was a child of woe, if I ever encountered one. And any student of astrology knows what sign that betokens.

"You are a Pisces," I said.

I thought she would collapse at the other end of the phone.

"What else do you see?" she cried.

"I see that your psychic friend is wrong." And with that the telephone conversation was happily concluded.

I could have been wrong, I suppose, but I wasn't, and I was being more psychic than astrological, since there had been a strong inner conviction—always the mark of the psychic—that I was correct.

In the pursuit of his thesis that the psychic denominator is not as rare as people suppose, Richard Ireland turned up a survey in Holland revealing an amazing number of persons who had verifiable, spontaneous impressions that reflected future events.

"The report showed in each case," he said, "that the individual who experienced the phenomena had in his lifetime more than one such experience. Apparently they were suppressed psychics."

While everybody, according to Ireland, has this potential, it seems to manifest itself more generally with creative people, people with a feel for the arts, which, he feels, reflect a definite intuitive flair. "Creative talent is like a great rainbow," he said, "each color representing a different interpretation of the same talent. An artistic person seems to be artistic in all aspects of art, not just in one phase. And the underlying structure of this creative talent is the psychic. Every psychic I have ever known of any proficiency has also been gifted in music, art, or some other creative talent.

"Therefore it would seem that the best personality trait for the psychic potential would be the artistic type. Psychics are sensitive people, and are sensitive to people's needs. That's why they are called sensitives."

He also speculated about the preponderance of women, not only as professional psychics, but as believers in the psychic.

"This sensitivity perhaps explains why women, more than men, seem to be endowed with the psychic. The man's conscious preoccupation as the bread winner often brings him in contact with abrasive circumstances, which forces him to become insensitive to others. And also, to support his brood, he has to keep his activities on a rigidly conscious level, with little chance to use the intuitional subconscious. And we usually lose what we do not use."

Obviously, not every psychic has to be a Paderewski or

a Michelangelo, or there would be a dearth of psychics everywhere. But if Ireland is right, anybody can develop his psychic potential if he will allow himself to become sensitive.

Any number of techniques to develop psychic awareness have recently come to the fore. Generally, these procedures concentrate on opening up the subconscious centers, which are presumably governed by the ductless glands, the pineal—the third eye—and the master gland, the pituitary. Presumably, man in his ordinary everyday function is on a measurable *beta* brain wave level, but as he uses his intuitive powers he passes to the superior *alpha* level. In the *alpha*, he dreams, memorizes faultlessly, and draws on his creative imagination.

In the Age of Aquarius, there are any number of groups teaching one how to get into the desired *alpha* for increased awareness, both of self and the world around us. They call themselves *Mind Control, Mind Dynamics, Alpha Dynamics*, but all are selling pretty much the same thing, a do-it-yourself technique to take one's self out of *beta* and into *alpha* at will, opening up a whole new world of inner space.

I had gone through a Mind Dynamics course myself in four days, and recognized the similarities to a Yoga experience. Through exercises in visualization and imagination, constantly repeated, the student is detached from his conscious *beta* mind and tuned into his *alpha* subconscious. As the techniques were repeated, forming subconscious brain patterns, I noticed in myself an increased tendency to pick up what people were thinking, and to anticipate situations or events.

One instance of this occurred as I was interviewing a teacher about the psychic Corrado. She had been telling me of his counseling a pregnant student in a paternity row.

"The father," she said, "didn't want to claim the child, nor pay anything for maternal care or child support, until Corrado advised her how to proceed."

It was a very sensitive matter, she said, as the father was exceedingly prominent in the Los Angeles cultural world, and nobody, particularly the girl who had borne his baby, wanted to see his career marred by a scandal.

All during her account the teacher had been careful not to mention the father's name. But I couldn't help being curious.

"I wouldn't dare tell you his name," the teacher said. "It would be scandalous."

But she brought out a picture of the child. He was about six months old at the time, and looked like any other baby to me.

"Isn't he beautiful?" the teacher said.

I agreed, and then said jestingly:

"He looks like —— to me."

The teacher threw up her hands in horror.

"Don't you dare repeat that name," she said.

I considered it a lucky hit at the time, but obviously I had picked up the name out of her consciousness, mentioning a man I had seen but once on the stage, and then from a distant seat.

I had seen other *alpha* students do as much or more in a series of tests given in the course windup. Given only an unknown person's name and address, Lennie Weiss, an average businessman in his forties, was able to drop into his subconscious levels and pick out eighteen different characteristics that were uniquely this person's—including a metal plate in the head and a wooden leg.

Another student, given only the age and address of a schoolboy was equally adept. "What is wrong with this boy?" he was asked.

As the instructor waited, the student began to "examine" from head to toe the body of the youngster he had never seen, putting him on an imaginary screen. Soon I saw him touch his hands to his eyes, and heard him say:

"He has something wrong here, I think his eyes are crossed."

"Not bad," the instructor said. "He has what they call reverse vision, he sees things backwards."

The subconscious examination continued.

"He has trouble reading, he's in a remedial reading class."

Actually, this could have been deduced logically, but it was nevertheless true, as attested to by a remedial reading teacher standing by who had provided the test case.

Still visualizing the boy on an imaginary screen, the student suddenly pressed his hands to his chest, and started coughing.

"I think," he said, "he is troubled with asthma."

The instructor held up a slip. There, plainly scrawled, was the word—"asthma."

On a more practical level, since it can be done at home, psychic Ireland proposes a do-it-yourself program for the development of ESP. "The proper mental attitude is paramount," says he. "The desire to develop extrasensory abilities must be strong, and perseverance must be present, for the ESP potential is realized only after diligent effort. Chase out superstition, fear, thought of social stigma, and don't think, 'It won't happen to me.' For it will."

Awareness of the psychic, he insists, leads to psychic awareness. "Become aware of psychic impressions which you are already receiving unnoticed from the psychic realm. Recognize the hunches, intuitions, feelings which seem beyond the five senses. Write things down, for this establishes a subconscious pattern. Establish a psychic diary and in it include dreams, hunches, spontaneous phenomena which appear to be psychic in nature. Record your dreams carefully on awakening, as some authorities feel that all dreams contain precognitive elements, and then regularly review your dream records to see if any of them has been a foreshadowing of the future."

Ireland cautions against trying to speed up psychic development, stressing a gradual development through applying newly learned techniques to the normal events of life. "The psychic element in man is similar to a muscle which has become flaccid through lack of use. Just as a muscle will grow strong through exercise and use, so the psychic abilities will develop if continuously used."

Ireland advocates certain aids, just as the *alpha* people establish a "workshop" for their visualization and imagery approach to the subconscious. "A good place to begin," he says, "is in the home, where the surroundings are pleasant. Do not be afraid to be wrong or to tell others what you perceive. They may become witnesses to your ability."

Playing cards are convenient testing material. And concentration is of the utmost importance, together with a feeling of confidence. "Try to discern the number and suit of a playing card that someone is concealing from you, or to tell its color—red or black—by merely concentrating on the back of the card. Try to feel the color of the card mentally as if it were a distinct impression—visualize red or black. Run through the deck this way, dividing the cards into separate red and black piles, and then add up your score. As you become more proficient, concentrate on the four suits—spades, hearts, diamonds, and clubs. Now make four piles as you go through the deck."

Ireland cautions not to expect too much at first. Some progress is being made if only a few cards are correctly placed in the proper piles. The experiment should preferably be performed at the same time every day, starting a subconscious pattern, and the neophyte should try to feel the color or suit just as the Russians visualized commands in their telepathy tests.

"As a part of developing the subconscious pattern, spell out an emotion—hate, love, happiness, anger—on a piece of paper and try to feel the meaning of the word, empathizing it, and letting the mind drift with the word wherever it goes."

As with the professional psychic, motivation is all-important. "If your sole purpose," says Ireland, "is egotistical, to get rich quick, or for other selfish or ignoble reasons, then your efforts will undoubtedly be in vain."

But once you have gained this ability, without hope of gain, it does have its gainful aspects. Presumably, as long as the overall approach has spiritual overtones, gain is only incidental, and no impediment to material success.

"How convenient it becomes," Ireland says, "to know if and when to buy life insurance, or whether or not a particular property is a good buy. With a well-honed ESP, we would not get into business deals that turn out unsuccessfully, or lose money in the market. We could cut costs in business, hire only productive employees, and market products in the best fashion for the best available market. As for the ladies, they would know where the children are at, what their husbands are doing, and when best to approach them for what they want."

It could also be done with Yoga, where the words money or gain are never expressed. In my own Yoga experience, with the benevolent spirit of the Emersons, Alcotts, and Thoreaus hovering over me, I meditated under the clear blue skies of Concord with only a seed thought to feed my subconscious. My mind picked up a picture of Christ trodding the dusty roads near Galilee, succoring the sick and bringing salvation to the strong, of a sorrowing Abraham Lincoln viewing the throngs at Gettysburg or picking his way among the dead and dying at Antietam. But what was first conscious visualization soon wandered off into unchartered land, and I saw Christ surrounded by faces I had never consciously seen before, and the agonized countenances of the dying turned gratefully to the Great Emancipator as a tear came to his eye. It was all very moving, and very real.

This was all many years ago, and I was in my *alpha* level, presumably, without realizing it. I suddenly found myself able to do many things with the mind that I had never done before. Reaching a writing snag, I could suggest to myself immediately before retiring that this problem would resolve itself when I awakened in the morning. It never failed. More recently, instead of fighting the typewriter, I merely take a walk on the beach, sit on a rock, look out on the waves for a while, allowing my thoughts to wander. The answer I am looking for is always there—at the tip of my fingers. Such is the power of the unconscious or subconscious.

Anticipating the Aquarian Age, Edgar Cayce, speaking of psychics, said that "first there would be the few, then the many." He was obviously looking forward to the time when man, recognizing the limitations of the rational mind in an unlimited world, would turn to his dormant psychic powers to cope with the absurdities of this badly managed world.

Beset at every turn by war, pollution, greed, and injustice, man seems to have lost touch with what life is all about—namely the enhancing of his own potential through self-awareness in a world whose greatness he is just beginning to glimpse.

If we are not to destroy one another before we realize this purpose, we must proceed with prudence and insight, the psychics say, to weld together a world of one mind and one heart.

It is all very simple, says Douglas Johnson, and the alternative is disaster.

"In arriving at our purpose, and pursuing it," says he, "we must learn to care about one another, for in uncaring lies the seeds of man's destruction—not only others' but his own."